Londoners

Also by Craig Taylor

Return to Akenfield
One Million Tiny Plays About Britain

Londoners

The Days and Nights of London Now –
As Told by Those Who Love It, Hate It,
Live It, Left It and Long for It

Craig Taylor

GRANTA

Granta Publications, 12 Addison Avenue, London W11 4QR

First published in Great Britain by Granta Books 2011

A CIP catalogue record is available from the British Library

1 3 5 7 9 10 8 6 4 2

ISBN 978 1 84708 253 4

Map on p.13 by David Atkinson www.handmademaps.com

Typeset by Avon DataSet Ltd, Bidford on Avon, Warwickshire

Printed and bound by CPI Group (UK) Ltd, Croydon, CR0 4YY

For Matt Weiland

CONTENTS

'What is the city but the people?'
— Shakespeare, *Coriolanus*

'No one, wise Kublai, knows better than you that the city must never be confused with the words that describe it. And yet between the one and the other there is a connection.'
— Italo Calvino, *Invisible Cities*

'If there is just one London, I have two arses.'
— A Thames River boatman

INTRODUCTION

I grew up in a small, seaside village in western Canada and most summers I travelled across the country to my grandmother's summer cottage on the shores of Lake Simcoe in southern Ontario. The walls were covered in classic cottage decor, including a series of felt pennants from every country my grandmother had visited during a European excursion in the early Sixties. There were newspaper clippings pinned to the wall — yellowed recipes and news items. In the back kitchen, which always smelled of turpentine, someone had tacked up an aerial photograph of London — England, not nearby London, Ontario. I spent a lot of time looking at that mysterious view. At the bottom of the poster was the famous Samuel Johnson quote I've now heard repeated, mangled and paraphrased many times: 'When a man is tired of London he is tired of life; for there is in London all that life can afford.' I didn't understand it at the time. The view of Tower Bridge looked grey and forbidding. It begged the question: 'What kind of person ended up in London?'

Years later, that person was me. I moved to London in the middle of a petrol strike in the autumn of 2000 — a time of panic-buying, political recriminations and worries about food distribution. I arrived on an overnight transatlantic flight from Toronto and emerged from Clapham Junction train station in the afternoon. The traffic was light. The sun was warm. The newspapers warned of impending disaster, riots and a return to the Seventies; as if this city could ever move back in time.

I knew no one really, but I had a contact. I was retrieved from the station by an Australian friend of a friend who had just enough fuel for the journey to my new home on a short street in Brixton without us having to get out and push the car. Here we were, two colonials coasting on fumes in London at the start of a new century.

From the window of my new room I could see the blinking light of the HSBC tower in Canary Wharf, then the tallest building in England. But what lay between was a mystery. So I turned to the *London A-Z* given to me by a friend who had lived in London years ago, who had been so sickened by the damp he chose Prague instead. I soon learned that for many the *A-Z* is an article of faith. Designed around the same time as the iconic Tube map in the 1930s, it is equally omnipresent in the city, used as much by residents as tourists. It doesn't simply show you the way home so much as prove that the rest of London, the parts that aren't part of your daily routine, still exist. In those first few weeks I saw it tucked into handbags and on the dashboards of cars; an essential companion to the city.

I was grateful for the gift, though its pages were yellowing and slipping from its plastic rings. I tested it out on the first night and flipped from my new home on page 93, east to page 94, then north to page 79 and east to Canary Wharf on page 80. It is an impressive spread for a new reader. The bottom half of the two pages are filled with a mess of streets, twisting and ending, some with illegibly small names. Some seemed to give up, disappear and fade back into the page. At the top of pages 79 and 80, the Thames curved around the Isle of Dogs and then made another 'U' around Blackwall Point. There was a descending list of wharves printed on the blue of the river – Morden, Enderby's, Pipers, Badcock's, Lovell's, Palmer's, Columbia – and I wondered if any still served a nautical purpose or if they'd become mere decorative names. Printed in the Nineties, my *A-Z* showed the demolished South Eastern Gas Works where the Millennium Dome now stands. Most *A-Zs* are half dead, because documenting a city as alive as London will always be an impossible task.

I walked around my neighbourhood. I lurched around, graceless, with a rucksack on my back. I looked at people's faces on escalators for a second too long. I hadn't yet become an urban otter – one of those sleek Londoners who moves through the city with ease. They're the ones who seem slow and graceful but are always covering ground;

who cross streets without looking back and forth; who know how to fold a newspaper crisply in the middle of a packed Tube train.

At nearby Brixton market I came across a stallholder selling cheap, bedazzled jeans and mobile-phone paraphernalia. He sat behind a desk covered in phone cards and posters that listed different rates for the different countries. The countries were given in three columns, set in the same size type. My country was there, but it was not, by far, the most expensive, just a name among names. I tried to buy a £5 phone card. Four pounds, said the man behind the desk. How much is that one? I asked, pointing to another £5 card. Three pounds, he responded. There was a system at work here. I hesitated before it, and he left me to sell a pair of jeans to someone else.

Later I opened a door to a payphone. It was covered with a full-length KFC ad, so I didn't notice the man crouching inside. He had just begun an ambitious inhalation on his crack pipe and our eyes met. He apologized and I apologized and he apologized again and I closed the door.

One day, while walking home with a friend, I looked to my left and saw the graceful movement of a pickpocket's hand as it slid into the pocket of my friend's coat. I looked into the pickpocket's face. He looked back and withdrew his empty hand. He remained expressionless, purposefully vacant, and he drifted back into a stream of people. He faded into passing traffic. It was like watching an old master, well versed in perspective and street camouflage, the latest in a long line.

Who were these Londoners? Not long after, a girl approached me outside Brixton Tube station. Her mascara was running; she had been crying for a while. Dressed in school uniform, she told me through her hiccups and tears that she was a long way from home. When I apologized and walked on, she followed and stopped me again, this time at the lip of the station. Her arm was on my jacket; a new sensation, a sincere touch. 'Where do you need to get to?' I asked. Her reply 'Staines' left me none the wiser. The way she said it made it sound wicked – a place where the mothers stand cross-armed by the windows until their daughters get home. She shivered and looked expectant, so I walked her to a bus stop, gave her a £1 coin and stood beside her, hands in my pockets. After several minutes watching double-deckers pull up and pull away, she scornfully turned away and walked off. My London self, I thought, when he finally arrives, will not be taken advantage of so easily.

I regularly felt lonely, duped, underprepared, faceless, friendless, but mostly a mixture of those on nights when I was pressed against the steamed windows of the 159 bus by grunting old men, big-hipped matriarchs or by a Londoner who insisted on making room for his fold-up bike. Moisture seeped into the dewy Routemasters; if I slipped my hand beneath the seat, I'd have plucked mushrooms. On some nights, after more of the city revealed itself, I walked home through a new combination of streets, attentive, watchful, aware of my setting. Not far from my rented room was the Southwyck House estate, also known as the Barrier Block, the most unwelcoming public housing estate in Brixton. The design was meant to minimize noise for residents but the result is a huge layered wall dotted with depressingly small windows. It's often mistaken for Brixton Prison. I became transfixed by it one night when walking by, drunk. What was scarier? The sodium lights and the small rectangular windows, or the personal touches, the shadows of stuffed animals? The Barrier Block looked stronger than the Bank of England, more powerful than Parliament; and who knew anything of the lives of the people who lived there? Why did my old *A-Z* feel more and more incomplete and bloodless with each day?

Most nights on the way home I walked past a man who said: *bruv, bruv, bruv, skunkweed, bruv, bruv, bruv* – and every night I waved him away, regretfully, as if to say, 'Sorry, but I'm managing.' Since our first meeting, the schoolgirl had staked out her ground on a stretch of pavement on Brixton High Street near a shoe shop. She walked in a slow circle, leaning up against the telephone box when commuters poured out of the station. I saw her almost every week, same tears, same uniform.

I learned to protect myself from the curtains of rain, the dripping archways, the faulty awnings; how to flick an umbrella back into shape, how to wrestle it out of the wind, how to go low when a passing umbrella goes high. I also felt the city assert itself against me. Waking up one night in an empty Tube carriage, as a cleaner tapped my leg, I thought, 'Why can't this train take me somewhere else?'

'Skunk weed?' the man asked softly. I walked past, head down. It was a test, this insistent voice, a way to measure my survival. My outer shell was hardening. But someone calling you brother, calling you bruv, even for a moment, it counts, doesn't it?

Sometime during those first months in London I felt compelled to learn more about the city, to go beyond my neighbourhood. I didn't want my experience to be limited to the first person singular. I felt a vertiginous rush when thinking of the multitudes that swelled London, at the vast array of experiences housed in the city. I never knew when it was going to come – the press of history. One morning I felt sick in the entrance to an old schoolhouse in Bermondsey which had been converted into flats. The woman I was dating lived there, and when I left her flat she was in the kitchen smoking a cigarette, drinking Red Bull and doing her stretches. In the lobby hung a black-and-white photograph of students who had attended classes there a hundred years before, all gazing towards the camera, heads raised and expectant looks on their faces, with no idea they'd some day be fashionable artwork. In that moment I sensed how brief my own London would be.

A week later, when I visited her at work at the Royal Ballet I picked up the tickets late after spending too long speaking to a human statue out on the corner of Floral Street in Covent Garden. He was on break and when I asked him how he did it, he said, 'You learn discipline in Estonia.' Then he smoked his cigarette and I could see a smudge of silver paint on the filter.

That night I watched a group of teenagers, mostly girls, spilling onto the street outside the Royal Opera House. They had come to London for the ballet and already, because it was so brief, because it had already gone for me, I envied them their first experience of the city, even the way they were nearly mashed by a black cab, naively believing it was going to stop at that zebra crossing on Bow Street.

I moved to Highbury, North London, and spent most of my time on the Holloway Road where the pavements are covered with orphaned office furniture. Past the chairs are the runny-egg cafes, the sex shops, an old library, a cycle shop, a Buddhist centre and the Turkish men selling cigarettes. Not long ago the London Metropolitan University commissioned a Daniel Libeskind building on the Holloway Road, but it didn't elevate the tone. The same wrappers and rubbish cling to it. I used the Internet cafes with their yellowed keyboards and a crowd of teenagers playing multi-player video games, and I noticed the download folders were full of documents left behind by others trying to persevere in London. One day I sat and clicked open Nigerian CVs, Kiwi CVs, Polish CVs, old London Underground journey-plan PDFs, instructions for interviews, a digital detritus left by people pushing through the city. All that accumulated education and work experience. Did achievement elsewhere mean anything here?

I moved back south of the river. My Highbury landlady said, 'I used to have friends who lived south of the river. Whatever happened to them?' as if a passport were necessary to make the journey. Again I was living with someone else's furniture, carpets and net curtains. The Portuguese shop beneath the flat sold custard tarts and dusty salt fish. Portuguese men congregated in the room at the back and occasionally the owner left the door open an inch, so I would see them sitting, hands clasped, speaking quietly, on mornings when I came downstairs for a puffed, doughy croissant. There are half-opened doors everywhere in London, and some days I glimpsed inside the clubs of St James's Square; I saw the paintings on the wall of the Garrick; the smoke hanging above the pool tables in Dalston's old Fenerbahce Social Club. There were only so many doors I could pass through in London, even if I knocked on them all.

My visa expired. The day slipped past silently. I checked with a lawyer, and she advised me to fly out of the country immediately so that I would not be an overstayer, a weighty term in the world of immigration law. I left immediately and slept on a friend's couch in Toronto. She asked me if I was going back, and how I felt about London. I contorted with each answer. I felt a mixture of love, ambivalence and loathing. Back in Canada, I remembered what it was like to live in a village, to walk under dark skies, to hear the rustle of trees and experience the consistent tempo, the pace, of life. It made sense when days had mornings and afternoons, and weeks had Sunday rituals. I understood that this is how life plays out. Growth, family, death. Yet all this can be dispensed with in London. It encourages defiance. I missed what it gave me, who it allowed me to be. In London, on the rare nights I could afford a minicab home, I rolled down the window and watched the lights on the Thames. Most late-night minicabbers reaffirmed their love of the city with the same view. I loved its messiness, its attempts at order. I loved the anonymity it afforded.

Most all of all I missed its energy. London is propulsion, it rewards those people who push forward. I remembered my disappointment at walking in New York and reaching the water, the point of turning around. In London, even on the days when my knees hurt, my hip hurt and my Achilles tendon hurt, I could keep going. I could push on.

I wasn't an Anglophile. My accent wasn't giving way to trans-atlanticism. I didn't want London as accoutrement, to be the guy who used to live there, advising my parents' retired friends on tourist itineraries. I just wanted to be back.

It isn't a two-way relationship. It's no use thinking this place loses any sleep over me. It disgorges people every day, sneezing black grime, heading back to other corners of the country or the far corners of the world. At the same time it was sucking in rich Russians in private jets. Packed 24-hour buses from Warsaw were arriving at Victoria Coach Station. The M25 was clogged with cars from other parts of the country filled with suitcases and potted plants. In the last ten years, the foreign-born population of London was busy doubling in size, reaching more than 2.2 million people, almost a third of the city. In addition to long-standing Irish, Indian, Jamaican and Bangladeshi communities, there were suddenly many new immigrants from Nigeria, Slovenia, Ghana, Vietnam, Somalia. London is an accordion breathing in and out. All these incomers crashed up against its great gleaming slippery wall, trying to get a hold.

Somehow I was given permission to return. Armed with a single piece of paper from the Home Office, I remember bending my passport open to show the Heathrow immigration officer this incontrovertible evidence that I belonged. It was masochism; it was happiness, purpose, a decision, a path. There's nothing like wandering around a city you've already left to define an internal change. I felt different: defiant, bold, victorious.

I didn't dare call myself a Londoner. But around that point I began to ask, who is? Who gets to choose? I began to feel as if I belonged. I guess secretly I was attaching another very inclusive definition to the word 'Londoners': if a person could get there, could stay there by whatever means possible, they could be a Londoner. It was then that the idea for this book began to take shape.

For me the geography, the architecture, the great mass of London facts and figures, all its history – these felt secondary to the lives of people here at the tail end of this first decade of the twenty-first century. I began to conceive of a book that might yield the richness of London now, a collage of voices that together would draw a picture of the city and find testimony in lively, demotic speech, as Studs Terkel and Ronald Blythe had done in their pioneering oral histories. I was inspired by books that focused on voices that were otherwise rarely heard, that relied on its subjects for poetry.

Anyone who wants to write about London works in the shadow of a stack of great books. There's no point in trying to out-Ackroyd Peter Ackroyd, out-Sinclair Iain Sinclair, or cram in more sheer fact than Jerry White's histories of the past two centuries. But perhaps there was a different history accessible to me. I wanted to find people who had dreamt of London, battled London, been rewarded by London, been hurt by London. Those who stayed for a day and then got the hell out. Those who had never left. Perhaps I could find people who worked with the stuff of the city, who made it work each day.

Every Londoner must have a story, I was told. But it's not true. Some people retract when they come in contact with this city, like salt on an anemone; they become lesser versions and pine for the country. But more often than not, the word 'London' stirred up great emotion. Asking them about the city, people grinned unabashedly, winced or sighed, or would roll their eyes or reminisce. London meant a new beginning, a hell-hole, a wonderland; too big, too foul; a safety blanket, point of pride, unfortunate problem, temporary mattress location; safety, salvation, life's work. A place to stack empty tins of lager. Stage, Mecca, my water, my oxygen. London as cell, jail and favour. London meant 'not living in England while living in England', it meant 'ignoring what my father said', it meant 'I hope I like the husband I'm going to meet at the airport.' Londoners cling to reserve, but find a reason to ask a question and their reserve is broken. Living history is thrilling, especially in an eloquent city, in a talkative town, in a place where people fought to get here, fought to stay here, fought to get out.

There were those who had reasons to love it and who still felt its power. There were those who had come from much worse, who conveyed in a gesture the deprivation that came before, the not-quite living, not quite able to be oneself, the low horizons, the shabby estates. The man who slashed the canvas of a lorry and leapt out to run towards London down the motorway. Those who still couldn't believe their luck, couldn't believe the variety of sandwiches they could buy at Pret. The new Chinese arrival who watched students march down the Strand and looked for tanks. Those who had quietly made millions. I learned never to be surprised at the variety of love for this place, which was often marrow deep.

Over five years, I interviewed around 200 people all over London.

Some interviews took months to arrange and lasted ten minutes. Other people I met on a lark, visited multiple times and interviewed for hours on end. After speaking to me, most said, 'There's someone you should talk to.' There was always one more person. I was sometimes bruised by the onrush of sound, noise and stories. London keeps talking; it unspools regardless.

I avoided the official voices of London. I didn't want local politics or a report from City Hall. I shied away from bland professional soundbites and the monotone of the (mostly) men who populate Speaker's Corner. I spoke to a few taxi drivers, those famed London talkers, but stayed away from cabbies who resembled professional interviewees, the edges of their stock answers rounded by years of performance. I sensed that a more pressing, varied, insistent conversation was happening elsewhere. In London, 'I know the answer' is never as exciting as 'I'm not sure but I may have found a way.' The historian's single perspective gave way to conflicting accounts. Tell me about the history of London, I asked one teenager. He replied: 'It started with me; it ends with me.'

In Victorian pubs and chain cafes, sitting rooms and offices, I listened to a parade of London voices from all the thirty-two boroughs of Greater London; from Buckhurst Hill in the east to Hounslow in the west, from Barnet in the north to Morden in the south. I ranged over some 600 square miles, but I still don't know the city. I get lost, I use another (smaller) *A-Z* constantly. There is only one definite I came away with. It was a statement made by a pest control officer I spoke to years ago who said, 'The bedbugs in Tottenham look just the same as the bedbugs in South Ken.' Anything else seemed too grand. Anything else could be contested by another voice. 'It's too expensive.' 'Try Tokyo.' 'It rains too much.' 'There's always Vancouver.' This city, after all, is eager to see you out. 'If you care about mortgages above all, get one elsewhere.' 'If you care about your health, there must be better options.' 'But I couldn't be anywhere else,' I was told. 'This place is mine,' I was told, often.

*

Whatever it is, *Londoners* is not a definitive portrait; it's a snapshot of London here and now. I never did manage to sort out just who is, and who isn't, a Londoner. True Londoners, I was told more than once, are true cockneys, and to become one of those you must be born within earshot of Bow Bells. Or: true Londoners are born within the ring of the M25 motorway. Or are those who have spent a great deal of time in London – at least 70 years, or 52 years, or 33 years, 11 years, 8 years, 2 years or, in one case, just over a month. 'But it was a very good month,' this new Londoner said, fresh from the north of England. 'I've totally forgotten Macclesfield.'

If you want true Londoners, I was told, they all now live by the seaside. True Londoners are extinct, another said. Foreigners can't be Londoners, a BNP campaigner asserted one Saturday on Hampstead High Street, before telling me a moving story of his own father's journey from Cyprus to London and the way this shell-shocked man took refuge and was welcomed in the city. It made no sense, given his political views. A true Londoner would never support Man U, I was told. 'The only thing I know' – and this I was told in a very loud pub in Cricklewood – 'is that a real Londoner would never, ever, *ever* eat at one of those bloody Angus bloody Steak Houses in the West End. That's how you tell,' the man said, wavering, steadying himself with a hand on the bar. 'That's how you tell.'

To truly experience the city, I was told, you needed to be a first-generation immigrant, for that's when London hits you, comes at you hard and you mould yourself to it: the mysterious eventually transforms into the commonplace. But then, some said a Londoner had to have an existing connection to the city to build on. They needed to reverse or improve the work of their parents.

Some Londoners are trying to loosen their ties to the city. 'Society in London is dreadful,' said a wealthy woman in an airy South Kensington flat. 'I won't have my daughters marrying into London society. The only real society these days is Austrian.'

A Londoner would never call himself a Londoner, I was told. On this housing estate the postcode is what's important, I was told.

*

The only definition of a Londoner I followed was the people you see around you. The ones who stock the Tube trains and fill the pavements and queue in Tesco with armfuls of plastic-wrapped veg. Whatever their reason or origin, they are laughing, rushing, conniving, snatching free evening newspapers, speaking into phones, complaining, sweeping floors, tending to hedge funds, pushing empty pint glasses, marching, arguing, drinking, kneeling, swaying, huffing at those who stand on the left-hand side of the escalator, moving, moving, always moving. It's a city of verbs.

It's been exhilarating to capture all these words, all the conversation, loose talk, asides, grumbles, false history, outright lies, wild exaggerations, declarations, mistakes, strings of anger hung with expletive, affirmations and sometimes revelations – so much that is, really, so little. The voices are here: wise and ridiculous, refuting and improving and refracting. Each of the people I talked to demonstrated the shortcomings of any *A-Z*. Each person added another layer of meaning to these streets.

Near the end I looked through my notebooks, the ones I had labelled 'London Chase'. I had filled at least fourteen, and my writing became increasingly erratic and rushed as names piled upon names, directions on directions, numbers on numbers. When I open them now I can see that the act of researching this book mirrored the act of living here. I developed within myself a complicated love. London Chase – it's exhilarating, frustrating, surprising, reaffirming. It's tiring, it's never-ending, it fills your life. That figure I'm chasing, out in the distance, out in the grey streets, always slips away.

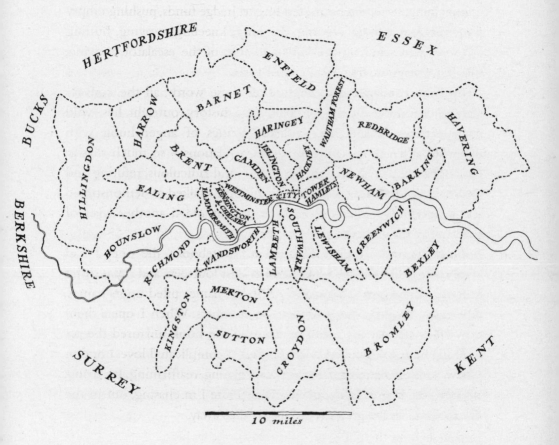

BUCKS
BERKSHIRE
SURREY
HERTFORDSHIRE
ESSEX
KENT
ENFIELD
BARNET
HARROW
HILLINGDON
HARINGEY
WALTHAM FOREST
REDBRIDGE
HAVERING
BRENT
CAMDEN
ISLINGTON
HACKNEY
NEWHAM
BARKING
EALING
WESTMINSTER
KENSINGTON & CHELSEA
HAMMERSMITH
CITY
TOWER HAMLETS
HOUNSLOW
RICHMOND
WANDSWORTH
LAMBETH
SOUTHWARK
LEWISHAM
GREENWICH
BEXLEY
KINGSTON
MERTON
SUTTON
CROYDON
BROMLEY

10 miles

PROLOGUE

SIMON KUSHNER

Former Londoner

When I first arrived I moved into a house in North London with a bunch of my mates. It was an old, condemned house that the landlord hadn't made any improvements to in decades. The wind blew straight through the walls and there was fungus growing on the wallpaper, and the garden at the back was just a rubbish dump. There were broken planks and bricks and bits of wood with nails sticking out and broken glass and a pile of rubble. It was your typical London garden, which in the winter is dead and in the summer manages somehow to grow about six feet of grass in the space of a month. Then it all settles down into a mush a month later when the summer ends.

It was a really dirty neighbourhood. The local council never used to collect the rubbish. Something that struck me about London was how you'll have the front entrance into the house and right beside it is where the garbage gets put. People leave their rubbish in front of their houses, right next to the front door. I thought that was just incredible. Or you'd see kids walking along with McDonald's, eating a Big Mac meal. As they'd finish, they'd drop the packet, drop the wrapper and drop the cup. They walked along leaving a trail of garbage behind them. There was rubbish everywhere.

London is actually a beautiful place when the weather's good; the mood is lighter and everybody's smiling. But for the other 350 days a year, it's miserable. You're standing there waiting for the bus in the rain or you're waiting for a train on a platform and it's freezing. Always a persistent drizzle – or if it's not drizzling, it's overcast and cold. My first winter in London I was so cold, that cold that gets into your bones. I remember getting into a hot bath, trying to warm up and being cold in the bath. Or I'd have cold sweats where I'd be freezing cold but my body would still be sweating. A cold London sweat.

Most of the time everything's grey, the clouds are low, there's no perspective. You can't see above the buildings, there's no horizon. You're surrounded by buildings all the time, you know? Your entire space is about one block in front of you and two blocks to the side, and the clouds are at the heart of the buildings. I've always found that if you live in a cramped place, you have cramped thoughts. London has that sense of being claustrophobic, and there's a general cynicism, a pessimism, that invades your thoughts.

Invariably there wasn't a decent supermarket within walking distance, so every day you'd get your daily supplies and carry them around with you. It was like a mission. What I hated the most was the homogeneity of the food. You'd go to any Tesco's and the food would be exactly the same: crap. The fruit and vegetables were terrible and the processed food – not all of it, the TV meals were actually pretty good – but the fruit and vegetables and the meat and the chicken, it just used to drive me insane. My last year in London I'd really had it. I used to walk into Tesco's and walk back out without buying anything.

I think for me the environment itself was toxic, you know? The lack of sunshine, the lack of fresh air. You clean your ears, you blow your nose and black stuff comes out. It's a toxic environment, it's not conducive to a healthy lifestyle. There's too many people fighting for space on the Tube, everyone's in a rush, everyone's in a bad mood. You cannot talk to a stranger. You see it when you're walking along the pavement in traffic and there's a million people out, like in Oxford Street when it's busy. Not a single person will get out of your way. You become affirmative in the way you move, in the way you walk. You have to adopt that attitude: that *I* am going to walk straight and *you* are going to get out of my way. Eventually it just becomes part of your normal way of living. You don't look anyone in the eye. You just look down. Once you've been there long enough you develop that mentality.

I became like that too. You *have* to become like that. I'd been there about five years and I was on a bus and I had to get off. There was a bunch of tourists standing next to the exit when the bus stopped and they weren't getting out of my way, so I was like, 'Get the fuck out of my way! Just move!' And I got off the bus and I remember standing there, struck by my own callousness. I would never have done that before. It'd taken me five or six years but I'd become just like every other Londoner. You live there long enough you will become like that. You have to, otherwise you miss your bus stop.

His voice crackles and is cut through with the digital fuzz of conversations held between laptops. It's overcast in Cape Town, he says, but the last week has been beautiful, high twenties, beach weather.

London was just more hassle than it was worth. Everything was too much, it was a fuss, a big struggle just to get from one place to the next. Having to negotiate the buses and the weather and the Tube strikes. I mean, I'm lumping it all together and obviously it doesn't all happen on the same day … but every day it *did*, and I just got sick of it. You know, the things that are amazing are the museums, the concerts, the exhibitions, those are the things I loved about being there and I used a lot of those resources. I used to go to galleries all the time. I went to all the festivals. But after ten years you've done all of that. You've done it to exhaustion and all you're left with is the awful public transport and the shit weather and the lousy people. It just became an exercise in frustration management.

And then it hit me like a lightning bolt. I was in Sainsbury's and I suddenly realized that if I stayed in London I'd be in exactly the same place in ten or twenty years. I'd still be waiting in the rain for the bus to go to the lousy supermarket for food I didn't like. I realized there was no happiness to be found in this city. Most of my friends from university had gone to London around the same time as me, and everybody had left except for two people – they stayed, and they love it there. These are two of my closest friends in the world but they are both somewhere along the autistic spectrum. What do they call it? Asperger's Syndrome. London is a city full of Asperger's people. They were just so backwards. If that is your mindset, then London is the place for you.

PART 1

PART I

ARRIVING

KEVIN POVER

Commercial airline pilot

There are certain times of the day when you're flying into London, and you're held – the skies are that busy – and it's just like bees around a honeypot. You'll be flying back in across from France, say, coming over north of the Bay of Biscay, past that nubbin sticking out south of Calais, and it's all nice and relaxed as you head for Heathrow or Gatwick. Then you hit the London frequency on the radio and suddenly everyone's jabbering away. There's a million and one voices on and the controller's not got five seconds to take a breath. You get a frequency, talk and then get off the frequency. They'll tell you what you need to do, and then you get out of the way. It's busy, you're gonna hold, everyone wants to get into London. Those planes are heading to London for a reason, and the people on board want to be there for a reason.

It can be absolutely glorious flying across Europe, coming into London on days when all the sea around the south coast is an awesome blue. If you're on the approach for Heathrow, out to the right you can see Wembley before the river, and out to the left you can see Wimbledon. You're flying over and then you can see the runway in front of you. So you've got Heathrow, Wembley and Wimbledon, and you're like, this is great. You come in and you pick out these views of these monumental areas and it's all there. Obviously it's all shrunk, if you ever visit Wimbledon it's a massive area – but up there it just looks small.

When you come into Gatwick they like to dance you around southern England, to keep you away from London City airport.

You can arrive from any direction but they'll feed you round and then you will end up south of Gatwick and you'll circle round the Mayfield area, they call it, round Tunbridge Wells, and then they give you headings to turn you onto the runway centreline. You're usually on the westerly runway, because the winds are that way. What you see is beautiful countryside to the left, you've got the South Downs and you can see the North Downs as well, the light and dark greens of the ever-changing Downs. And then you see the city out to the right-hand side, and on a clear day it is magical. You can just see everything so clearly, you've got the beacon on the top of the HSBC building at the centre of Canary Wharf, and from there you can work your way across the city. On a lovely day when all is calm it's almost angelic. You don't touch the thrust lever, you keep the engine at 58 per cent. You coast down as if on rails, tickle the control column back, grease it on.

But London has crosswinds. Nothing's stable. Nothing's set. It can be tough work too. If it's rough you might duck into the grey clouds at 15,000 feet, into the mist and murk, where you can hardly see two hundred metres in front and you have to follow the white beams of the leading lights, just follow their intense glow right in. Some days you might hear a cheer and a load of clapping when you land. After that you might get ten seconds, or eight seconds to slow to sixty as soon as you're on the ground and then they're telling you to vacate the runway. It's London. Someone else has got to land.

RAYMOND LUNN

On arriving from Leeds

I came to London about seven weeks ago, from Leeds. I'd finished my degree and wondered what I was going to do. I'm an ex-offender, I've committed crime in the past. I was actually a career criminal, made my living out of crime from the age of 10 to about 22. I'm 37 now. So it's fifteen years since I've last been in trouble with the police and once I graduated from university I thought, right, I need to challenge what's affecting my life. What was affecting my life was my past and the law that says that an ex-offender has to tell any prospective employer about their previous conviction. My conviction was for attempted armed robbery on a post office, and I got three years for it. That conviction's never spent. I will always have to tell anybody who ever asks me about that conviction. It makes it very difficult to find work. So I came to London. London attracts people to it who think, like me, that the streets are paved with gold and that if you come to London your life will change. It's well known, is that dream. It's been going on for hundreds of years in London.

I arrived in Victoria Station at six o'clock in the morning, at the coach station, feeling quite optimistic. Feeling that at the end of the day I'll be in some sort of hostel or something. I had my backpack stuffed with my clothes, a few books about crime and rehabilitation – Michel Foucault's *Discipline and Punish*, Zygmunt Bauman's *Wasted Lives*, Descartes – and an old laptop. And my dissertation as well, my actual dissertation from university. That's basically it, because I'd got all my possessions down to a minimum. I think I threw away about twenty black bags of personal things and I gave away forty of my academic books to the British Heart Foundation and cancer shops. That was a massive weight off my shoulders. It was almost like I'd gone into a Turkish bath and been rubbed down and gone out clean. Suddenly you was new.

It was cold and overcast when I arrived. I wasn't sure where I was going. I'd printed off the names of quite a few different organizations to get in touch with, but it was early in the morning and I ended up talking to this old man who was homeless. We went for a coffee and sat back down on the ground outside Victoria Station. This guy had been homeless since the 1970s and he's one of those homeless where that's his life. That's what he's chosen to be. The sort of person you'd gladly give a pound to if he asked for it. He didn't seem to be an alcoholic. But he had quite a lot of ailments because of being on the streets so long. He told me about a place around the corner from Victoria Station where the homeless get breakfast. I think the doors opened about 8.30, so we sat talking and then went to this place. That's when I became scared.

The people who were there – alcoholics, drug users, foreigners – were definitely from the bottom of the barrel in terms of where they were in life. There was one guy in front of me who ended up sat on the ground pissed, and when he pulled up his trousers all I saw was severe bruises, yellows, blues, blacks, reds. Then there was the background noise, lots of little arguments and whispering. I had quite a good backpack, and I had clean clothing on, clean nails. Whereas everybody else had a sort of dirty street look. I became paranoid at that point, thinking my bag's being eyed up, I'm being eyed up. I was petrified in terms of getting my phone out. You'd see people with cans of lager and other alcohol in their pockets.

Eventually the doors opened and they let in five at a time. By that point I didn't want to go in. But I was told that they could point me in the right direction of getting accommodation or assistance. So I went in and it was cavernous, painted drab colours and there seemed to be these little corridors going into all sorts of different places. I just followed it round and that's where the servery was. I think I got three sausages, four bacon, two eggs, tomatoes and beans for about £1.50. It was brilliant. But the staff seemed to treat the clients like schoolchildren: keep in a line, don't do this, don't do that. They'd obviously been through it every day, but for me it was demeaning. When I told them that I wasn't an alcoholic, I wasn't a drug addict and I didn't have any substance abuse or anything, it was like they didn't want to know. I'm homeless but I'm not eligible for their help because I don't have any support issues. So that was the first drop, the first hit in the stomach.

I then got a Tube up to Camden Town. I went up there to look for a place where I could get onto the Internet. I have a Twitter account, a Facebook account, so I had all sorts of different connections with organizations what could possibly help. I found a Wetherspoons pub near Camden Lock, so I got myself a pint of cider and tried to forget about the stress and worry of the morning and become optimistic again. I got online, started typing on Twitter what was going on. I had all sorts of different ex-offender organizations watching me on Twitter, so I put it on Twitter: I'm homeless but I've not got an alcohol problem or a drug problem. Nobody's willing to help me, blah, blah, blah. I rang some organizations and I got the same response. Because I had no needs as such, other than needing housing, nobody was prepared to help and I became angry. I did. And then out of the blue I got saved via Twitter. An organization based in Camberwell, South London, were watching my tweets and they said, come in the following day and we'll do an assessment and see if we can help you. I was absolutely over the moon.

I knew it was very likely I would be sleeping on the street that night, but that didn't bother me too much. I had plenty of warm clothing. I was walking round Oxford Circus for a bit when it started getting late, and I came across Cavendish Square. I climbed over the fence and found a fountain with benches round it. Well, there was another two people on the benches. They never said anything. I never spoke to them, and I got myself onto the bench opposite them. We couldn't see each other because of the fountain. I thought that was quite good and I was knackered. My backpack had everything in it so it was heavy, I'd been walking around all day, I was grateful for just getting the backpack off my back and my boots off and giving my feet some air. There were beautiful buildings around the square, typical London, large turn-of-the-century build-ings, some modern, some not, but it was quiet because there was no bars or pubs or anything. Occasionally you'd hear a van or a car or whatever. And I then heard these little rustling sounds. It was all the little mice going up to the fountain and the bins to the side, and I was grateful that it was mice and not rats. I ain't got a problem with mice.

★

He leaves his Guinness behind when he excuses himself to smoke outside the pub. A rickshaw passes him on its way to Soho Square. Through the window I can see him scanning the street, looking left, looking right. He returns to the table, sits down and runs his hand over his close-cropped brown hair. He's got bags under his eyes.

When I woke up the square was open. There was a guy with another guy, a physical trainer doing exercises, which isn't what I wanted to see first thing in the morning, no thank you. And I sat up and watched the sun rise and just took in everything around me, the day starting and London waking up. The traffic began to get busier and busier and then I started thinking this backpack is way too heavy, so I decided to take my books out and place them neatly on the bench so if anybody walked past and fancied a book they could take them. That's what I did. Hopefully somebody's got some absolute joy out of them. The best possible scenario is that somebody who's never really thought about crime and punishment found them and that's made them aware of something they weren't aware of before. If somebody saw a person like myself who was an ex-offender as an equal, not as a second-class citizen or somebody who should be for ever punished, but as someone who can be productive in society – I'd be very happy.

The next day I made my way to Camberwell. I found the offices. Sat there nervous. I could see they were a little bit suspicious. I was there with my backpack, and even though I'd slept rough that night I was still clean. Not the typical homeless guy, probably. But once we'd gone through the assessment, they said, yes, we're going to help you to find accommodation. But it would take a few days, and it became obvious that I was going to be on the streets for a bit longer. They told me it was important that while I was on the street I was found by spotters. They go searching for homeless people and register their details and you're only classed as officially street homeless if you've been found by the spot team three times in a week. I took in all the advice and thanked them for letting me store my laptop within those premises because it would make me a target.

Now I was waiting for phone calls, waiting to be found while I roamed the streets for the next however many days and nights. Camberwell's got a crime problem at night so it was a danger for me to be there. So I went a little bit further towards the river, to the park at the side of the Imperial War Museum. It seemed to be out of the way of any sort of issues, gangs or anything like that. I was tired by the end of the day, it was dead, nobody around. I just thought, what am I going to do with myself? It was a case of having to just sit there and wish your life away, watch the day disappear and night come and go. Later on, when it was really late, I managed to kip down under a tree. It was very uncomfortable, I was waking and falling asleep, waking and falling asleep. And then I was woken at five o'clock in the morning, I think it was, by the spot team. They gave me some leaflets about where I could get food and a shower, reminded me I needed to be spotted three different nights, and let me be.

It's always better, once they've found you the first time, to end up back at that location because they then know where to find you. So that night I went back to the Imperial War Museum and drifted away in a daydream. Time in the moment feels for ever. Why was I here? Where was I going? Sometimes I'd daydream that things would work out; but sometimes the nightmare would come in and go, no it's not. Somebody's going to mug you and stab you. Somebody's going to do you in.

There's a pub near the Imperial War Museum and it sounded quite close and quite loud. That would piss me off – not the loud noise, but the people enjoying themselves. It weren't long ago I was doing the same thing and suddenly I'm homeless. You start thinking negatively about them, because you start believing that they have negative thoughts about homeless people and you're a scrounger and you don't deserve the help. All you can hear is their laughing. I found myself becoming a sort of separate species to them.

I started watching pigeons and magpies and squirrels, they would help you drift off into a different thought process. The crows always have back bits missing. They're a bit scruffy in London, aren't they? In Leeds they're all quite smart and dappy, but not here. They're hard here. At one point there was fifteen magpies in one tree, going up and down, dropping off the tree, doing something, and one would be arguing with the other. And the pigeons, they want to rule the world. They are hatching plans as we speak and you can see them look at you as if to say, yeah, we'll get you! You see one without a leg and he's still going on, you know, I've got you!

You become enthralled by nature because you're there for hours, you start to see that they have personalities. They argue with each other. They fight each other. Watching magpies arguing with crows is brilliant. The crow seems to be the big boy, but the magpies always keep on coming back going, 'Ha, ha, you haven't got the white bits though, have ya?' Know what I mean, eh? Your imagination just runs with it and it's funny, you feel you're touching nature or you're just a part of it. And then the night closes in and you can hear the traffic decreasing and the pubs getting louder and then getting quieter as people are going home. It's at that point you think, now's the time to go to sleep.

A few days later I got a call from the homeless organization, who said they'd spoken to a social letting agent and they had a property in mind for me to look at. I felt happy, because I was becoming desperate. I wanted to give in and go back to Leeds. I went up to Cricklewood to meet the agent who was going to show me the studio flat. To be honest I wouldn't have cared if it was a shed, I'd have said yes.

The flat was one room and in it you've your fridge, cooker, sink and a couple of cupboards on one side, a window on the other side and a bed, a foldaway table with two chairs, and a separate bathroom and toilet. I thought, ideal. This'll work. So I said yes. I was told I couldn't take it until the next day, but I was able to leave some bits from my backpack in the studio flat. I took out my writing books, my dissertation, some clothing, some boots. I wasn't sure what I needed while I was still on the street, so I kept a lot of things in the backpack. I was just happy that it was lighter and more manageable. I then went back to South London feeling very happy and optimistic; things were going to change. I'm going to get sorted out, I'll get a job, I'll get this, I'll do that. But I was starving as well.

I knew that one of the sandwich vans comes round the church up near Waterloo Station around ten o'clock at night. So I made my way to the church. On the way I bumped into two homeless English guys. They'd walked from somewhere near Norwich to London in three days. They would beg and then buy alcohol, and what struck me was their generosity. They had two sips between them and they gave me one. One of them was a Geordie, and they're funny people anyway, but the stuff he was coming out with, I mean, I just couldn't stop laughing. They hated London, so they were going to walk to Eastbourne or Brighton. This one guy, a Falklands veteran who'd been shot, he showed me the scars. You could see they were bullet holes. After leaving them I felt really sad because this guy had donated his life for the protection of our imperial wealth and is now bloody homeless on the street. He'd chosen where he was now, but I'll never forget the humour and I'll never forget the generosity. They asked me to go with them. I said, no, no.

At the church I could see people within the grounds. There were these Roman pillars, a bit of shelter and that. They were loud. They were drunk. I went up to this girl who I'd seen in the centre and asked if this is where the sandwich van comes. She went, 'You can fuck off an' all!' I just thought, you don't even know me, I don't even know you. I sat on a bench outside and thought, I'm not moving. This quite big lad, thickset, came up and just started talking. We found out we were both from Leeds and he loved hearing my accent, he hadn't heard it for a while. So he invited me into the group while we were waiting for the sandwich van. I was introduced to everybody and he asked me if I wanted a drink. I thought, why not? It was my last night, I'm with a load of British people, they all seemed to be very close and I'll be all right. They must be allowed to because there's a bench which is made of ceramics which is a dedication to some of the homeless people what've died. They all had their own little bits and they were quite proud of the fact they kept out the Eastern Europeans. It was like, this is our territory, this is homeless territory. So I got amongst them and I drank two cans of very strong cider and they made me laugh, some of the stories they were coming out with. I was saying nothing about the fact that the next day I could be in a studio flat. The sandwich van come, we got a load of sandwiches and boiled eggs and stuff like that. We went to the back of the church and we got a fire going, a little timber fire, and then a fight broke out between a girl and one of the lads. It was nasty. There were no punches or anything like that, just dragging each other round the floor and things and in normal circumstances you'd get up and do something but not in that situation and everybody said, no, leave it, they'll sort it out. I was tired, very very tired, I fell asleep.

I woke up the next day feeling absolutely rotten and I could smell the horrible smell of stale, high-strength cider. Everybody had gone – and so had my backpack. My last night on the street and my backpack goes. I can't say it's them because I have no proof. It could have been anybody. I panicked initially, then I got quite philosophical about it and thought, fuck it, I'm getting a place today. They've got nothing. And I don't even know if they took it. I went to the police and said my backpack was missing. Just fill out a form, they said. We'll get the pigeons what did it. That's who probably did it, I'm telling you. The pigeons.

JANE LANYERO

On arriving from Uganda

I was still at the university in Uganda, we were writing newsletters about the war in my area. We cited some atrocities that had happened and took pictures of it and I put my name in there, saying, oh, we've got the evidence, and blaming the government. It blew up to be something really risky, so I had to leave the country and come over. I was 22.

At Gatwick I was handed a train ticket, with directions to take me from the airport to a bed and breakfast in Harrow on the Hill. Good enough, I could read and write. But I'd never been on a train, I didn't know what the train of London is like. You're told to follow the Circle Line, then change to Metropolitan Line, then change to this line, when you get to this station you can change to that platform. I said, God, be my help. You go up, you come down, you come out … I didn't know. I was scared to ask because you see all the white people around and don't know how to approach them. You say good morning to someone and they just look at you. Or everybody's sitting with their newspaper, reading to themselves. Ah, is this what this place is all about? I didn't talk to nobody. And it was so cold! I came in July, but I felt very very cold.

I had my papers and directions to take me to Harrow on the Hill, they told me the house number. But I had no clue that houses had numbers in one direction. I'd be going one way and then find that I was going the wrong way. I think I left at 9.30 in the morning and I got to Harrow on the Hill at about eight o'clock in the evening. Eight o'clock! It's not that I stopped anywhere, but at Victoria Station alone it took me four hours to get from the mainline trains into the Underground station. Then the Underground train, even when it's coming, I felt too scared to get on. I waited for the first train to pass to see what the people are doing and then I waited for the second one to pass too, because I still didn't know what to do. I said to myself, let me see how they do it: they're very confident, they just walk and go into it. But I didn't know, is this door going to open or not? Because you see the door opening and sometimes they're pressing buttons ... It was so scary. Never mind the gap!

The most frightening thing is that I was given a date to report back to Gatwick for a refugee interview. I could not sleep for one night thinking about my journey. I wasn't even thinking of my interview, I was just looking at the nightmare of the journey back to Gatwick.

But the people at the bed and breakfast were very welcoming. When I came in, the manager said, 'Are you Jane? I've been expecting you – what happened?' I told him, my goodness, if only you people know what I've been through.

JOHN HARBER

A tourist from America

For the first time in my career, I took two weeks off at one time and flew over on a Saturday night out of Atlanta, Georgia. I got to Gatwick the next morning, and I could not understand the man at Immigration. I had to ask him to repeat himself. He said, 'Are you here for business or pleasure?' I said, 'Yes.' I couldn't understand what he said. So he said, 'Well, which one is it?'

I rode the little train into Victoria Station and then a van picked me up and took me to the hotel. I was surprised at the number of Chinese people and Indians I saw. But from what I understand, a lot of people immigrate to modern Britain.

I took a bus past Westminster Cathedral, past Westminster Abbey. I went to Trafalgar Square and tried to figure out why the crowd was there; it turned out they were having a Darfur protest. I saw Nelson's Column. We drove down Whitehall Street and went by the Cenotaph, and – God, there's just so much history. You see these pictures of the Queen Mother and Queen Elizabeth putting a wreath there at Remembrance Day, and just to say I've seen that, I've been there – it meant a lot.

I went to an evensong in St Paul's, which was just incredible. You got to sit under that dome. That's one of the great churches of the world, one of Christopher Wren's churches built in, I think, 1666, isn't that right? And going into Westminster Abbey where every monarch except two have been crowned. To see the coronation chair, that's just too much.

I walked through Soho and came out at Leicester Square. Was it maybe the last year or so, when they found a car bomb on a street near Leicester Square? When I heard that I was like, oh my gosh, I've been there.

I went by the Royal Opera House. I went up to Covent Garden, where the old Punch and Judy shows were performed. That's where the first few scenes of *My Fair Lady* were filmed. Did you know that? And the British Museum – I could not believe that it was free to get in and see the Rosetta Stone. I was able to go right up to it. I mean, it was behind glass, but I was able to go within a foot or so of it. If I'm not mistaken, there was a passage on the Rosetta Stone that was translated into three different languages and that was the key that unlocked some of these lost languages. I remember reading about that when I was maybe 10 years old and to think that thirty years later, I could actually see that – that's too much to take in. I was able to see the Elgin Marbles, which made me think of the Parthenon in Athens. I remember how the horses' heads were carved.

I went to the Tower of London, saw the Crown Jewels and went into what I guess they call the Jewel House, and saw the White Tower, if that's what they call it, and just thought about the wives of Henry VIII. They were in those little bitty tiny cells. Sir Walter Raleigh was in there. I went up the hill, they called it Scaffold Hill, where they would behead them and I think some of that stuff might be embellished a little bit, but still it's really interesting to see.

I went to a little restaurant the first night I was there and had like a chicken and mushroom tart. I was not familiar with the tipping etiquette, I did not know whether to tip or not. I ate Chinese one night and, I'm kind of ashamed to say this, but I went to Pizza Hut one night and it was quite good. The hotel I was staying in had one of the best breakfasts I have ever had in my life. I'm not a big beans person, but they had the broiled tomatoes and I mean … you could easily skip lunch.

A few people would ask where I was from. I'm a native of the state of Virginia, and in Westminster Abbey I was able to go in a chapel to see Queen Elizabeth I. That's who Virginia was named after – did you know that? This was just too much to take in. You know, I've been to her tomb.

Living in America, we don't realize how much open space there is here. Go to an old capital like London that's been there for hundreds or a thousand years and you'll see the difference. I won't say it's cramped, but I saw how compacted it is. If you had a lot of money it would be a fabulous place. You could have a big apartment or a big house. But I would imagine the people that I saw probably all live out in the suburbs and probably spend an hour, hour and a half, commuting in to work in the city.

One thing I did notice in London is when I would come back into the hotel at night, my face would be kind of tingling. Apparently the air quality is not the best there and there seemed to be a lot of – well, I won't say pollution, but maybe coal dust or something there?

FARZAD PASHAZADEH

On arriving from Iran

I left Iran in 2007. Always I wanted to run away, to come abroad. My brother lives in London, he used to tell me it is not what you imagine. It is not perfect place, but I wasn't satisfied with what I had in Iran. It's not because of the finance, but because of the freedom. And I heard that in London homosexuals are so free, they can go anywhere they want. They are not scared of anyone. They can be very open. There are lots of bars and clubs which are specifically for gay people. Always I heard about that.

I had a visa for Thailand, so first I went there. It took me seven hours' flight from Tehran to Bangkok. It was my first time in an airplane. When the plane took off, everyone took off the scarf. I'd never seen ladies with all their scarves off and I thought, oh my, what they are doing? I'd heard about that and seen it in the movies, but I'd never seen it in reality.

In Thailand, I met up with an old guy who made passports. He made Austrian passport for me, and he highlighted my hair, eyelashes, everything. I couldn't believe it: I was looking like Europe! I looked like I'm Austrian. He took a few different pictures, and one week before I'm leaving, he showed the passport to me. It was an Austrian passport and the name was Daniel Primmer. He said, you have to practise the signature, you have to learn how to sign it in the airport. If they become curious about you or they think it is a false passport, you have to do that.

He mimes signing a piece of paper again and again, then laughs. It's hard to hear his soft, accented voice over the clatter of the Waterloo Station concourse – high-heeled shoes, platform announcements, mobile-phone conversations. To my left a couple of pigeons waddle towards the orphaned remains of a muffin. 'Daniel Primmer,' he says, and practises the signature again.

Me and one of the people I met there, who had a German passport, we flew from Thailand to Sri Lanka. That country was the worst country I have ever been in my life. Really nothing interesting about there and so boring. After one week I left Sri Lanka and went to the airport to fly to Charles de Gaulle in France. I'd been in business lounge about one hour and then they called us, the flight to France. There was a guy who checked the passport and when he asked for mine I was a little bit nervous, my hand was shaking. But he checked it, waved me through and I got on the plane. When I arrived I took a bus to central Paris. Most of the French didn't want to speak English but I say, how can I go to London? Someone told me Gare du Nord, the station, and always I will remember a very nice lady, I don't know where she was from, but she was with two children and she took me to Gare du Nord station. I bought a ticket for 500 euros, first-class Eurostar to Waterloo Station. The train was leaving in one hour. Finally I am almost there, it was the last step, my journey's going to be finished. I passed through French customs and then the UK Border Agency guard checked my passport, put it on the scanner, and straightaway said, 'Come with me.'

I thought, oh my god, everything's finished. We went to the office and a massive dog came around me and was sniffing me. I had a very bad feeling. I never have this feeling before in my life. I waited for a long time. Finally a guy came and he asked, where is my baggage? He was bald and had a quiet voice. I said, they took my bag, they searched my bag, they couldn't find anything. And the guy gave me a form which was in German language and he said, you can fill it in and then you can go. I couldn't do that. I couldn't speak German! They said, how are you an Austrian national but you can't speak German? I said, I'm Austrian but I was born in Greece and I grew up in Greece ... They didn't believe me. I was petrified, I was scared, I started to cry. They said, where are you really from? I said, I'm Iranian. And then they took me to a police station.

The UK Border Agency gave me to French police, who were so so rude. They didn't give me even water and I was there for hours. When the interpreter came they said, oh, you are Iranian, how old are you? I said, I'm 16. He said, you are not 16. I say, yes, I am 16. I didn't want to tell them that I'm over 18 because I heard that if you say you're over 18 they will behave different with you. The interpreter couldn't believe me and he said something French to the police officer and the police officer slapped my face. They took me to prison for twenty-four hours – in France, if they catch you with the foreign passport not belonging to you, they take you to prison for twenty-four hours. It was horrible. I've never been somewhere like that. So smelly. People were making horrible noise, they were screaming, shouting. Next day a social worker came, picked me up from prison and took me to a hostel for refugees. I bought an international calling card, phoned my brother in London and he said, you have to go to Calais. I didn't know how can I get there. So I ran from the hostel and went to the Gare du Nord station again. I went to buy a ticket, I said I want to go to the Calais. They told me to take the Eurostar, but I know that to get Eurostar you need a passport. So I went outside and said to the first taxi, I'm going to Calais, and the taxi driver said, 'Calais from Paris, no, no, no.' To the second taxi I said, I'm going to Calais. He say, 'Yes, how much?' I said, 200 euros. He said, no, six. I said, four. He said, okay, come. I paid 200 euros at the beginning and 200 euros when we got to Calais.

My brother had paid someone to bring me from Calais to the UK. The guys who will do that for you, they've got hiding places in Calais – under a bridge, near the train tracks – where you go so they can find you later, in night-time, when they can put you in a lorry. So they took me under a bridge for first night, hungry, tired, depressed, under the bridge in Calais. It was nearly winter. It was very cold. I had two or three jackets, two, three jeans, still I was freezing till morning. Most of the others were Kurdish. They were all refugees. They were waiting there for a chance to pass from Calais.

It was one of the worst nights I have ever had in my life. When the lorries passed they made a horrible noise. We hide from police. It was very cold and horrible. I couldn't sleep until morning, it was so freezing. When we went to that area to get breakfast I met a few other Iranians and they said, why are you staying with Kurdish people, come with us. They had a small place and they had a few shelters they had made with wood and covered everything with plastic, which was very nice and warm. Much better than under the bridge. It was called the Jungle.

After one week, a guy told us to come to a petrol station near the bridge very early the next morning. We did, and it was very quick. In ten minutes a lorry was stopped there, the driver was in the petrol station, and they called four of us, saying, you, you, you, you — go! We ran towards the lorry, got in the back and we all lie down between the stuff. We hid and tried to be quiet as possible. Soon the lorry started off and about fifteen minutes later we arrived at the ferry.

I knew a few people who had been in Calais for about six months, each time they reached the ferry they'd been booted out of the lorry because they've got this kind of sensor that can find them if they breathe. So we just hid between everything and prayed. I was saying, oh my god, my god. It was small space, and one guy was so fat he could barely fit. Really there wasn't anywhere to hide. We tried to hide between things so if someone opened the doors they couldn't see us. But if they came up even one step, they could see us.

The lorry had a plastic and canvas cover and we had a blade to cut a little bit to see what's going on outside. A little later we saw that we are in the ship, and they came and chained the lorry wheels to the ship and someone was speaking French and then English. We could hear the ferry make noise. [*He makes a foghorn sound.*] We were so happy, we were. Especially me.

It took us about forty minutes to get to Dover. From there, the lorry started to drive. After a while, when the lorry had stopped at a petrol station and it seemed like the driver had gone inside, we broke the canvas on the back with the blade, jumped out, and we all ran away. Two of us this way, two that way. We thought maybe someone was going to follow us, but when we jumped out of the lorry the driver was just coming out of the petrol station, and he started running away too. He was running away from us! I think he was scared, because there were four of us and the driver was just one person. Anyway we were running on the highway, the cars at very high speed, they pushed horn and we were scared. We crossed the highway and saw there was a village nearby, past some farms, so we ran towards that. We ran through the farms very very quick because we knew mostly the police check and there are cameras. We were running like horses! I've never run like that in my life. I could be Olympic runner.

When we reached the village, I called my brother and he told me, 'Get a train to Waterloo Station, someone will come and pick you up.' I found a hotel and I went to the reception. I said, I want to get the train to London. She said, you can't go from here, you have to go to Peterborough by taxi and catch a train there. I still had some euros but I don't have change, so I found a taxi and gave him forty euros and said, please take me to Peterborough. I don't want change for it. In Peterborough, I bought ticket to Waterloo Station, and when I got there one of my brother's friends came and picked me up in front of the McDonald's.

I was so dirty, smelly and my beard was grown and I was much skinnier. And I was so exhausted, you know. And of course I was scared. But I couldn't believe it: I am in London.

When I came here I was nothing. Still I'm nothing but now I've got a personality. I've got documents in my pocket. I've got bank account, which I never had in my own country. I live in a nice flat. I don't have perfect things, but I'm very very grateful. And always I will tell to people, London is something different than other parts of Europe. Here is a place where they give you two wings to go higher than other people. When I compare myself with my friends in Iran, I'm much much higher than them. I had lots of trouble, lots of problems till I get here, but now I'm happy. It was worth all the struggle, it was worth it to get to this position now where I am. If I had to decide again, I would come to London again.

GETTING AROUND

EMMA CLARKE

Voice of the London Underground

I started off doing some very highbrow stuff for the BBC – poetry and prose reading, you know, dramatic stuff. Then I kind of blurred my way into comedy. My dad saw an ad in the local paper about a studio near us that recorded commercials. It never occurred to me that anyone actually had a job doing voice-over. It seemed like a really silly thing to do for a living. It didn't seem like a proper job, but he said I should go and send them a tape, so I did and they invited me in for a voice test. I was terrible. Shocking. Because when you read radio ads you have to speak in such an upsy-downsy way; nobody normal speaks like that and I just couldn't get over my embarrassment at first.

So I went away and I listened to commercial radio and transcribed the ads and practised them to find my own style, my own voice. I learned the different conventions of a voice-over artist: a certain way you do lists, a certain way you do price product commercials, and so on. You know, say it's about a garden centre and they've got a Christmas special on – you'd say *candles, potted plants*, and so on. [*She slips into her dramatic voice – it is crisper than the other voices in the pub.*]

You have to know how to do the light and shade and give each product a different bit of zing. You don't want items to run together. It's not about the words, it's about the client's marketing objectives. Instead of blasting through a list of words it's really the marketer saying, 'Here's the range of products we have on offer. Look at our marvellous range.' But you have to imply that in the inflection and tempo you use. You really learn what's in your vocal kitbag and you explore your own voice.

I practised for two years. In the meantime I ran a theatre company which specialized in writing and performing training playlets for businesses and services. There was heavy stuff we did about anti-aggression and violence, dealing with people who were dying in their families. Hospitals and doctors giving bad news to patients, lots of very difficult interpersonal stuff. That was my job.

Outside of that I was practising voicing, because it's a highly stylized way of speaking and to be a really good voice-over you need to know when thirty seconds is up, when twenty seconds is up. You need to develop your internal stopwatch to a tenth of a second, a hundredth of a second in some cases. You have to know the timing. I went back after two years and said, could I try again? They listened and then they started giving me work. It developed, more came in, and I had to give up my theatre company.

A few years ago, London Underground approached a production house I worked for and asked them for recommendations. This production house suggested three men and three women, including me. London Underground took it very seriously and they tried out these different voices in focus groups, over an eighteen-month period. I think there were about six lines we did for the test: 'Mind the gap'; 'The next station is …' They gave each voice a code name; mine was Marilyn. Anyway it was a rigorous selection process, and I'm not sure what qualities they perceived from my voice, but they chose mine. I've often wondered if they'd called me Brenda or Ethel whether the punters would have chosen me.

I was in a pasta restaurant in Barnes in south-west London when I got the call. I couldn't believe it. I thought, you're taking the piss. To be honest, it had been going on for so long I thought they'd given it to someone else – but no, they were still testing and testing. I kept it quiet. I'm not a person to go, 'Guess what I've got!' I just wanted it to occur when it occurred. More months passed because they couldn't decide on the scripts. They really cared about getting it right. The first session we did took about an hour and a half to record the station names and 'Please don't leave your bags unattended' and basic safety messages, 'Move along the carriage' and stuff. Because there isn't a huge amount to record. Once you've said 'The next station is Oxford Circus' – you know, how many ways can you say it? They did ask for variations on Marylebone. They couldn't decide how to pronounce Marylebone, whether it was *MAR-le-bone, Mary-le-bone, Mary-lee-bone*, or, most bizarrely, *Mary-la-bon*. So I had to voice all alternatives. I think they chose *Mary-le-bone*.

We went line by line, because the different lines in the London Underground are owned by different parts of the organization and they needed a sense of continuity, an audio through-line. I have a fondness for all of the names, I really do. I suppose I especially like 'Piccadilly Circus.' I like the rhythm of it: 'Piccadilly Circus.' My favourite is 'Theydon Bois' (*thay-don bo-is*). That was great. 'Mind the gap' was straightforward, though we tried it several ways. I felt I didn't want it to sound too scary, didn't want people to think I was some sort of awful dominatrix wearing thigh-high PVC boots. Because there's a balance between warning somebody of a potential danger and scaring the living daylights out of them.

It was all done in Received Pronunciation – no London accent. It was about clarity, about encouraging the people who would hear the announcements to understand it straight off and have no doubt. I think they're right to have done it the way they did. I love regional accents, but their concern was that foreign visitors might not understand a regional accent as well as they might Received Pronunciation, so it was a safer bet to go with RP. But I don't talk in RP normally. If I use this accent for my work I'd never get booked because very rarely do people want this accent. They only want my normal Northern accent if it's playing the part of a person giving a testimonial about an earthy, down-to-earth product. You know, like fence primer. It's becoming more fashionable to use regional accents in national campaigns. A Northern accent would be rustic, trustworthy, no-nonsense. A cockney accent would be cheeky, wide-boy.

I also recorded all sorts of fail-safe announcements for all the Tube lines, so if there was a technical problem they'd be ready. 'This train will not stop at ...' God, you know, I was very conscious when I read those lines not to sound like I was gloating, or like I sounded smug. It is important to sound clear and empathetic, authoritative and somehow nurturing at the same time. You can do that. It's subtle but when you hear it – when you paint with that many shades – you hear it straightaway. Like if I was to say 'The next station is Oxford Circus,' [*she stiffens, her jaw tightens, and the resulting sound is hollow with a brittle almost nasty edge*], it's crisp and clear but not a lot of soul in there. But if I was to say it again this way [*her face softens, her eyes grow larger for a moment; the sound is now warmth and honey*], it's welcoming, it's embracing. It is a difference in tone, in consonantal attack. There's all sorts of things you can do. Like with the plosives – *p-uh, b-uh, t-uh, g-uh* – you attack them. When you need to sound crisper you're straight on them. Whereas if you're doing a softer read you blur them. And the way you use the resonators in your head. For a crisp, clear, corporate-sounding version you use the resonators in the top of your head. Whereas you use *theeese* kind of sounds when it's warmer. If you're going to do it properly you need to know all this stuff and put the voice in the right place.

So I tried to do it as welcomingly as I could. I did think, actually, in what circumstances would people hear my voice? How would they be feeling when they heard my voice. Would they be glad to be in London? Would they be scared to be in London? What will people be experiencing when they hear my voice? What will they be coming from or heading towards? It's quite a weird thing. I've done hospital radio and it's weird to think people would have listened to my voice as they were dying. It's a very strange feeling. You invisibly accompany people. You're the soundtrack to their lives when you're a voice-over artist. When people are on hold I think, god, they're going to be really pissed off with my voice. That was a concern with the Underground. I really hope people aren't too irritated. I'm sure they will be. When they've had a hard day, when the Tube's late, when it might have had a technical malfunction and it's me telling them over and over again that they'll get there soon.

It's funny, because when I got the call from London Underground I was at the restaurant with a guy I was seeing at the time and he said, 'God, I'll hear you everywhere.' He wasn't saying it happily. We split up after that. He has since told me he is haunted. It is scary: you're having a bad day and you get on the Tube and there's the voice. Poor guy.

NICKY DORRAS

Taxi driver

London taxi drivers are renowned for their encyclopaedic knowledge of the city's messy tangle of streets and byways. Since 1865, they have been required to take the famously difficult Knowledge of London exam, informally known as 'the Knowledge', in order to operate a black cab. I meet one off-duty driver sitting in a faded Bugs Bunny jumper at a cafe near Great Portland Street station. His London cabbie badge is attached to a keychain which is attached to another chain hanging around his neck.

'Everything's happened to Nicky,' he says. 'Inland Revenue review, licence nearly taken away, firemen cutting me out of the cab when I was hit by a lorry up on Baker Street.' The pain in his neck and arm abates over the weekend but reappears once he's back on Monday, so he's down to three days a week.

Years ago he used to own two racing dogs. They raced at the track where the Brent Cross shopping centre now stands. He sat next to his father's friends in the stands – they thought of themselves as the last of the Jewish gangsters, peeling pound notes from a stack the size of a football. London was slow back then, he says, London was dingy. About the only flashes of colour were the bibs of the dogs as they exploded down the track.

★

When I started doing the Knowledge, they gave you a little book with twenty-six runs on each page. You was meant to take yourself to the first place and work out your route to get to the next place. The first run, which everybody knows, is Manor House to Gibson Square. It's just off of Liverpool Road and Upper Street in Islington. So you worked out how you did that and then you had to learn bits and pieces that you saw on the way and around each area. In those days you had to go back in fifty-six days and they would give you tests on the first five pages. So you had like 130 runs to study in two months and if you did okay, they would say to you, come back in twenty-eight days and they would test you on anything in the first ten pages, and then twenty, and then eventually it was just a free shop. And they didn't ask you the route that's down there. They didn't ask you Manor House to Gibson Square. They would ask you something close by with a different name. They might say, take me from Woodberry Down to Myddleton Square, which is just on the other side of the Angel, so it would be the same route, but slightly different. And you had to know the bits at both ends.

I rode around on a little moped every day. Still got the marks on my arse. Some people are totally incapable of doing it, but most people can. You just have to force it in until eventually the map appears in your head and you can sort of see it. The first six months it's like a piece of poetry and then eventually you get it and you can see other things and other routes as well so that you can cut across from one to the other. You've really got to give it your attention. It's like a well. You've got to pump it every day. So if you're doing The Knowledge and then you take a two-week holiday, you come back and you've forgotten everything you've done in the last six weeks.

There were several places that were alien to me. So what I did was, I went for a test one day and I just couldn't figure this one out at all. The guy asked me one of these places, so I went through and I picked out all these runs that I thought were a bit alien to me, mainly in south-east London, places like that, and I used to keep practising.

I bought myself a tape recorder and every day I used to record them runs into the tape recorder and listen to them. Every day. I know that sounds a bit hard to believe, but it's true. I'd memorize them, because then after you've done the run, you write it down in a book, all the streets, and then after I'd been doing it about six or seven months I thought, I can't clear these ones, these ones I'm a bit unsure about. So I made a point of learning all those like a piece of poetry and doing them every day until I was confident that I could do them.

Most people in those days used to have a partner, so if me and you were doing the Knowledge, you'd hold the book and I'd call it and you'd say, yep, yep, yep, yep, and after you'd been doing it four months, they're fed up with you. They don't want to hear you any more, so you have a tape recorder that doesn't get fed up with you. As long as you put the batteries in it, it was okay.

Some of the guys would do memory tricks. So they'd go down Harley Street and the three roads that run across, they'd remember that by Don't Want None. It was DWN. Devonshire, Weymouth, New Cavendish Street. So you'd think, what street is that? Don't Want None. Weymouth, there, you've got it.

When I did it, I think it took me just over a year from start to finish to do, which was pretty good. Now, as I understand it, there are so many people trying to become cab drivers, that they give you the book, tell you to go away, and when you've learned it, come back and then they'll start testing. So it might be a year before you do the first test.

None of it's W. H. Auden, I can tell you. But eventually the mists do start to clear and you can see it.

EMILY DAVIS

Cyclist

Everybody has their own London and they don't very often move outside it. So I have Hackney and Stoke Newington, Islington and Covent Garden and the West End, which I feel very much are my London. And then I have whatever parts I'm working in. Anything else is an adventure. We went to visit friends in Catford the other day, where I'd never been in my life, and we set off through the Blackwall Tunnel and realized in fact it's no distance at all! But once you cycle round London, you take much better control of it than on the Tube or even the bus. You work out your own routes and you know exactly where you are and you know how long it's going to take you to get from one place to another, and you're not dependent on the vagaries of the transport system. I think there is something about controlling your own route and deciding whether you're going to turn left or right and will I cut across the park or will I go round? All those things give you a sense of ownership that you don't get when you're on public transport and somebody else is delivering you to the second point.

There are areas I probably wouldn't go by myself late at night, including areas not far from where I live. But that's to do with that sense of ownership when you've kind of mapped your city, then those mapped areas you feel somehow you're entitled to, whereas I'm sure if I lived in some of the areas that I personally now wouldn't go to at night, they would be fine for me as well. I don't think there are areas that are particularly dangerous. I think it's just unfamiliarity. [*She stares out the window of the cafe in Holborn.*] I find West London a strange and alien environment. It doesn't scare me, but I just find it a world apart somehow. There's a sharpness or something, and that isn't really who I am. I think there's a brittleness about it that doesn't appeal to me. I'd rather have this clutter round me, a slightly more human and warmer energy.

My husband and I went for a bike ride around the Olympic site the other day. I find it impossible to believe that London will be capable of achieving all the things that the Olympic committee are pretending it's going to be able to achieve. And I don't mean the Games themselves, necessarily. I'm sure all stops will be pulled out and the Games will be fine and they'll be efficient and they'll work and there'll be a lovely opening ceremony and there'll be a lovely closing ceremony and nothing terrible will happen. So I think all that will be okay. What I find it hard to believe is that they will be able to restore the site in the way they say they will to make it this great.

But I find it hard to believe because there is always an expectation that we will never live up to the promise. There's an English thing – and maybe a London thing – about never living up to promises. I think London will continue to muddle on and some things will work and plenty of things won't work, and somehow that combination of the working and not working is what gives it a particular energy and a particular life. If everything worked it would be like Canberra. It would be dead in the water. And if nothing worked it would be a third-world city where literally it would be like Haiti, or whatever, but this combination of not being able to get everything to work that we say will work seems somehow to give it an energy that makes it more appealing perhaps than a well-run, efficient city. I mean, if you're always striving for success you end up with something like America, and nobody wants to be like America, really.

CRAIG CLARK

TfL Lost Property Clerk

I arrive at Transport for London's vast Lost Property Office near Baker Street station when it is loudest, between eight and nine in the morning – when all the lost mobile phones, programmed by absent owners and sealed in their

individual brown envelopes, begin to chirp and ring and speak in novelty
voices and vibrate and arpeggio on the racks where they are shelved, each with
its own designated number. The chorus gets louder every quarter of an hour,
until a last burst of sound at nine o'clock, and then most alarms go quiet for
the rest of the day.

Say a pair of false teeth gets lost on the bus one day. Someone notices
it, gives it to the driver, the driver hands it in to the depot. Each
depot then sends it on to us and we log it on a computer system
that we use called 'Sherlock'. Then we ask people who ring up what
they've lost, and we input it into the computer and look for matches.
It takes a bit of initiative sometimes. Things can get lost here.

Careful. That's a sword, look. A Samurai sword. I don't know when
that came in. Half the stories we don't know about. We get so much,
it's hard to keep tabs on everything. Pretty darn cool, though, ain't it?

Umbrellas – we've got umbrellas. We've got Puffer fish, iron, false
teeth, gorilla suits. There's a satellite dish. You want to see the fox?
There's also a bridesmaid dress upstairs. And we reunited someone
with a whip at the end of the week. She came in to collect it. It was
more of like an erotic whip. If there's something quite interesting the
property team will bring it upstairs and show us. Sometimes when
there's something cute like a baby's dress or something, everyone's
going *ooooh.*

You learn about trends working here. There's a social aspect to
it, you see what's in fashion with women in the summer because
there'll be a ton of berets coming in or what's popular reading, like
the Dan Brown books when there was that big craze with him, or
the latest *Harry Potter.* You notice if the *Evening Standard* are giving
away a free book or something, you get tons of them in; if we have
an influx of six copies of the same book on one day you realize: it
just came free with the *Standard.*

In the summer you get lots of Ray-Bans coming in, trendy
sunglasses. And you get more touristy stuff in the summer as well,
guidebooks, keyrings, that sort of junk basically. And cameras. We

have to ask what the pictures are, because everyone's got a Nikon digital camera or a Sony Cybershot, or something like that. So the best thing for us to do is to go through the pictures. One chap called and said, I've lost my camera. I said, I think I may have found it, I'll just go through the pictures. He didn't sound too keen for me to do it. I asked him what pictures are on it and he said, pictures of my honeymoon. Me and my wife on the beach. I said, okay. There were. And then I sort of went one too far and there were, uh, the proper sort of honeymoon pictures.

Christmas is not a fun time. We get lots of presents come in that are wrapped up, and we have to unwrap them. We have to know what it is because Christmas paper is Christmas paper, you know? It's all got Christmas trees on or Rudolph on or something, so we have to unwrap it to tell what it is.

Once someone rang up and said, I left a slice of gateau on the Tube today, I was wondering what are the chances of it coming in? Apparently it was a really nice slice of gateau. I had to be honest with her. I said, no, we don't keep food, we'd just be infested with rats, this place. It takes about three or four days to get to us. Honestly, somebody had it for their lunch. You get people ring up about their packed lunch as well, they'll leave it on the bus or something.

Another time a briefcase with £10,000 in cash came in. I think it was left on the Tube, and when we opened it up, there was a whole lot of stuff in addition to the money. We found some information that could identify the guy, including his street address, and the police got involved because it could have been a crime. That's a lot of money in a briefcase. So they did some investigations and found the guy and rang him up and said, have you lost anything? Yes, £10,000. They said, we've got your £10,000 here mister, do you want to come and pick it up. He said, I can't right now, I've got my Meals on Wheels getting delivered. His Meals on Wheels was more important than his £10,000. So he had to come in later. It was an elderly man and he didn't believe in banks and he carried his cash with him everywhere.

*

Any property that's lost we make an active effort to return it. If there is, say, a passport or a driver's licence, we'll send a letter saying we think we may have found your property, call this number and quote this reference number and we can send it anywhere in the world. We use a courier service. You have to pay for the courier service, but it doesn't matter where you are in the world. It can be reunited to you. We send a lot of stuff back to America, Australia, South Africa ... Not a lot of people from Australia agree to it because they find it's cheaper to buy their stuff again.

We do get angry people and we get mad people turning up. We had a guy who turned up and he was topless in the summer, okay, and he said he'd lost his T-shirt about an hour before. We also occasionally get drunks come in, or crackheads ... Once these two guys came in and said they had lost a swan. I think they were hallucinating.

And we get a lot of people angry about paying the restoration fee. Generally it's £4, but for mobile phones it's £6, cameras £10, laptops £20. And then if it's lost in the back of a cab they have to pay a fee which is based on the value of the property. We have to follow that, because the drivers have to hand it in to a police station first before it comes to us and that can take a minimum of an hour being in a police station. They potentially lose a fare, so it's an incentive for the drivers to do it. And they do do it. They are really good, really good. We get lots of property back from taxi drivers. People seem to get a bit annoyed about paying for it but it costs us money to retrieve it.

If no one shows up, after three months we give most things to two charities: British Red Cross and Salvation Army. The higher-value items are auctioned off but the money goes back into the running of the operation. There's no profit made. Things like mobile phones and laptops, we get someone to come in and wipe all the personal data off it before it's auctioned off. The walking aids and things like crutches and wheelchairs, they go to the Third World. So there's a nice thing about that as well.

We have lists of people's enquiries and we search to see what's there.

One time, I found a Tiffany engagement ring, so I kept trying this woman who had asked about one for about a week. It's a huge thing in someone's life to lose that. That must be horrible. She wouldn't answer her phone, she must have had about ten missed calls from me. I left her a direct number, because I was in the office and I would be always by the phone waiting patiently for it to ring. And when it did ring I was like, yes, it's you! The relief, the joy, was brilliant. I said, if you can provide the certificate that has the serial number engraved on it, then we'll give it back to you. And she did! I said just ask for me when you come here because I knew everything about it and it'll save confusion. So she came in, and we went through it all. She was a little bit nervous when I was reading it; I had to tilt the ring to the light … and I was nervous about it because I didn't want her to have come in and then have to say, oh sorry, it's not yours. But on the final digit, I was like, yeah, it's yours. She broke down in tears when we gave it back to her.

Just yesterday a man rang up because we hadn't unfortunately found his wedding ring after three weeks. After twenty-one days we stop searching because it's a significant amount of time and things generally only take about four or five days to get to us. He'd gone out and bought a new one and he didn't tell his wife. After twenty-one days we send a notification letter and he didn't have an email so we sent a physical letter and he rang up and was like, don't send it to my house, my wife doesn't know. But it was too late. We'd done it … he'd got the days wrong or something. Or that was it, it had already gone to the post room to be sent. He'd rung in the afternoon and we do all the post first thing in the morning. So we were like, sorry, but … We don't know if his wife found out. I guess if you hear a massive scream in the morning in the next couple of days, we'll know.

People have such a bleak view of London. It's not portrayed as a happy, smiley, honest place, is it? Especially in today's climate, when you read every other day in the *Daily Mail* about muggers and just a portrayal of hell. When actually there's a hell of a lot of good people here. It's a testament to the honesty of Londoners and people in general who hand things in.

I spoke to someone from Mexico who was reunited with their camera and they said, this just would never happen in Mexico. It would be stolen. And even like in America, people are fascinated. This is the only place in the world basically. We're not aware of such things happening, well, on this sort of scale.

That's what I like about it as well, because you do know there are good people out there and we're trying to do our best and people are helping us. The volume just keeps increasing, year on year, more stuff is handed in. I don't know whether that's because there's more visitors. I'd like to think there's more people being honest, which can only be a good thing for society really. If I had a pound for every time someone said to me, 'Ah, my faith in human nature is restored,' I probably wouldn't be working here. I'd be loaded.

NOEL GAUGHAN

Driving instructor

I love roundabouts. I absolutely think they're the best invention and I don't care who invented the pen, the biro; whoever invented the roundabout, they should be up there on that plinth that they've got going on in Trafalgar Square. You can have a little bit of fun with it, you know. Will I go? Will I not go? The other car might go in my lane. There's a bit of a dance going. It's like a samba. Because in this city, sometimes you just come to a sudden gridlock and you think, well I'm waiting for him, he's waiting for me, he's waiting for him and you've got everyone looking at everyone – who will make the first move? And you begin to move and he begins to move and then you stop, and everyone's being really polite. But every day you get somebody who doesn't really care, a young lad and he doesn't give a monkey's. People are petrified of the Hyde Park roundabout in particular. I love it and it's a little bit of a challenge sometimes because you get people who, not because they're bad drivers, they just have no idea where they're going. So they've come in and they've got their satnav or TomTom going on and it's shouting at them to go one way and they're thinking, no I think it's over that way. They're not quite sure what to do, so they'll swing one way and they'll have a look at the TomTom and they'll swing back. It's quite hilarious.

In the car you learn so much about people. Once you get started and people relax, it's kind of like being a hairdresser. People tell you stuff. You hear these wonderful stories about people's lives and some of them are heartbreaking. Years ago, I was very nosy. I'm not so nosy now, but still I hear yarns and sometimes you feel like you've had a mental workout. But you learn so much. I get a lot of business from Tottenham. People who are driving illegally and at some point they get to 40 or 50 and think, perhaps I'll get a licence. The trouble is, you can't pick them up from home because people assume they have a licence because they've been driving for years, going in and out of the house, and the neighbours see.

And then you've got the Australians, they're like little English people. They never want to go home. They'll say, I want to go back, I hate this country. And then you say, why not go back? And they say, it's a lovely country, I don't want to go back, I want to stay here.

Then there are the Americans who don't quite understand the system. You go to some parts of the States, I think in California you do the test in the car park because it's too dangerous to do it on the road and the reason it's too dangerous to do it on the road is because everyone does tests in the car park. So they come to this country and they're used to big, wide roads, not much traffic, everyone going in the one direction ... But here they go down small roads and wonder – why's that car in my way? And they'll try and push you off the road. So there's a bit of a challenge.

You get a lot from Eastern Europe. They're quite funny, they always seem to be in a hurry. They have the Polish plates and they're flying around, they don't want to stop because they're always rushing off to see some Polish movie, whatever it is, and they don't know how to stop. And they're always doing stuff in the car, they're either reading a paper or they're texting. That's London for you now.

Sometimes I get young Bangladeshi women in full hijab. I used to think they were all downtrodden and what a sad life they lead, but they get in the car, they're very funny, very witty, very educated, you know? They tell you about what they're going to be doing in the next twenty years. Most of them feel very proud. I had one who was a normal sort of young girl, 18 or so. She looked much younger. Very smart. She had a very old-fashioned father, so she was only allowed out twice a fortnight: once to sign on the dole and once to do a lesson with me. Every time we were four or five minutes late returning home, he used to go mad. So literally her whole life was then through me. She was only supposed to look at Bangladeshi movies, she wasn't allowed to watch anything else. But we had a little chat about *EastEnders*. I never watched it that much, but you get a grasp and play along with it. As we were driving, she'd ask me, did you watch it? And I'd go, yeah, loved it. Because you couldn't say no! And then she'd go on about this and this and this.

Anyway, she just disappeared one day, completely disappeared. I got a phone call about six or seven months later. She'd got married to a hubby who'd come over from Bangladesh. She was pregnant, and they were going to call the child a big long name I couldn't pronounce, but with Noel in the middle. It was absolutely fantastic. So there's a little chap in East London, a little Bangladeshi kiddie, with a proper name and he's got little Noel somewhere in the middle.

Once I had a pupil from Thailand, a young woman. We were in East London, in Poplar, and the pupil had pulled out. This chap just whizzed past, blocked the road in front of us, and got out of the car waving a great big knife. I thought I'd better get out of the car and stand between him and the pupil. He was shouting, 'I'm going to kill her, I'm going to kill her!' I said, 'You can't kill her because she hasn't paid me. If you kill her, then I won't get paid.' And he just looked at me and thought, this man is fucking crazy, and he didn't know what to do. I said, 'You drive off and I won't call the police,' and off he went. It never dawned on me to get his number plate. I wasn't going to call the police. He was what I would call a typical East End boy and I just think he had a bad day. He was a young lad, driving round with a little knife just in case some learner driver pulls out in front of you. And he thought I was crazy.

My pupil had only been in the country about six months and she just thought this was normal, that this is what it's like in London. She was from Thailand, came over here as a student. I got back in the car and said, you okay? 'Yeah,' she said, 'let's go.' She thought it was part of driving in London, someone comes out and, no big deal, threatens to kill you.

When you've finished a test or they're gone for ever, that's a very weird thing because you're very close to somebody and you've got to know them really well and you're not quite sure how to say goodbye to them. I normally say, be gone with you. That's what I say, be gone with you now, go away. [*He sweeps his hands out, a large gesture of farewell that almost upends the pepper grinder in this Turkish cafe in Dalston.*] And then I usually go up to Woodford and around Epping Forest, which is proper driving. You can actually go out there and not get stuck in traffic. I'll have a nice little drive, listening to Johnny Cash and not stopping at every set of traffic lights. It's real driving when you get out there. So that's what I do, I go up to Epping Forest, drive round the roundabouts. I do love roundabouts. I go out of my way to find roundabouts. If you can do roundabouts really well, you can drive.

NICK TYLER

Civil engineer

I studied at the Royal College of Music and spent seven years as a freelance musician. I play the oboe. Which was a fantastic life, but not so good for paying the electricity bills. I thought I ought to do something to earn some money and went through a period in industry before realizing that industry's terribly boring. So I negotiated with my company to let me out and I did a Master's course in transport. Now I sit in a university where I'm paid to think of extraordinary things, that's what I do. Somebody who's paid to run Transport for London has more prosaic things to think about, so they tend to come to me with specific problems. The transport system is a bit like the melody that goes through it all. Sometimes it's going to be dissonant and sometimes it isn't. People like me try to design dissonance out of it.

In London there's a lot of transport. There's 273 Underground stations, 17,500 bus stops. The gap between the buses stopping at them will be at most ten minutes and often it will be only a few seconds. [*The look of incredulity on my face passes without notice. He pours red wine and continues. We've walked from his office at UCL to a French restaurant just off Carnaby Street.*] There's a vast amount of transport moving. It's very hard to see in any other city anything at that sort of level of transport. Paris has nothing like that.

In the programme in which I teach, the first day we say, what do you think is wrong with this city? Talk to some politicians, talk to some people, talk to the engineers and come back to us. Then we do a bit of teaching, and at the end of the fifth week, we close all the lectures off and say, okay, now you're going to tell us what you think we should do with this city. Of course it's going to be pretty naive, but it's got them to realize that in the world there are messy problems with bits and pieces and all sorts of things that interact, and that's what they have to grapple with.

At the moment we're building some Tube trains in the laboratory so we can test how people with wheelchairs might be able to get on if we did something to the infrastructure. Last year we built some mock-ups of stations and bits of stations: we had a life-size train to test people going through doors. The environment is difficult for wheelchairs. There's no question about that. Most wheelchairs are designed to be pushed around inside an institution. So if you started to think about a wheelchair that could go on a Tube train, what would you design?

If we could make London easier to walk in, it would be great. It would be really beneficial to think about how one does that. Because walking is the most natural way to move. If you think of transport on a personal scale you have the opportunity to understand what the environment looks like, what it feels like. Walking makes a city human, so cities ought to be for walking and yet we don't really see walking as a means of getting around. The thing about pedestrians is that we tend to think of them as traffic. So we model them as rather like cars, but actually we want people to stop. That's a good thing. People stop and they talk and they turn to go into streets: they're not like cars. We don't want cars to stop, but we do want people to stop. Finding some way to represent how we enjoy stopping is a really important issue.

Maybe we need to think a lot more about the quality of what we're doing. To a certain extent, part of the quality is, do we ever stop? John Betjeman said, look up. I think one of the beauties of London is if you do that, on the whole, you will find something interesting to look at. If you look at the old maps of London from across the Thames, there are two famous views. One was in the sixteenth century and one was in the eighteenth century, and you see that Wren's vision was that all the churches paid obeisance to St Paul's on Ludgate Hill with its dome. That's a phenomenal vision. If you think about it, this is a guy who could not get in an aeroplane and look at this place from up above. This is a guy whose idea of height was 1.3m above the ground, basically. Phenomenal. So all these churches pay obeisance to St Paul's. They're telling a story, and what a sense of space that delivers.

One of the great things about London is detail. If you go round the back of Baker Street station, the road by the Planetarium, there's a block of flats from the 1930s or whatever. If you look at the top of that, there's a whole set of train parts stuck in the building. Genuine train parts – the buffers and couplings and stuff like that. I think this is what John Betjeman's about in many ways. Spend a few seconds to look up and say, those things are there, that's very interesting. Why? What? How? All those sorts of questions. If you were to stand in the middle of Oxford Street and look very fervently at the top of the roof line, people would come past and they'd start trying to see what you're looking at. It's always a great game. If what they looked at was bits of trains or bits of something or whatever, maybe somewhere in their life something expands. Maybe we need to design a city around making sure that stopping is part of it.

Whenever I come back from a trip and we fly over the centre of London, this is what comes to mind: what a fantastically green place London is, what enormous history there is, what a huge variety as you fly over. You go over the barren stuff in the East End of London, over the Palaces of Westminster, over the parks and all that. You know, they have no idea of this, but the people in the aircraft that are flying down that flight path every ninety seconds, or whatever it is that they do, they could be getting a phenomenal education in the cultural set-up of this city. It's the most fantastic way to understand it. And I almost think as I sit on this plane, I want to tell you about this. Forget all this crap about seatbelts, I'm going to tell you! I'm going to tell you about this! This is *my* city and I'm going to tell you why I love it so much and what it's about. I wouldn't be able to, but that sort of magic about it maybe you can only see from the sky. We tend to see people who are living and working here as they get stuck on the Tube, on the buses, on pavements that don't have enough width, in traffic jams. They get stuck in that sort of detail

and forget that actually all they're doing is moving around inside
some sort of mythical philosopher's stone, which is this wonderful
city. It's a phenomenal place to be. I find lots of places exciting places
to be, but somehow London delivers that piece of fifth dimension
of which how we move around it is part. It's not just a question
of whether we've got red buses or green buses or whether they've
got articulations or not – it's not about the minutiae. It's about a
place where people can live, where people's ambitions, people's ideas,
can thrive and we have a transport system which enables them, if
they so choose, to make their ideas work. That's why it's been such a
successful city for so many centuries.

SEEING THE SIGHTS

DAVID DOHERTY

On Buckingham Palace

He sits in his tidy ground-floor flat in Fulham drinking tea and watching the evening light fade. He doesn't reach to turn on a lamp, so by the end of the conversation he is sitting in near darkness. There is a boxed set of Band of Brothers *under the coffee table, and on the windowsill a photograph of Doherty astride a horse in full ceremonial garb.*

I've been to New York, I've been to Washington, Texas, San Diego, LA, Beirut, New Delhi, Sydney, Perth and Adelaide. I've been to Ireland, France, Spain, Italy. There's only one London. That's it. We are what we are.

I've ridden around the streets of London, driven around the streets of London, walked around the streets of London. You can't help but be a person of your time and you can't help but be connected to your place. Wherever I go in the world, they immediately know where I come from. There's no question. I'm a Londoner. Not a cockney, because that's all a load of cobblers. The last cockney was born so long ago they couldn't be around. The ol' bells ain't struck since the ol' king died so I don't think there's any danger of too many cockneys about, but you'll get plenty who tell you they are. The reality is you're either from the east, west, south or north of London, and that's it. But those differences can mean the world.

The beauty of London is that we've got such a rich heritage of people. My parents were from the south of Ireland before they came here. Friends of mine came from Paris during the war, or some were Jews from Russia who came before the war, and so on and so forth.

You can't help but notice how other people live. You can't help but listen to what they say on the streets. You see how they adapt their lives to this place – east, west, north, down south, and you've got that river in there too, slicing through. That's what makes London such a great place to live. The only thing that is truly Londonish about London is that it's all bits and pieces of everybody else.

I'm from the west. I grew up in Fulham, in what my mum considered to be a posher part of Fulham, which was sort of West Kensington. I think I was there for seven months, eight months before we moved to Fulham Court, which is right in the centre of Fulham. From there we moved to Bishops Road in Fulham, which is now £3 million houses but in them days were council houses. And then we all grew up and went different ways.

I never really left Fulham until I joined the Army at 17. I'd never been to Whitehall before. I didn't have a clue what the Household Cavalry were or the Life Guards. All I knew was we'd go every year to the Royal Tournament and I'd see all these soldiers and that's what gave me the idea to be a soldier.

The Life Guards are the most senior regiment in the British Army, not the oldest but the most senior. They escorted Charles II into London when he came back from being overseas in exile. Oliver Cromwell had died and a troop of cavalrymen or gentlemen cavaliers went down to meet him and that was really the beginning of the Life Guards. So they've had this superior sort of feeling.

I didn't have a clue about the history. Where I signed on in Great Scotland Yard I walked out into Whitehall and there was a whole crowd a hundred yards down on the side. I thought, what are they doing? These blokes on horseback, I wonder what that's all about? I never realized that six months later I'd be sat up there on a fucking horse. I didn't know about Horse Guards Parade, I didn't know it was the official entrance to Buckingham Palace and all state occasions, all state visits go through there and come back out. I didn't know American girls used to come on spring vacation and dress up in boots and try to fuck the daylights out of the Guards. I didn't know we could drink on guard. Queen Victoria came through there one day and the guard were drunk, so she said every afternoon at four o'clock the guard must be inspected by an officer. So at four o'clock an officer rides down the Mall from Knightsbridge Barracks on his own to do the four o'clock inspection, and after four o'clock they open the bar. How was I to know that?

The reason I joined the Guards was very simple. The commanding officer said to me, 'What do you want to do?' It was the first time anyone had ever asked me. I wanted to learn how to drive, which was a real big deal because no one in my family drove. No one had a fucking spare tire, never mind a car. And I wanted to go abroad. They said, 'Right, look through this book' and they gave me a brochure on all the different regiments in the Army. The one thing that stuck in my mind was this guy sitting on top of an armoured car looking through a pair of binoculars with a palm tree behind him. I knew palm trees meant desert or coast. Little did I know it was just a fucking drawing. The officer said to me, 'You like that?' I said, 'Yeah, who's that lot there?' He said, 'That's the Life Guards.'

'Where are they?' I asked.

'In Hong Kong.'

'Right, can I …'

He said, 'Yeah, if you join them you'll get posted to Hong Kong.'

'Will I learn to drive?'

'You'll learn to drive.'

I said, 'Right, where do I sign?' And that was it. I could have had an easy life, a million girlfriends, I could have learned to drink like all my mates did. I could have learned to smoke drugs, could have got nicked for breaking and entering, I could have been a bank robber or thief or murderer or fucking nutcase or whatever. But I didn't. I joined the Army.

But then later they said, 'Right, Doherty, we've reviewed your education qualifications and we've decided that we don't want you to go to the armoured regiment, the armoured side of the Life Guards.

You won't be going to Hong Kong or Singapore or any of these other places. We're actually going to post you to the Household Cavalry squad.' I said, 'Oh, that sounds interesting. Where's that?' I asked.

'They're in London.'

I said, 'Ah.'

'You're going to become a member of the Life Guards Squadron up there and you're going to do ceremonial duties for the next three years.'

That's exactly what happened. After that wonderful dream of learning to drive and going abroad, I wound up sitting on a fucking horse in London.

Second night in, down at training, outside London near Guildford in a place called Pirbright, we were put in this big room, twenty-four men in a room, all getting to know each other. Wear this, wear that, stand up, sit down, shit. Yes, shit. Go shit now, have a shave, have a wash, no time for yourself. This nice man, a squadron corporal major, he came in and his name was Swift. Big tall man, had the forage cap, the britches, the boots, the riding crop. He called us all into the NCOs' room in the middle of this spider of blocks down in Pirbright.

We were the newest there. He said sit down on the floor and he got out two packets of fags. He handed them around. He went round the room one by one asking the guys, 'Where are you from, son?' Son! He relaxed, he took his hat off, he undid his shirt a little, and he tried to get to know us – Baden-Powell, Boy Scouts, let's sing the happy glee song, and all that shit. Anyway, coupla stories went by and he come to me and said, 'Where are you from, boy?'

I said, 'I'm from Fulham, sir.'

'Oh, you're a Londoner are you? You're a know-all then.'

Straightaway I thought, fuck me! I said, 'I don't know about that, sir.'

He said, 'That's what I mean. You're a fucking know-all. You think you know you ain't.'

He tripped you up.

I was the only Londoner in the troop of twenty-four men. They all thought I knew everything but the reality was they knew far more than me. I lived in a space with a 2-foot-6-inch-wide bed, six foot long, with a locker, and in the next bed was a fellow from Newcastle, a Geordie, who used to wake up in the morning at reveille, and I'd look round and he'd go, 'How you gannin'?' And I used to think, what the fuck's he talking about?

Once you'd passed out of the riding school you became what they called the Mounted Dutymen – one of the chaps, no longer one of the recruits who got the shit kicked out of them every night. It was like going back to the time of the Charge of the Light Brigade. Behind the facade of Wellington Barracks we went back two hundred years. Blokes walked around in riding boots with britches and spurs, caps and whips. Everyone wore a uniform in there. You saw a guy with civvies and he was an officer visiting the place or somebody in on leave, but during the day you never saw anybody in civvies. For me it was like being on a movie set. I thought I'd gone to a different world. All of a sudden from being a hunch-shouldered mod living in London, to this. You had a uniform for this, you had a uniform for that, you carried this, you saluted this way, you turned right that way. It was a completely different world.

At Pirbright you weren't that close to officers, you didn't get to see their uniforms and all the rest of it. Now all of a sudden you saw these San Browne belts all highly polished, one or two service ribbons, you saw the crowns and the epaulettes on their uniforms and the real gold braid on their peaked caps. Their beautiful ironed shirts and there's us dirty poor bastards scrubbing to get an iron together. They had batmen to look after them, orderlies to serve them their food and grooms to groom their horses, which I became in the end. I myself became a groom. But it really was Victorian, Edwardian times.

I spent the three years doing ceremonial duties, out on watering order with the horses early in the morning, going through the old Covent Garden, the old fruit and veg market. We'd ride through there in the morning and the men would stick carrots in the horses' mouths. They'd stop and talk and all that. I didn't have a clue about it, I was a Fulham boy. All of a sudden up there at half past six in the morning sitting on a great big fucking eighteen-hand horse and leading another one. Blokes looking up at me and saying back to them, 'All right, boys.' These big tough bastards who have been out loading lorries since two or three in the morning. Rough buggers and they respected me. Whether they like it or not, a lot of Irish people in this country still got an inferiority complex because they were always getting the shit kicked out of them, whether it was verbally or physically. Fortunately that's changed. Now Irish people are the flavour of the month ever since *Riverdance*. Prior to that it was 'no blacks, no dogs, no Irish' in London. My mom and dad – certainly my mom felt there was some animosity towards the fact she was Irish. All of a sudden it was like we were rated, we were reckoned, and all of a sudden I'm riding a horse. I'm not riding a dog, not riding a pushbike. I'm riding a great big bastard that will kick the shit out of you and eat you for dinner.

Our base in those days was Wellington Barracks opposite Buckingham Palace. Knightsbridge Barracks was the original cavalry barracks. It had been flattened and rebuilt but wasn't completed until 1970. I joined in 1967 so what they did was move our regiment – the Life Guards and the Blues and Royals, the other side of the Household Cavalry – to Wellington Barracks. They built a riding school on the actual barracks parade ground itself, just in front of the Guards Chapel and we lived in the barrack blocks above the beautiful Regency facade, columns and all the rest of it. Nice from the outside, but when I was there the place had been condemned for eighty years. You couldn't light a fire because all the flues had collapsed inside and it would cost too much money to fix them. So we survived the winter wrapped in fucking blankets, drinking tea from the cookhouse, and sleeping with a blanket over our faces because the rats would come out and bite the shit out of us. This is in the centre of London across the road from Buckingham Palace – the lap of luxury in this country.

Here is the Queen's personal bodyguard, sovereign escort, in helmets and horses and swords and silver cuirasses and boots worth a fortune. When you got on top of a horse you were worth the National Debt. But at night you were sleeping in this fucking old iron bed with a dodgy old mattress and a blanket over your face so you wouldn't get bitten by the rats.

There was an awful lot of men in London in those days that quite liked guardsmen. All these wealthy men wanted the attention of these young troopers, these young soldiers, these guardsmen in their red jackets and plumes and bearskins. I thought, 'This is an odd sort of carrying on.' You've got to remember this was before they legalized homosexuality. In 1970 it was legal between consenting adults; prior to that it wasn't. It fucking definitely wasn't in the Army. I knew nothing. I thought homosexuality was a sexy word. I didn't know what it meant. But then I also thought prawn cocktail was something you drank. My brother told me once, 'I had a prawn cocktail.' I thought, how can you fucking drink prawns? That's how ignorant we were.

The more I got into becoming a regular trooper in the Life Guards, the more I got to know about what they called the Old Sweats, the blokes who had been about a bit longer. You started to learn a bit about what they called 'tyking'. A tyke was a man who paid for your company. Like a guy pays for a woman – they were called tykes. What would happen was something like this. A good pal of mine was on £6 a week. He had to support a wife. He used to go with a barrister to Lincoln's Inn Fields, a real swanky part of London. They would cover themselves in oil or grease and they did Greco-Roman wrestling. My mate always had to lose, with the barrister kneeling on his shoulders with an erection. This is what I was told. For that my mate got twenty quid. When you're getting £6 a week and someone's spending an hour a week wrestling around on the carpet with a barrister, you got to say what the fuck's going on here, it's going a bit odd.

London does strange things to a soldier.

*

The first time I came down the Mall? Fantastic. I hadn't fought a battle, I hadn't fired a round in anger at anybody. But it was a great feeling. It's the Queen's official birthday. Everyone's there to cheer her on, say lovely, happy birthday, all the rest of it. You're one of eleven men riding down the Mall and the whole world is looking at you. You daren't look left or right. I could see the Queen. In those days she used to ride. She would ride round the troops, the footguards, and go back to the saluting position. We would ride past her and we would see her up close and personal with all her medals and sashes on and all the rest of it. There were no smiles, obviously, she didn't say 'Hello boys.' But then she would ride back and be immensely proud of her troops because we'd just trooped the colour for her and although it's gone on the same every year, every year's exciting.

When it's all over and the Queen's left the parade ground, the sovereign's escort, which is the Household Cavalry, rides out. One division rides in front, one division rides behind. In front of that division are the massed bands of the brigaded guards, five regiments of guards. There's five bands playing and they're marching and they're playing their music. In those days both sides of the Mall was absolutely thronging. You couldn't get a razor blade between the people down the whole length of the Mall. People were shouting, waving flags, and you're riding down the Mall behind the Queen and you've got your sword, your horse, your helmet. Unbelievable. You're a movie star.

It's diabolically hot. The leather skullcap used to shrink. As it got hotter you had to keep shaking your head, otherwise it grips so tight blokes pass out, blokes faint. And then it was over, you'd done it, you'd achieved, you'd done the Trooping of the Colour. You'd really made it. I suppose it's like an Olympian standing on the podium. Even if it's a bronze it didn't matter. The flags went up, people cheered and waved, and you rode down that Mall. It was a fabulous, fabulous feeling.

BRUCE SMITH

On Big Ben

I've always been drawn to London. Always. Why is that? Was it Ben Jonson, the playwright, who said, 'When a person's fed up with London, he's fed up with life'? I believe that, I really do. There's just something about London, it's addictive.

In the 1980s I was living in Hertfordshire, in Potters Bar, and you didn't really get Class A drugs there. You would now, of course, but then I had to come to London to score my drugs. As soon as the crack of dawn, I wouldn't even clean my teeth, I'd get on the train to King's Cross. If I hadn't got the money, I'd borrow it from someone, beg, steal or borrow, whatever. It'd be commuter time and if I was high, great, it would be a lot easier. If you're sick and you're clucking, it's not a very good thing to do, to get amongst other people. But you find a way, so I'd get up to here, to King's Cross. It was a very good place to score drugs.

At the time, I was with this woman who was working as a graphic designer for a soft-porn publisher in Soho. Like me, she had a habit, she was using heroin. The area had this kind of like Bohemian feel about it. There'd be pubs where there would be artists and poets and these guys hanging round and they'd be basically getting out of their heads, not on booze, but on Class As. I loved it.

In Charing Cross Road there was a notorious chemist that was used just for one thing: to buy your syringes and get your prescription drugs. There'd be all the usual things in there which chemists would sell: soaps and what have you, but nobody entered there for anything other than prescription drugs or syringes. So you go to this chemist. You score. You get your syringe. What do you want to find next? If you were lucky you'd find a McDonald's, but you'd go to the public toilet, so you'd go to Piccadilly Circus toilet and you can bet no one went there for the purpose of relieving themselves. They'd go in there to fix. I remember the first time I went in there, I think I was about 26, 27, and it was just people standing around fixing. There were junkies who'd been at it for years, maybe 50, 60 years old, and their veins would all be worn down. So they'd be fixing up in their groin right in front of you. Today, if I walked into a toilet I'd be appalled by it, but then it was like, wow. Look at this guy having a hit there in front of me, quite openly. To an addict, it's as welcoming as a beautiful blonde woman in the party giving you the come-on.

No personal details, he says quickly. He drinks coffee in King's Cross. Occasionally he plays with the zipper on his fleece.

I didn't think I had a problem, but there I was shooting up all different kinds of stuff – whatever you'd put in front of me really. The denial was so strong, I'd be looking at some old guy shooting up into his jugular or in his groin, you know, and I'd be thinking, I'm young, I don't hang around here much, I just get the drugs and go back to my girlfriend's office in Soho. We'd have a hit in the comfort of this office and I'd think, mmm, I haven't got a problem because here I am in an office, got a beautiful girlfriend. You know, I'm kind of working.

I finally quit in 1989. Early in my rehabiliation I was offered a flat in Russell Square. It was a first-stage treatment place for recovering addicts. I stayed there for eighteen months and then they said, you've completed the course, you've been a good boy, you've stayed clean, we're going to give you a council flat, social housing. And I said, fantastic, where's it going to be? Expecting somewhere like, I don't know, Mayfair or Clerkenwell, somewhere nice. You'll never guess where they said: King's Cross. They gave me a flat in a street which was full of really sleazy hotels, junkies and drug dealers.

I'd wake up in the morning and the first thing I'd see would be a deal going on, or there might be a prostitute going about her business in the middle of the square. It was quite common to turn a corner and there might be a hooker there giving a blow job to a punter. It was that bad. Or you'd be stepping over a junkie. I've done some pretty desperate things, but one day I saw this street addict bend down and fill his works with water from the gutter. I don't know if he was cleaning his works out or using that water to shoot up with, but either way that's pretty bad. That was right outside where I was living, and I thought, my god, I'm so pleased I quit taking when I did, because we call that a 'yet' in recovery – it's something we haven't done, but it's out there waiting for you if you continue.

In all these years, I didn't spend a great deal of my time with my head up. I'd just see a lot of London's pavements. It's like that old song by Glen Campbell, 'Rhinestone Cowboy'. I knew every dirty rotten crack in the sidewalk, you know what I mean? I knew where they led to. You're oblivious to buildings around you, really. If they served a purpose in as much as that building had something to give you, maybe you might take an interest in it, but I'd be oblivious to like, I don't know, anything like aesthetic, anything beautiful. I'll give you an example: Big Ben. Wonderful big clock, but I never gave it a second look.

In recovery I found myself living in Brazil for four years. I was teaching English as a second language and some of the most common questions you'd get are, so, you're from London, have you ever seen the Queen? Have you seen Buckingham Palace? What's Big Ben look like? They ask you these kinds of questions. There was a student who was studying architecture and he used to talk about Big Ben to me. He'd say, Big Ben's a beautiful clock, isn't it? And I'd say, is it? I don't really know. I've never really looked at it. It wasn't until I came back home four years later. I was driving round Big Ben, I had my sunroof open, I had my wife and kids in there, and I looked at Big Ben and it was as if I'd looked at it and seen it for the first time. I thought, fucking hell, he's right, it's a beautiful clock. And it's the first time I'd really actually seen it. A big phallic building, four wonderful clockfaces, you know, gold, shining, all lit up and I thought, how comes I never saw this before? The reason is because I spent a great deal of my time with my chin on the ground.

When I lived in Brazil I used to think, my god, I've got to get back to London soon. I'm missing it and I'd come back here and I'd find myself walking round the streets and seeing things I took for granted before, like Big Ben, knowing it was there, but not really being aware of its presence. The difference is I'd come back from Brazil and I'd be looking at Big Ben and it would be as if I'm touching it and I'd be looking at it and I'd be counting how many dials it's got on there. Maybe it's something in me, I don't know.

There's so many addicts out there who won't quit taking drugs because they believe there's no hope. Big Ben is like a symbol of hope to me. Every time I see it, it represents some kind of hope to me. It's like a spirit, an embodiment of my recovery.

PHILIP AND ANN WILSON

On the Tower of London

PHILIP: To become a yeoman warder, you must have served twenty-two years in the armed forces, have reached the rank of staff sergeant or above, and have been given an exemplary recommendation. I am at the Tower of London to entertain and inform; and, when my day is over, I don't have to go far to see my wife: we live in the Tower. We've got a village green, a doctor living beside us and plenty of neighbours. But no one believes we actually live there. 'What's it like?' 'Have you got electricity?' We hear all of that. And try ordering a pizza. We share the staircase to our flat with the public, but it's very private up here. Our grandchildren think we live in a castle. In some ways we do.

ANN: It is a bit strange coming through the Tower with shopping bags. We've heard about the ghosts. I'm not so interested in history, but it's seeped in over the years. People ask about the Tower and I somehow know all the answers. I couldn't think of a more unusual place for us to be. We've even had murder mystery parties here. It's been an interesting journey that's brought us here. When I first met him, there were these three army men in a pub. Two of them were very tall – most men serving in the Guards were, back then. I thought, 'Well, as long as I don't get the short one in the middle with the ginger hair.' I did. We were married five months later. I made the right choice. We've always had good banter, since we were first married and he was stationed in Berlin. We still chat when he gets in. His yeoman uniforms do take over the house. The full one has tights and knickerbockers. He's a bit of a clothes horse, too. He likes his bow ties. He's got more cufflinks than I've got earrings. But I get a cup of tea in bed every morning before he leaves to guard the Tower.

TIM TURNER

On 'Londin'

People sometimes ask me, 'Oh, so where are you from?' I say, 'Oh, I'm from Londin.' They can't hear it when you say it but it's not the same place. It's a subtle difference but it's very important to understand it, especially if you're not from here, especially if you're just passing through. It's a different word. It's like when you move here you're introduced to this charming, attractive person, well versed in history and up to date with all the music, and you decide to meet up, but when you get to the pub their really odd twin sibling is sitting there instead. You can see the similarity but you just think, wait a minute …

What is my life like in the city of Londin? I get on the Tube at Elephant and Castle. I get off the Tube at Bank and go to work. The next day I get on the Tube at Elephant and Castle. I get off the Tube at Bank and go to work. The next day I get on the Tube at Elephant and Castle. I get off the Tube at Bank and go to work. The next day

I get on the Tube at Elephant and Castle. I get off the Tube at Bank and go to work. I don't think I know what an elephant is any more, I can't really summon a mental image of an elephant. I hear that word and I just start walking towards work.

I'm hated. I work in finance. I wear a collection of terrible ties. My work is constant. If I describe it in any detail I will literally have to fall asleep, I will just have to put my head down on the table and sleep and hopefully dream of another kind of job, a job where I never once have to say the word 'mortgage'.

I'm not living in a London of big pleasures and tourism and Russian billionaires and Saatchi Galleries and the London Eye, but Londin. I guess it's a cross between London and Londis, really. You're not exactly at Waitrose, you're not even at Sainsbury's, you're not even at Tesco. It's a bit shit in Londin, but there are little pleasures, like walking very quickly and listening to my headphones; like the taste of that ready-made pasta they sell at M&S, with chunks of feta the size of miniature golfballs; or like the big southbound platform at Angel station. There's so much room on that one platform. I was there the other day and I thought to myself: why did they make this platform so ridiculously big? It's wonderful. It was like I was on holiday in Londin. You could run up and down it, ride an animal up and down the platform. Ride an elephant. Elephant! Watch, I'll start walking to work. I've said the word: *elephant*.

I had a friend who used to live in South London but she moved back to Huddersfield a couple of years ago. She called me the other night and told me she'd joined a choir. I said to her: a what? She said: a choir. It was like a word beamed in from another galaxy. Why would she be in a choir when she could spend that time working? How would 'singing in a choir' even work? Why would she even think of stepping away from her desk? I suppose I could join a choir if they held their rehearsals in the aisle of M&S where they keep their takeaway pasta meals. I could just swing by during dinner time for about three minutes before going back my desk and then sit there and hum, but otherwise ... I suppose there are choirs in London.

Maybe one day they'll start one in Londin. The Londin Men's Choir.

Then I had this image of me trying to sneak off to a choir rehearsal or something, something in London, sneaking towards London from Londin, and just about getting past this enormous sleeping beast, just like tiptoeing past. But then the Elephant awakes. And then the Castle awakes beside it – tag team! – and the two of them block my way. You can see it, can't you? With his trunk, like, swinging down. I don't know what the castle would do. Can castles be aggressive? I guess they can when you play chess.

I'm going to move to London some day. When I'm rich and have finally cashed out and don't have to ever, ever, ever again say that I work for a bank. I'm going to cut all my work ties into little pieces and throw them in the Thames and then I'm going to take all this money I've earned, all the money people think I've earned while selling my soul, and I'm going to move from Londin to London. I'm going to go up to Elephant and Castle for the last time and get on the Bakerloo Line and travel north. I'm going to go to Westminster Abbey and the London Eye and when I'm in one of those pods going up to look at the city, some tourist from Munich or Idaho will say to me: oh, is this your first time in London? And I'll be all like, yep. And you know what? London is everything I expected it to be.

He is called away to a table surrounded by men in suits, covered in empties. He nearly forgets the tie he's left coiled by the salt shaker and the menu. He's left behind a small stack of pound coins and an empty glass.

EARNING ONE'S KEEP

RUBY KING

Plumber

I came to London to go to dancing school. It was the early Eighties
and I was the first black girl at my college. And I came to London
deciding I was gonna be a huge star. I remember walking down
Oxford Street going, 'I'm going to be a star. Excuse me: I'm going to
be a star. I'm gonna be … Excuse me: I've arrived.' [*Laughs.*]

But the funny thing is, after the first week I was on the phone
crying to my mother going, 'I hate it, everybody's horrible.' Because
I couldn't cook! Couldn't cook, didn't know how to do anything.
When I lived at home, I used to cook for my family, and do Sunday
roast, and do all of that kind of stuff, I'm the youngest of six. And I
came to London and I had to do *everything* myself. I lived on roast
chicken and roast potatoes, that's all I could do, because you could
put it on one plate and put it in the oven and hope for the best. So
after a week I'm [*sobbing voice*]: 'Please let me come home …' and
it was like, 'No. No. This is what you wanted, you wanted to go to
dancing school' – because I'd gotten in to dancing school – 'and stay.'
And she said, 'Try and stay until half-term. If you don't like it after
half-term, then you can come home.' So I stayed up until half-term
and I came home, and I was like, 'Yeah, I need to go back.' And she
was right. I never went home since.

I've been singing and performing for twenty-odd years. I'm never
the romantic lead, I'm always the fat funny girl. In *Fame*, I played
Mabel Washington. In *Carmen Jones*, I played Frankie. So it's always
the character roles, and I love those roles. I did a film, years ago, called

Knights and Emeralds and I played the rubbish baton-twirler girl. It was an all-black marching band and I was the one who couldn't do it. And then I did a film called *The Tall Guy* with Jeff Goldblum.

I have done my stint of being a slave. You know? I've done my spear-carrying. I did *Porgy and Bess* and it felt *good* … because we were all black and we were all there together. But to be a slave.… I'm getting a *little* too old for that shit. So I said to my agent, 'I don't want to be a slave any more. Because it'll just make me really unhappy, and I'm done with, "Yessir" [*Deep South accent*].' Didn't wanna do it.

So after I finished *Porgy and Bess*, I was like, what do I do? Do I do plastering? Shall I be an airline pilot? Ah. … No! I didn't get far on that one. I just thought I'd look great in epaulettes! Trolley dolly? I thought, nah … I'm not that patient with the tea. And dealing with shirty, horrible people? I do that anyway. Then I found this plumbing course and it really suited what I needed.

There's no female plumbers. There's absolutely no female plumbers. When we talk about it, everybody wants a female plumber. I would prefer to have a woman stumping through my house than a guy stumping through my house.

Every job is different. I never know whether people are going to accept me, I'm always mindful of … you know, they open the door and I see it in their eyes: 'Errr …' I think I'm quite an open, quite an easy person. But if you don't know me, all you see is a black woman with dreadlocks, you know, me in overalls with a headscarf and my locks sticking out. And for some people, that's threatening. But I was like, 'I'm gonna turn up at their house, full-slap, with a really sexy outfit on.' Gonna be like: 'Ommp!' [*Laughs.*] And hook up with lovely bored housewives. Lots of housewives and neither are they lovely or bored. Probably bored but not interested in me! [*Laughs.*]

Everywhere I go, I think, I wonder how their plumbing is in the kitchen … And I look to see what the plumbing is. Then I figure out whether I could have done it neater and hidden those pipes a little bit better, because the whole idea of plumbing is that it's available, it's there, but you can't see it. And it needs to be neat, and clean, and tidy. That's why I think women are better plumbers than men.

With old houses, you've got the old lead pipes. It's a nightmare to cut lead pipe, because you have to hacksaw it. You can't just use your pipe-cutter. So you're trying to hacksaw away at that and then connect lead pipe to copper pipe, and it's really difficult. I hate it. But I've always loved lead pipes, and I just think, I wonder how long ago that was put up? It was in Victorian times when they started doing all the pipe work and you think, wow, what must it have been like without the sewers? It does intrigue me, but when you get into a house, all I'm thinking about is they want me in and out as soon as possible. I need to see what the problem is, I need to assess it and I need to get on with it, so you don't have the opportunity to sit and think about it, all you're doing is problem-solving. And you need to problem-solve.

I prefer to work with other people but I've got used to being on my own. I take my radio, listen to Radio 7. Which also surprises people because I say, 'Do you mind if I put my radio on?' and they go, 'What are you going to put on?', thinking, you know: high energy [*she makes noise of pumping music*]. And I go [*posh voice*], 'Radio 7, it's got great plays.' And they go, 'Oh, okay.'

I find it easier to concentrate when I've got something talking at me. And then they don't have to listen to me breathing. When I first started I caught myself in the mirror jumping up and down going, 'Fuck it!' And then there are times where I just say, 'Calm down. You need to calm down here,' but I'll just say it quietly: 'You need to calm down, Ruby. You're not going to get the job done if you don't calm down.' And then I calm down, and then the job's done, and then I go, 'Well done, Ruby! Good job!' I did a job a couple of weeks ago and I had to do brickwork outside cos somebody had sledge-hammered ... Terrible, terrible botched job. Polish workers had done a runner from this job, didn't complete it. They put bits of pipe together that were broken. And when it was leaking they just covered it with cement, hoping that would solve the problem. And of course it didn't. So I had to go and fix it, put it back together again. And I had to do the brickwork and I'm like, 'Never done brickwork, I'm a plumber!' And so I pulled it apart, put it back together again, and it was one of the best jobs I've ever done and I'm like, 'Yeah, good job, good job.' The woman had gone out and I was like, 'I can do it, I can do it.'

I do like my plumbing, I love it actually. And I love the fact that when people used to ask what I do, and I'd say 'I'm a singer,' they'd go, 'Oh, wow, that's amazing, that's amazing!' And now, when I say I'm a plumber, people still go, 'Oh, wow, that's amazing, that's amazing!'

KAMRAN SHEIKH

Currency trader

He is tall, maybe 6 ft 3 in., and his eyes are large, magnified, watery. We meet in a cafe near his office, not far from Bank station. The commuters walk swiftly past, umbrellas under their arms. 'The Fire of London', he says, 'started in Pudding Lane, which is two minutes' walk from here. That's where the baker was and what happened? Fire.'

I'm a technical analyst of emerging markets. Most people understand technical analysts as IT-related but in this particular field it's more trend analysis and the price-section analysis of markets. I look at price and I cover Eastern European countries, and also Brazil and Mexico. Basically it's a little bit of everything. I have got five screens in front of me, three at face level and two on top. I have two PCs. One PC has three screens so I can open multiple windows because there are multiple programs running. I can open them with different screens and watch the live prices coming in.

On one screen I have a list of all the instruments I watch. I do about 20–25 financial instruments, which are a mixture of bonds, currencies and stock-market indices. I monitor not only those but also slightly non-related markets that I like to watch. I'm not covering the American stock market but I like to see its direction because it affects emerging markets. Although my role is mostly Eastern Europe I like to see the yen, dollar, euro. Everything else is fine but I like currencies. I think the currency market is a very active market. London is the world centre of currency, I don't know the exact figure but it's something like ... it's in trillions of currency traded every day. It's huge.

I feel a part of that trade. Being a small part of something really big, it makes me quite happy. Every big bank in the world has an office in London, every financial institution has an office in London, and in London time they trade very actively, those currencies. London time is key. London is key. So it's all active. The other items like government bonds and other instruments are quite dull but the currency market is active and there's volume and there's something always happening.

If it was a human being, government markets would be a very old, ugly woman. On the other hand the currency market would be a very attractive blonde. Stock markets are something in between – more deep. I would see the stock market as a thinker, an intellectual person, so you can go inside the mind and there are sectors and sub-sectors that can be divided. Everywhere there is something happening within one market. When I say the currency market is an attractive blonde I mean that she can hurt you badly. She is very flirtatious and unfaithful. She can make you feel great, take you to heaven, and make you really hurt as well.

I was born in Pakistan but I spent most of my childhood, up to 13, 14, in Libya and other Middle Eastern countries in the middle of the Sahara. We were literally in the middle of the Sahara because my father was a geologist and he was working on water projects that would help build irrigation in really rural areas.

My father was at work, my mother was at home. My schooling started quite late so I was kind of just alone. That formed my personality in a certain way. I also had some trouble with my health, some eye problems. I had retinal detachment – I have a genetic reason for that, Marfan Syndrome, which makes me tall and causes eye problems. I lost one eye because of retinal detachment. They did surgery but they couldn't fix it. And then I had retinal detachment again in the other eye, but they operated and it was saved.

We lived for a long time in the middle of nowhere, in such a basic town there was no sewage system. Inside the house the toilet was fine, but it went outside our main door to a hole in the ground, which was obviously covered. Once every week or two weeks a tanker would come to suck everything away. That used to be the most exciting thing for me – to see the tanker coming.

Outside the town there was nothing, just sand and desert plants, so it was very depressing. I didn't see rain. I don't remember seeing rain even once in those ten years. That's what everyone complains about in London, especially English people who were born here. But I love walking in the rain, it has a beauty no one notices. It has freshness, it brings freshness. The air gets clean – it's fresh, it's life. The desert is closer to death. This is life because rain falls, grass grows. This is something people don't appreciate.

When we moved back to Pakistan my father was getting involved in the stock market and I was quite attached to my father. I used to discuss with him what happened in the market, how it happened, all these things. Those days there was no Internet so he used to go to the local stock exchange in Lahore which had trading hours of ten to two or three o'clock. The trading took place in the Karachi stock exchange, but he used to go to the broker's office who had a screen with the rates and everything. Again, very basic. Each day he'd come home and tell me what happened.

This was my first exposure to the markets. I started to write prices down. I selected 100–200 companies and every day after school or college I used to spend an hour or two and I used to make a big register. I made columns and I used to write the price every day. I wanted to know how prices moved. Then I thought it might be a good idea to plot it on a chart so I bought graph paper and started putting it there. I just got into it. That was my hobby and passion.

Until 1999 I worked in Pakistan. I was working in a brokerage firm that was based in Pakistan but was doing business abroad in America. The problem was this business was not regulated in Pakistan so more firms started to pop up, take money and then disappear – a lot of frauds and those sorts of things. I really wanted to make a career in this field. So in '99 I moved to the UK.

Before coming here I sent letters to about 100 companies, writing about what I have been doing in the last five years and what I want to do and that I want to make a career here and what are my chances, what are my prospects. I got about sixteen or seventeen replies. Some people said you'll have no problem finding a job here. Some people said a one-eyed person is better off in the kingdom of the blind, stay there and do what you can.

I had the feeling I would get what I wanted. After I came here it was completely different. Here nobody cares what experience you bring from Pakistan or anywhere in the world. Nobody gave a damn. So I found a job at a fried chicken restaurant in South London, near Sutton. Chicken was a job that was much harder than I expected. It doesn't look as tough when you go in to buy chicken. Working there was not good. Everything gets dirty, the smell of the chicken is everywhere, the customers are nasty, and everything is greasy. The back area, you have to clean it. After working there you don't want to eat there any more. The bus ride home was terrible. It was really, really depressing. I was tired, frustrated, desperately wanting a change. This is what I experienced in the first few years. Loneliness, while living with 7–8 million people but still being so lonely, not having friends. And what would I eat? Fried chicken. I would take something from the restaurant.

I didn't forget that other part of my life. During all my jobs, in factories and chicken restaurants, one mistake I made was that I always told people what I wanted to do, what I had been doing, what

I planned to do in London and that caused me a lot of trouble. In Pakistan, we have a big respect for educated people, so if you tell somebody you're educated, people will respect you even if you're doing a tough job. I had this same expectation here. Each time I was working in a fried chicken restaurant or a factory or anywhere I shared this – I always said where I was going when I had an interview. I told them this is what I plan to do, this is my background, this is my main profession, my passion. This is what I had been doing in financial markets, I'm doing some exams and improving my qualifications, I'm looking for a job in this field. After that they got really nasty towards me.

I was living in Morden, the last stop on the Northern Line. Mostly I lived in rented rooms in a shared flat. One place was with two guys, one a teacher in a college and the other a Nigerian working for ExxonMobil. It was just basically nothing – we used to see each other if we ran into each other while waiting for the toilet or in the kitchen. Everybody was in their room.

I joined the Society of Technical Analysts of the UK. They hold a monthly meeting for about 150 people and they invite a speaker, a prominent analyst, who speaks about the market or techniques. So I started coming to those meetings. That was an opportunity for me for a change, working at the chicken restaurant or the photo shop I worked at after. To dress up nicely, to put on a suit and tie and come sit with people, London people, completely different from where I was. They were mostly white English, I think I was the only Asian there. It so much increased my confidence, just putting on a better outfit and talking with professionals working in the City. For a while I feel that I'm a part of this different world, and I listen to the lecture. But after the lecture the painful part starts.

Afterward there is a gathering where people socialize with each other, networking, and I thought it might get me some contacts with people and help find me a job. I'd say I was not working as an analyst at the moment but I was looking and I had a history of four or five years in this field. They would ask me where I had worked and when I would say in Pakistan, then they were not too interested. It was extraordinary for them that someone from there would be doing those sorts of things. But one guy was interested, he even introduced me to his boss, who was the speaker. He asked me, what is your main area of interest? I said I'm most interested in currencies, dollar and yen exchange is my favourite. He smiled. He started talking about it but I was not in touch with the market, I didn't know what was happening. So I started thinking, who am I? Do I belong here? What am I doing here? It was depressing, and when it finished I used to walk the streets. I didn't want to go home. Where was I going? Back to Morden. After a year or so I stopped coming because I realized it gives me less pleasure and more depression and disappointment.

A cousin in Morden told me, are you living in a fool's paradise or what? Put your mind on what you are doing. Even if you are sweeping floors, put so much effort and dedication into it you can grow from there, and one day you might have a cleaning company. You can always excel in what you are doing. But I felt that you can't find success until you have an aptitude for what you are doing.

I kept applying, and when I found out about this job I was living in East Sheen, working in a pawnbroker and cheque-cashing place. This was a huge feeling of insecurity. I had three interviews with five different people, and finally when they confirmed the job it was the happiest day of my life. I was a technical analyst – junior. Sorry, I was a trainee. But I was very happy, very very happy. What they offered me was a lot lower than what I was expecting. Because they knew during the interviews what they were getting, although I tried to present very differently. The HR person was very clever. She got an idea of my circumstances, how desperate I was, so they offered a lot less. When they told me I was definitely happy. There was the moment they said I could negotiate. I could have got a lot better but I was so afraid of negotiating. I just asked for a little, little more and then said, it's fine, fine, don't worry.

I was so happy. I was not believing it. It was after so many years – the confidence had decreased so much that even after one month on the job I didn't resign from the pawnbroker. At first I told them I have to go to Pakistan because my father is sick so I'll be gone for two weeks. Because I was thinking it can't happen, it can't be, it's too good to be true. It was just a false thing. It will not happen. My father's sickness was the best excuse I was able to come up with. And then after two weeks I came back and said I was sick.

I don't know. Those years had really damaged my thinking and approach and made me so insecure. After one month I thought, now, that time has passed and I still have a job, I'm still here and it seems like it will continue. I finally resigned from the pawnshop. They had been calling me all the time telling me come back, what is wrong?

I remember my first day going into the City, I woke up in East Sheen and put on my suit. I took the train from Mortlake Station to Waterloo, changed to the Waterloo and City Line and came to Bank. The office is on King William Street, across from Bank station. I went to reception, signed in, told them I was starting work there. I came upstairs, saw the receptionist at my floor, sat there and after a few minutes my boss came and he took me to the place I was supposed to be.

He introduced me to everybody in that section. It was so overwhelming, so much confusion, so much pressure. People were joking and talking as they welcomed a new colleague. I was trying to interact with them but I was so nervous. I had so much anxiety. I don't know, I just … I was under so much pressure I don't remember that first day.

I sat at a colleague's desk who was away on holiday. The IT department had to set up my desk and computer. It was so good. I had a nice big desk, so many screens in front, two keyboards, a mouse – too good to be true. I had started a new life, doing what I really love: so many digits flashing on so many screens. I like the feeling of seeing them. A live market has a feeling of life to it: each time a number flashes in front of me a deal has taken place, and usually the minimum number is $1 million. They are constantly flashing. And they are flashing in London because we are the centre.

RUTH FORDHAM

Manicurist

We are standing in a drizzle out on Farringdon Road near her shop. She smokes a cigarette as buses roar past and black cabs splash the puddles. A police officer stands looking stern at the bottom of Ludgate. She has just finished her 1.30 appointment. At the end of the session the woman thanked her, spread her hands wide and admired her nails. Although she spent her first twenty years in Germany, she has adopted an East London accent. 'When I try to speak in a German accent now,' she says, 'I just sound confused.'

I'd just come out of a really messy marriage, getting divorced, and I mean, when I left my ex-husband I left him, literally: two suitcases, three binbags of clothes, a sunbed – obviously a girl has to look good – and a Dell 500 DOS5 computer. I was like, yes, I can conquer the world. I knew that I wanted to run my own business and I've done nails before, mobile work and sitting in the car, living in Essex, driving twenty-five miles just to do one manicure for £7. I was chasing my tail. So to me, actually being in the city and all of a sudden people coming to me meant (a) no more travelling time, and (b) money. We were just coming out of one small recession so people had got fed up with having nothing. It was like women going, I'm going to treat myself. So, you know, I got in at the right level. I got in before the Chinese took over with their little, you want this, you want that? All for £20. And I think it was that freedom. Yes, I've got a job. I'm actually self-employed. It's unsure so I have to be on the ball and I had no option. I had to make it work. And it was all about that, and the adrenalin kicked in.

My first day at work was January 1994 and I got off at Blackfriars Tube station and I walked and there's a little short cut there, before they put all these big buildings up and as you walk up the stairs you see St Paul's. My tummy went over and I just went, yes. I've arrived. I just knew. This is where I want to be.

Very green, as in naive, you know. Ah, there's lots of mistakes you can make. Taking a booking with no deposit is one and then people not turning up. That was a lesson quickly learnt. Another lesson is don't believe everything people tell you. You've got a set of nails on and someone says, I was sitting by the settee and they fell off. Hello? What do you mean, they fell off? You know, I was looking down, they was on the floor. Wow! You got spooks! But in those days it was my confidence that got knocked because I thought, I'm not good enough. You're obviously challenging my work and then within a few weeks you sort of realize that it had absolutely nothing to do with that. It was people wanting something for free. They've gone out and done the gardening. They'd gone out and done loads and loads of different things, and then blamed my workmanship.

I mean, I'm just a nail technician, what do I know? And then every year it got easier because every year I learned a little bit more and I just made sure that I went on every course that was available. If there was something to learn, I learnt it. If there was something to change, I changed it. Because I just thought, I'm going to make a difference, but no one's going to take the mickey either. And so far it's worked.

I've got clients I've seen for the last fifteen or sixteen years, so to me a lot of it hasn't changed, but I suppose it must have changed. Because it's gone from doing nails for ladies that lunch or the ones that were in that financial bracket who could afford it, to actually now secretaries have it.

I've got Germans, Dutch, South Africans, Americans, pole dancers, table top dancers, lap dancers, a lot of Romanians, Latvians, Eastern Europeans. I've even got some English people come in the odd night. I deal with anyone. Crossdressers, you name it. They usually come in when it gets dark. You know, it's like visiting a brothel in some ways. They walk up the street, look both sides and then come in. It's brilliant. Barristers, the legal side of things. Misguided solicitors, obviously. She should be a bloody karaoke singer, her. A record comes on and we start doing nails, the next thing we're both singing away and it gets louder and louder and louder. It's quite embarrassing really. Yeah, just deal with everybody really. There's no boundaries where nails are concerned.

They all have different temperaments, completely different personalities. South Africans, you either get really laid-back South Africans or you get really uptight South Africans. You either get the ones with attitude or the ones who are absolutely brilliant and great fun – lots of humour – or the other extreme is the ones that, you know, as you're doing something they're watching you and then they'll pull their hand away and you're like, I've only filed one nail. We're only one-tenth of the way there – give me a chance, you know? Or you get the ones where you've finished and they've got to check, you know. I think it's a power thing, just to let me know. That's the South Africans, the ones that have had maids and the ones that have had a privileged upbringing, all of a sudden they're paying for a service, therefore you become the service girl.

It's a bit like a psychologist. I'm sure people shout at him and tell him he doesn't know what he's doing. He just thinks to himself, do you know what, for two quid a minute, you can think what you like because at the end of the day you're a pound note walking out the doors.

Then you've got the Dutch. They're a bit harder going. Trying to get a smile out of them requires a bit more effort and you have to really balance between humour and sarcasm, there's this really really thin line and you sort of say something and go, oh shit, I shouldn't have said that. I say, I'm so sorry, I'm hormonal, and just carry on.

And Americans, the more west they go, the more laid-back they are. Then you get the New Yorkers who try to be chilled, but oh god, you're trying to do someone's nails and they've got a BlackBerry and then they've got an iPhone and a mobile phone and you just go, right, you've got three phones, one pair of hands, I'm going to have one hand at the time, how are you going to deal with those three now? And then all of sudden the phone rings and they go, do you mind if I take this? Oh, not at all, you go ahead. So I just sit back and back away and they speak. Then they say, I hope you didn't mind? No, that's all right. If we run over, I'll just charge you a little bit extra, that's all right isn't it? All of a sudden the phones get all put in the bag. Works every time.

Eastern Europeans, they've got a hard time, or feel they've got a hard time being accepted, so they are trying very hard to integrate. That comes across as a real effort. It's really hard to explain unless you're sitting in front of someone who desperately wants to belong somewhere and is not quite sure. Half of them don't even want to be here, you know, they got sent by companies abroad and like, oh yeah, London, great, and when they get here, they could be at the top of their game and they'll say, I'm Latvian. Bloody immigrant. Could be an immigrant with a BA honours degree or something and it's people's prejudice that then makes them behave differently because all of a sudden they feel they have to defend their nationality or the reason why they're here. No one should need an excuse why they're here. They're here because they want to be here or work sent them. You know, you should never have to make apologies why you're somewhere.

And then you've got all the English. I love them. Oh god, I love them. Well, they're just really strange people. They're trying very hard not to be uptight and they take themselves very seriously, and they get stressed very easy. The Italians – ah god, the Italians! They're in a rush all the time. And it's like they've got this phrase, 'I've just come for a quick manicure, how long will it take? Half an hour. I'll just have a quick one.' Right. Let me reinvent time then. So we have a standard thirty minutes and then a quick thirty minutes.

The recession was awful. Goldman Sachs announced, just after Christmas 2008, the redundancy of 600 people. To me, when I've got a client base of about 300, right, when you've got 150 coming from Goldman Sachs your client base goes down to 150, that's 50 per cent of your business wiped out within the redundancy period, so you know it's coming. So you're sitting there and you're going, right, these people are going to leave now. What am I going to do? I need to recruit … I have to go and find a replacement. And it was horrible. It was horrible. What did I do? Revamped my website. Made sure the key words were right and I just kept thinking to myself, right, okay, no one's recruiting. Job agencies are not doing anything, so I know what we'll do, we are going to just survive and I believe in positive thinking. I believe if you greet a smile with a smile, you get a smile back. If you greet a frown with a frown, you're going to get someone either give you a bollocking or frowning back. So I can't sell services if I'm down in the dumps because the people just go, I ain't going to see her, I'm depressed enough as I am. I want someone to not entertain me but I want someone to actually take the pressure.

As people were looking for different jobs they weren't feeling too good about themselves, so then they thought I haven't got much money. I haven't got this, I haven't got a holiday. I know, I'm just going to get my nails done. So all of a sudden a different group of clientele. People that actually live in the city, like Smithfield. Covent Garden, you've got a great big council estate and people on social security have more expendable income than anyone else. Trust me. They have got more money available than anyone else, so anyone saying never open up a nail bar on a council estate is absolutely wrong. You keep your prices low and you actually, if you want to be like a churning-out-morer, you just get in there and do that. But, you know, it sort of changed and people said, okay, I can't have this, I can't have that. I know, I'll go and have my nails done. I'm going to go for a sunbed. I'll have a facial. I'm going to have a relaxing time at home by taking away the £300, whatever it cost me, to get there. They were using their spending money here without having to spend the flight money.

London has been a trading city since 94 AD or 92 AD. You had the Druids. You've got the Thames is a river that brings things in and it's almost like if you live near a canal, if you live near a river, if it's got a port it brings people in. It's the first stop for immigration. It's the first stop for migration. People coming in, going out. And it's a bit like you'll never see Trafalgar Square without a pigeon, no matter how hard the Lord Mayor tries. They're going to be there. You're not going to stop London. You're not going to stop the flow. The essence of London is trading.

It's almost like I know where Shakespeare got his inspiration from. He watched Londoners and his plays reflect the times of what was going on. Like Othello, you know, the Moor? At the end of the day, this man is an immigrant. And now it's immigrants coming in, immigrants going out. I just can't understand the word 'minority'. I'm German and no one's going to build me a school. [*She laughs.*] It ain't gonna happen. So I might as well just get used to it.

When I first came to England, Petticoat Lane was Jewish. Petticoat Lane had Jewish tailors, it had Jewish merchants. Everyone was Jewish. We had the Indians, but they have now decided they've made enough money, and they've moved out to the nicer bits. Now we've got Eastern Europeans coming in and selling their toot and it is toot. You literally just go, that's crap. You look at a pair of trousers and you just go, that leg's longer than that leg. Who was this modelled on? Heather Mills? Without the leg? Honestly. Who was the model for these trousers? A three-legged octopus or something? Because that's just not going to fit, sorry. And then the sizing. Oh, it's European sizing. Hello – I'm from Europe and if that is a size 10 then I'm size 0. No way. It's just great. It cracks me up.

And people say, oh, it's cosmopolitan. It's such a crap word – 'cosmopolitan'. What is it? It's a magazine, as far as I'm concerned. Go back to old-fashioneds, it's all nationalities. It's global. It's not just cosmopolitan, you know, where it's just one city or a few cities thrown together – it's global.

MARY FORDE

Publican

The Schweppes lemonade is going flat slowly, bubble by bubble, in a pub in Kilburn. There is a smoke-stained Irish flag hanging limply behind the bar. The orange strip looks yellow, the white strip looks yellow, the green strip … yellow. There is Polish music coming from the CD player behind the bar; a double CD set, 50 Irish Rebel Anthems, *sits on top of the stereo. There are two sides to the pub, two entrances, two bars.*

I was doing office work and I was just fed up with it. Same thing every day, and one year was the same as the next. I'd done a bit of bar work in the years gone by, and I just thought I'd take a chance on a nice little pub.

When we opened I was such a nervous wreck I could hardly sleep. My sister and brother-in-law were a great help the first two weeks even though they'd never done any bar work before. And the barman was staying for three months, so at least I had somebody I could ask if I didn't know something. Somehow I got through the first six months, and I began to think the next six would be a little bit easier. And that's how it's worked out, really.

You need to have a good sense of humour to run a pub in London. And you need to be able to keep calm in whatever situation. You know, yobs and all that, and trying to deal with the youngsters who swipe phones and stuff like that. You just don't know what people get up to, honestly. And when people get drunk, you have to ask them to leave nicely and not get all uppity. That's what I always say to the staff: anybody out of order, deal with them pleasantly and they'll go along with you 99 per cent of the time. If you just shout 'Get out,' that's when they get upset. Come back tomorrow, come back next week, whatever, you know, when you sober up again. Otherwise there'll be rows and stuff. There used to be an awful lot of that in pubs years back, but touch wood, from when I came here we've never had anything like that.

This bar here has mostly Irish and English, and they get on really well together. They call this side the English bar and that the Irish one. I reckon all the English, years back, used to drink in this side and all the Irish used to drink over the other side. But now you get both drinking on both sides. There's a little space we cross over there to go to the other side, they say we need to see your passport; passport control they call this. Oh, there are some people who drink only on the one side, they'll only cross it to go to the toilet. Some of the boys, they go over there to the toilet but maybe they'll stop outside the door to talk to somebody and someone will say, you're on the wrong side, you haven't shown your passport. They have a red card over there and sometimes they show you the red card, get back on your own side. It's very funny, they have a good craic over that. It's all a bit of fun.

LOVING ONE ANOTHER

ALINA IQBAL

A love story

When I was younger there were certain things I wasn't allowed to do. In the early Eighties, for example, I really wanted a miniskirt but I wasn't allowed to wear one. It was because my father thought that it was not modest and it wasn't fitting with our culture. Or I wanted to do ballet lessons, but because within Pakistani Muslim culture dancing is associated with prostitution, I wasn't allowed to. These things matter when you're a kid.

As my sister and I got older and approached adolescence, my dad became more obsessed with policing what we were doing. When I was 12 years old, I was coming home from school and my dad picked me up in the car. He was furious and I didn't know why. It turned out he'd read my diary, and in my diary I'd written that I had a crush on a boy at the bus stop. That resulted in my dad not letting me leave my room, apart from to go to school, until I was 18 years old. So I spent my entire teenage years in my bedroom or going to school. I wasn't allowed to go out with friends or have any semblance of a normal life.

It is not uncommon for Asian girls to be policed in that way. Rationally you may think, this is ridiculous, I should stand up to this – but you internalize these feelings of responsibility. There's an Islamic concept of honour called *izaat*, which means you cannot bring shame to your family. The consequence of you doing something wrong is that your entire family or your tribe is shamed. It sounds ludicrous to other people, but that notion is so internalized from such a young age that it's very hard to flip that.

I went off the rails at university. My whole social life changed. I was in Manchester and it was the early Nineties, the tail end of the acid house club scene. I got involved in setting up illegal warehouse raves and everything that goes along with that. So I went from never going out and not leaving my room to setting up techno parties in warehouses, and I did that for probably three or four years. I had a crazy time. I was lucky to get my law degree. All I did was party for years, basically.

Once, while I was at university, my parents came to see me and said there was a possible match for me. I broke down in tears and actually my dad at that point told my mum to back off because I needed to finish university. My dad said no, we're not going to force her to meet anybody, let her finish her studies. So he did stand up for me.

When I was 23 I met the person I considered to be my first serious partner. I was beginning to settle down by that stage, and I was much more comfortable with myself. I met Ryan through friends. He was at art school in the same city, we became friends and ended up going out with each other and then we were inseparable and we both moved down to London together.

It was a great time. We were both in our early twenties. I had just started my career. I was doing a really, really tough job and had long hours. But I loved the work that I was doing, I'd moved into Brixton with my best friend, and we had a nice flat. Before long Ryan was spending all his time in my flat, and then we just casually decided to move in together and get our own place. When you're that young you don't really have bad experiences to make you nervous.

All that time my parents didn't know that I had a boyfriend and that it was a serious relationship. We thought we were going to be together for ever and we didn't really think about it until after he'd moved in. Then we realized there were all sorts of practical repercussions. I had to have a special ring tone on my home telephone in case my parents phoned, so he wouldn't pick up the phone. We often kept the curtains drawn because I used to be paranoid that my parents might suddenly come unannounced. The few times that my parents made planned visits we moved all of Ryan's stuff out of the house. He had to go round to a friend's house. Thankfully, he didn't have that much stuff. Or I'd have to lie and say it was my stuff, which was weird because my dad would ask why have you got a really top-spec video camera – Ryan was a video artist – and I'd have to lie and pretend that I'd just got into making films as a hobby. I had all these convoluted lies.

All the paraphernalia that you have in a relationship: photos of each other, notes we'd written to each other, all of that had to be put away. It was tough. I did it for seven years. To someone outside they'd think, that's crazy, how can you live like that? But you just get used to it and I've always had to live like that. I was essentially leading a double life.

I've become much more used to leading this life, but in those days even if we went on holiday I'd be really petrified in case my parents had found out somehow. A lot of the time I'd have anxiety attacks as I came into an airport. Oh god, my dad's going to be there. Because I had no idea how my father would react. I had no idea whether he'd be okay or whether he would disown me, which I thought was probably going to happen, or whether he would go as far as – I know this sounds ludicrous – hiring someone to come and find me and harm me. I don't think my dad would ever do that, I've just been affected by representations in the media about honour killing, which is actually very very rare. But definitely that fear was there.

Ryan's parents couldn't understand it. His mother would get drunk and then say to me, 'It's because you don't think your parents will think my son is good enough for you.' She couldn't understand that had nothing to do with it. I just couldn't reconcile being with the person I loved and also not tearing my family apart. Also, because I'm the eldest child there's a particular responsibility. If I'd done something to bring dishonour to the family, it would have brought dishonour to my brother and my sister. I was worried that if I rebelled and told my parents then they would come down even harder on my sister and force her to marry someone, so I thought the best thing would be not to tell them.

The funny thing is, my sister's recently got engaged to a non-Muslim guy, and after a lot of heartache my parents have accepted it. So she's maybe started a precedent.

In my twenties my parents set up a match with somebody and it was disastrous. I was secretly living with Ryan, and you can imagine how awful it was for him to watch me go back home to meet somebody my parents wanted me to marry. At that point Ryan proposed to me because he just didn't want us to be in this situation. But I thought at 25 I was too young. I didn't want to get married yet. So I went back home and I had to meet this man. Oh, it was awful.

Firstly what I did was deliberately dress myself down and make myself look much worse than I would do normally. I didn't do my hair for days and days. I wanted to make myself look as physically unattractive as I possibly could. I wore this pink jumper that had baggy elbows and holes in it and a really unflattering pair of black trousers and an old pair of spectacle frames that made me look really geeky. My brother helped me. He said, 'Yeah, you can make yourself look even worse.' So he made me look really bad. Then this family arrived; when you have an Asian match you meet the entire family, not just the man that you're being matched with.

My mum made a faux pas as soon as the family arrived. There was a younger man and there was an older man who looked much older, balding and with middle-aged spread. Naturally my mum assumed it was the younger boy that I was being set up with. She said, oh, it's very good to meet you. Then the family said, no, it's this one, the older one with the middle-aged spread. My mum just looked horrified. I couldn't believe it had just gone from bad to worse. This guy had no social skills whatsoever. He was still living with his parents in his late thirties and I'd had this whole other life. I could not really settle with anyone like that.

The final nail in the coffin came when the family started talking about work. They were a really traditional and religious family. The father of this man said, 'Well, clearly after they get married, Alina will have to give up her job to keep house.' My dad was furious. He said, 'I haven't put my daughter through university for all these years for her to give up her job to become a housewife.' So my dad again, unusually, stuck up for me and forced them to leave straightaway.

Since then they haven't mentioned a match again. And my relationship with Ryan ended. It went on for ages and then the strain ended up … you know, we split up for lots of reasons. We split up because the relationship ran its course and we were young when we got together. But one of the factors was the strain of having to live a double life.

My parents occasionally make mutterings but I'm 38 now and they realize that it's unlikely I'm going to find someone through the traditional arranged way. So it's become less of an issue now.

They don't think I've been romantically involved with anybody. They really do believe that. They just think I've been immersed in my job and that I don't want to be with anyone or I've been too fussy, and I think as far as they're concerned I probably will end up being on my own and not having a family. Actually I think probably my mother would hate that and my mother's changed a lot over the last few years. She doesn't care who I end up with. She just wants me to be with somebody and to be happy.

My father, I think, would much rather see me be on my own than to find out that I want to be with somebody who's non-Muslim. As far as he's concerned that would be two of his daughters marrying out and he'd have no more standing in the community. He says a lot of people don't talk to him any more because he's seen to be irreligious. He feels like he's lost face in the community. It matters more to him what strangers think than what makes his children happy. That's hard to defend and makes me respect him a little bit less.

It helps to live in London. It would be horrible to be in a smaller environment. For me, London's very anonymous. No one looks at you twice if you're a mixed-race couple, whereas if I leave London I get stared at all the time.

Whenever I think that it's been tough for me, I realize it could be much tougher, actually. It's very hard for some girls who are in London who live in smaller communities. I've done a lot of work in London with the Bangladeshi community and it's difficult for young girls there to negotiate any kind of life of their own because the community's all around them. Class and education make a massive difference in terms of how you can negotiate these things. But what's striking is that with all the opportunity I've had, I'm still leading a double life, and I'm a bit older than these girls. So you can imagine for girls who aren't in my position it's going to be ten times worse really.

It's almost as though it's incompatible to be British, Asian, Muslim, a girl and to be in a mixed-race relationship. As though the narrative is always that it ends in tragedy. But it's not like that. Lots of us negotiate our relationships. They have to be very carefully managed but what we're trying to do is negotiate our way to a situation where we can have both. Where we can have our family and have the partner we choose to be with. I still think that's possible for me. I really hope it is.

I have a new partner now, and we're about to move in together. It feels exciting. We met and fell in love here in London. That makes a difference. I feel a sense of freedom here. I'm away from prying eyes and am allowed to get on with my life without any interference. All sorts of people with all sorts of stories find themselves in this city. I am able to show my partner some of the best aspects of my Pakistani culture like the food and the films and the music. He can share in the things that have shaped me. Things feel different now, I think it's because I'm older. I can imagine going home and just telling my parents, look, I've found a guy. He's not Muslim, but he's decent and he's good and we've got a lot in common. I mean, I don't want them to find out but if they do, it's not the end of the world. But it's at times like that I get cross, because it's a choice that many people don't have to make. If you're an Asian boy you wouldn't have any of this happen to you at all. It wouldn't even be commented on. It's just if you're a girl that you're expected to behave in certain ways. It feels horribly unfair. It *is* horribly unfair.

I don't want to lose my family. If it comes to that, it would be a hard choice – but I'd choose being with my partner. I feel like I'm getting on a bit now and I deserve to have a bit of happiness in my life.

PETER DAVEY AND MILAN SELJ

A couple who met on Parliament Hill

MILAN: London can be a horrible place if you're alone. I came here twelve years ago and started with a small company, so I didn't meet anyone through work. But then I took a walk and there he was.

PETER: It was 3.30 p.m., August 14, ten years ago on Parliament Hill. I was walking the dog when I saw him in the distance. I made eye contact and smiled.

MILAN: After the smile, I was so gobsmacked I said hello. He was just wearing a pair of shorts, no shirt.

PETER: We both walked on, stopped, looked back, then walked towards each other.

MILAN: Some people meet their prince on a horse. Mine came with a dog.

MISTRESS ABSOLUTE

Dominatrix

A new, unopened electric toothbrush sits on the windowsill of her office, not far from Vauxhall station. Handbills pinned to a nearby board advertise monthly slogans for her club night: 'The Hunt for Pink October'; 'The Darling Butts of May'. She is wearing boots, jeans, a black top and red fingernails, and as she sips her tea she leaves small half-moons of red lipstick on her white mug.

I wasn't happy. I thought, I've got my three-bedroom house, I've got my corporate job, I've got my boyfriend with two cats – and if this is all there is I might as well top myself now. I knew there was another side of me lurking somewhere that wasn't being looked after, *fed* is I guess the best way of putting it. I studied people from a very early age. My earliest drama teacher used to make me sit on park benches and watch people, which I used to love doing because then you look at how they walk and it's actually stood me in very good stead for what I do now, being a professional dominatrix – because when people come in you have to size them up pretty quickly. You have to listen to what they say and read two or three layers into it and you have to – if they're bound, gagged and in a body bag you have to look at the twitch of their eye and figure out if they're in ecstasy or whether they just really want to get out.

Everybody has a sub and a dom side. Once I was going to do a public humiliation session. I'd got the guy's phone number and everything. I'd turned up at Bond Street Tube station, where we agreed to meet and we were going to do some public humiliation out in Selfridges area. He would be on his knees while I'm shopping, which is always quite fun. And I'm waiting at the Tube station. I phoned him and he's not picking up his phone. I'm thinking he's not going to turn up, he's not going to turn up. Great, I've just got myself here. He's chickened out. And then this guy comes over and says, 'I'm really sorry, have you been waiting long?'

I said, 'Yes I have. Get down on your knees and kiss my boots.'

He got down on his knees and kissed my boots and got back up and said, 'Right, where are we going then?'

I said, 'As you know we're going to do some shopping and then I'm going to have a cup of tea and you're going to be sent on some errands.'

'When are we going back to yours?'

'You know there's none of that happening today.' But then I started to wonder … So I said, 'How much deposit did you pay me?'

And he went, '£50.'

I said, 'You're not the person I'm supposed to be meeting.'

And he said, 'No.'

But he'd come over to me, spoken to me, and got down on his knees when I told him to and kissed my boots in the middle of Bond Street Tube station. And he didn't even know what a dominatrix was.

London is one of the kinkier cities in the world. I don't know why. It has more fetish clubs, more mistresses, the biggest fetish clubs. The difference in different countries is amazing. The Germans are really into rubber. They arrive early and leave early. I know it's a gross generalization but it's true and it's so funny. The Dutch – I stage-manage an event out in Amsterdam – there's lots of big buff men and they arrive and they all take their clothes off and fuck and go home. The French are all really rude. They're just disrespectful. They'll come up and grab you. '*Maitresse!*' Get your hands off me. They all think they're Gérard Depardieu. The Americans – if you go to LA most of the mistresses in LA want to be in films, really. A lot of the mistresses in San Francisco are very leather-bound. They have a lot of societies there. It's quite regimented – ethical leather. The Czechs make good doms. A lot of them do cross over into the sex side of things. They come here to make money and they'll just make it. They don't have the same British reserve, not that the British girls have that much reserve either, actually. There is a different mindset behind it. Then you've got the Japanese doms, the Oriental doms. That is a whole other culture in itself, you've got the Japanese girls and manga culture. Each country is different, it's very tribe-like.

The British are very fortunate to have so much going on. There's just so much to choose from: you can go to a school event, a body modification goth club, a straight play club, a small club, a munch. A munch – I hate the name for it – is for people who are into fetish, you go and meet up and have something to eat and you just talk about your kink and that sort of thing.

London is big enough so that you can keep a bit of anonymity but it's small enough that you can go to a club and see people you know. In London, I can go to the Oxo Tower in rubber for lunch, as I did on my thirtieth birthday – a rubber pencil skirt, a rubber blouse, a rubber corset and high boots. You can go and do that and some people might bat a bit of an eyelid. Being a Londoner, nothing is going to faze you. There's a complete mix of people here so if you see something weird and outrageous, well … it's just London.

If London were a person it'd be Mr Ben. Do you know Mr Ben? There were only thirteen made when I was a child. Mr Ben would go into a fancy-dress shop and the owner would give him an outfit to try on and he would become whatever outfit he put on. He would put on a space outfit and go on a space adventure and give the outfit back at the end. You can reinvent yourself in London. You can be who you want to be, which is why Mr Ben came to mind, because it's that ability to change. Put something on and it will change you. I'm going to wear this and I'll become a different person.

Each experience, each street has different stories, different chapters.

Different areas have different feelings. I'm much more comfortable in South London than I am in North. That's just me personally. I've always lived in South London. There's one dungeon in North London which evokes a lot of happy times. It's closed down now. It's actually near where I have my nails done. Everytime I go up and have my nails done I think, oh, I must … oh, it's not there any more. Different pockets of London have different feels to them. That's not something you can verbalize, it's just a feeling. I'm sure the feeling I get will be slightly different from someone else's. But then you wouldn't have the specific good memories of whipping someone's ass in Kentish Town.

JAY HUGHES

Nurse

This kind of work is as far removed from the kind of nursing that I was trained to do as you could possibly get. It's far closer to working in a bar than being a nurse. Being a nurse on a ward, it's all very task-orientated. You have to do this, then you do this and your day's pretty much mapped out from start to finish. With what I do, somebody opens the doors and let's see what comes cartwheeling through.

I think the first thing you realize and it happens pretty quickly is that sex is a great leveller. Regardless of class and culture, sex is kind of sex, no matter who you are. Pretty much everybody does it and I've seen people from the age of 14 to people in their eighties. Coming to the clinic is getting more normal, which is great. I mean this is what we work for. Women are always much better at it anyway. But I think that's because girls grow up knowing that they're going to have to get their breasts examined. They know they're going to have to get their smear tests. They're realistic about it. Men in general will wait until there's an absolutely calamity before they do their first visit and then when there's a serious danger of something falling off, that's when they'll come and see you.

What they want is the magic bullet, you know, the tablet they can have the day after this unfortunate thing has happened that's going to make all the problems go away and it's not really the antibiotic they need. Mostly what they need is something that's going to erase their memory and you can't fix that. Working in the City that's pretty much most of what I see, especially during Christmas party season.

Well, you know, you've been to a Christmas party, I'm sure. This is where it all happens. This is where 'ooh, I've accidentally had sex with the secretary' happens. So much insanity goes on at Christmas parties. People who have been taken to lap-dancing clubs because it's what everyone in the office was doing, you know, and are convinced they've caught HIV because they've touched a pole somebody was rubbing against. It's tough. Physically there's absolutely nothing wrong, but physical problems you can deal with really quickly. That's okay. The psychological stuff is what takes the time.

From early December until the tail end of January it is absolutely insane where almost every man that comes in will tell you an almost identical story. It's really quite amusing. It's the office party. People go out and get absolutely bollocksed and have inappropriate sex with each other. I've had people in the past come and see me in absolute hysterics because this has happened to them and they were working for the police. They were vice squad and they've managed to have sex with somebody inappropriate at the Christmas party and thought it was funny. Well, not funny – ironic. As I said, sex is a great leveller. Everybody makes exactly the same mistakes no matter how old and how wise you are, in London you're always just that one beer away from inappropriate sex.

The Christmas party stuff kind of tails off January time. February bimbles along, it's a bit too cold, but after Valentine's Day you will see lots of people coming in for emergency contraception. You know, the morning-after pill. Lots of that. Around the same time you do get the odd person who's discovered they're pregnant after the Christmas and New Year shenanigans. And then, you know, March, April, May we just kind of tick along, nothing really sensational happens during that time of year. You get people coming in because they've just got random problems. But then the summer months, it's all sort of fallout from the summer holidays; everybody's been off to Ibiza and shagged the entire island, been shagged by the entire island. And then there's the Pride festivals and music festivals. Then again it tails off a wee bit before it all starts building up to Christmas.

You get quiet people that really don't go out all year and they just go absolutely crazy at these Christmas parties because they don't really drink all that much and then all of a sudden they're confronted with this vast amount of free alcohol and just completely lose their total identity and have absolutely no idea what's happened to them. If there was no alcohol in this city I probably wouldn't have a job.

GETTING ON WITH IT

NIKKY, LINDSAY AND DANIELLE

Students

It's raining outside a school in South London. A police officer speaks to parents at the school gates as the children drift out in packs. The screens on their phones start to glow. Phones of all sizes are returning to life. Rucksacks, fingerless gloves, hair clips holding down the unruly hair. Black kids in groups, white kids in groups. The drama room has a reassuring familiarity with its black curtains, lighting booth and the stacks of chairs. This afternoon the room is set out for a debate. Two pairs of chairs at the front, rows of chairs for the other competitors from other schools and a table that holds packs of cheese and onion crisps and plastic containers of Fruit Shoots. As a few of the students enter and eye me suspiciously, a little aggressively, I ask them what they think a Londoner, or anyone coming from somewhere else to live here, needs to know to live in the city.

NIKKY: Learn how to read the Tube map. Definite.

DANIELLE: That is a good one. Actually there's a lot of things. I want them to be clever. Like, if they come to London they'd probably be scared of London because of all the media things they hear. You hear like, you come to London, you're gonna get stabbed. If you see a black person on the street, if he's got his hood up, you've got to be running and that. Whereas because we live here we know how it actually is, so we're not scared and we're not wary all the time. Obviously it's good to be wary sometimes, because anything can happen at any point in time, but we're not majorly scared. I'm only scared that if somebody lives

123

outside London and comes in, they're not going to be streetwise. They're going to think everything's magical out there, like you can run around and everything's fine and that, but it won't be. I think it's important to be streetwise.

LINDSAY: How to cross the road, basically, properly. It's so busy and you see how many people get run over and killed, it's just simple things. Like, don't worry about learning how to do algebra; learn how to cross the road because you're going to need that more than you're going to need algebra in life.

NIKKY: Keep your valuables to yourself and be aware. Yeah, London does teach you to be aware of things.

DANIELLE: Don't stare at people. If you see something that's a little bit out of the ordinary, most people's first reaction is to stare at it and that. Don't stare.

LINDSAY: I know why my mum said, don't stare, when I was like 4. Now I know why.

DANIELLE: If there's a big gang, right, normally you turn just to have a look at them and see what they're doing and that. But because we live here, we know it's best not to give them eye contact so there's a reason for them to say something. We don't have to be scared and put our heads well down and walk past them scared, we can still continue our conversation with whoever we're with – just don't stare.

PAULO PIMENTEL

Grief counsellor

When I started doing this work, all I could think of was the Harrods IRA bombing in 1983. I must have been about 16, I still didn't have my driving licence. It was a Saturday and my sister was a Saturday girl in the men's department of Harrods, and my dad came to wake me up because I'd been clubbing the night before or something – I was a bit of a rebel. I said, where's mum? He said, she's gone down to Oxford Street. I switched on the news and they said there's been a bombing in the men's department at Harrods and then I thought, I'd better get down there. I tried to call the department, there's no answer, and so I drove my dad's Mini like a lunatic, without a driving licence, down Park Lane. We lived in Marylebone, and I was listening to the radio and they said there's a suspected bomb in Oxford Street. And I thought, bloody hell – my mother and my sister on the same day.

Of course Harrods had evacuated and I didn't know where they would evacuate to. I couldn't get down into the Knightsbridge bit so I went round the back and I saw these people in this warehouse and I thought, maybe they evacuated there. I went in and there was my sister standing there. She was in terrible shock. I said, you're coming home with me, got her into the car, went home and then had to find mum. There's a bomb going off in Oxford Street and we can't find mum and of course we didn't have mobile phones so there's no way of getting in touch with each other. But before we could leave, my mother turns up at home. I said, there was a bomb scare. She said, oh, was there? You know, completely oblivious to it all. The four of us sat down to dinner that night really quite happy that we were the four of us together. We thanked our lucky stars.

Later, when I started doing this work, my sister told me that she had seen a man's head being blown off, and she'd been living with that for an awful long time with no support, nothing.

That day with Harrods affected me for a long time. It's one of the reasons I took on this work.

Not long after the 7/7 terrorist attacks, we set up the 7th July Assistance Centre. The phones just went ballistic, absolutely ballistic. It was like opening the floodgates, the helpline had to go 24-hour. It took about two or three weeks for us to adjust to it. Of the people involved in a trauma, only between 5 and 25 per cent actually develop PTSD – Post Traumatic Stress Disorder. Everybody else is okay to get on with things. But often they need somebody to talk to, somebody to scream at when they get angry, to talk with about all the guilt that they're feeling. They'd go into minute detail about the Underground, about the smell of blood, the smell of the dust, the smell of everything.

In fact it could have affected so many more people. It's alarming how, you know, it's *only* fifty-two people that died, when you think of the size of London and the size of those Underground trains – each one carries up to about 1,000 people. So it could have been much more horrific. But a lot more people were affected because their lives changed. Their lives changed totally.

Many of our bereaved clients were in between their fifties and eighties, a time when a lot of them had retired, led reasonably peaceful lives, and then suddenly they're hit by the loss of their son or daughter – it throws absolutely everything into disarray. Imagine if somebody went out to work, called last night or two days before, everything's hunky-dory and then all of a sudden you don't know where that person is. You know they're in London. You don't know where they are. You try to get in touch with the authorities. They can't tell you anything. You can't get hold of them on the mobile. Then all the mobile networks go down anyway, so you can't get hold of anyone. And then the networks are up again, you still can't find that person. You know … just that is a trauma in itself and then finding out that the person's actually died, their limbs are missing, all sorts of really grotesque stuff like that. What do you do?

The problem is to be able to cope with all that and do your day job and be a partner/mother/father at the same time, explain things to kids who have no idea. A lot of them do know unfortunately, but they shouldn't have. You know, why do people do this? Of course, it's for ever. They're going to die with it. And sometimes they'll need to talk about it. My concern is that there'll be days that are real shit for them, and just to know that you can pick up the phone, get somebody at the end of the line, to come in for one or two counselling sessions that may save their relationship, may save their employment, may save their relationship with friends, family, you know? Because also there will be these cutting remarks from people: oh god, you still think about that? And it hurts when you're suffering and when you've suffered so much, for somebody to just dismiss it like that.

I've spoken to a lot of people who said, I wish I'd died on that day because my life has changed so much and I'm not able to cope with it any more. People don't understand me any more. If I'd died they would have been able to get on with their lives without me. Which is really hard for people to say but it's the way they feel.

We've been through two world wars, we've been through IRA bombings and now we have this 7th July bombing and we can't cope any more – what the hell's going on? You know. Take the Madrid bombings in comparison to the London bombings. The 11 March 2004 bombings on the trains in Madrid caused a government to fall. Everybody saw that it was the fault of the government's foreign policy. It became very political and the bereaved and survivors became celebrities. Here, it didn't move the government. We just want to forget about it, forget it ever happened. You're supposed to get on with your life. You know, the stiff-upper-lip thing.

The truth is, the British have changed an awful lot. I come from a Latin culture, which is two hours' flying time away but a world away, and I tell you, the British have become much more in touch with their emotions in recent years. There never used to be any of this kissy kissy thing. Now everybody kisses each other – all over TV, men are kissing each other, women are kissing each other, everybody's kissing each other. We've gone completely the other way, which I think is really good. I remember when I started school here, my dad would drive me to the school and I'd say, don't kiss me outside the school, it's like horrendous. But in Portugal we kiss everybody.

The Sunday following the 7th July – 7 July 2005 was on a Thursday – on the Sunday there was a planned march through the Mall. People actually thought, is anybody going to turn up? But thousands of people did turn up, saying we will not be beaten. They will not win. It must have been a security and logistical nightmare for the police, but it was phenomenal.

You could be hit by a bus, you know, you could be in an accident. You could fall down the escalators at the Tube and crack your head open. All sorts of horrible things can happen to somebody, so do you stay at home and just wrap yourself up in cotton wool? The likelihood is that most of us will die from something else not terror-related and there may also be a certain sort of humour about it, you know, because we are living in London.

One day in the Haymarket there was a car with a bomb about to explode and I had walked past that car literally about two minutes beforehand, before the police came and took it away and dismantled the thing. I remember saying, 'How funny. Can you imagine, the project director is bombed to death in a terrorist attack? The *Mail* would have had a field day.' We just thought it was hilarious, and just then some people walk into the office. We're cracking up laughing and they say, is this the bereavement service? They expect us to be always sitting there in mourning. But it's completely the opposite, because if you didn't laugh your head off you'd be crying your head off.

LISTON WINGATE–DENYS

Personal trainer

I grew up in the East End, so most of my friends did a martial art, or boxing, or ju-jitsu. I used to live on a council estate, so most of the kids did something. [*He laughs.*] In our little area alone, we had seven world champions at something, at some stage. Wen chen kai, karate, judo – actually, it wasn't judo – ju-jitsu, a form of cage fighting which used to be done underground, back in those days, it's not all the glamorous stuff it is now. But mainly karate. Some of the people that lived in that area, they were destined to fight somewhere, and instead of doing it on the street, they took it somewhere else.

It was quite a strange place to live – lots of pockets of different types of people, so you had blacks, you had Irish, you had Chinese. My mum had come from St Lucia in the mid-Sixties, when Bow, Mile End and all that was a dumping ground for West Indian immigrants looking for work, either on the buses or in the hospital. It was a long, long journey to get back home, so a lot of the people who came from the islands just stayed here. Mum, her first job here, she was a cleaner, as most of them were. And then she was a machinist; she was very good at that. And then she worked for Tower Hamlets as a home help. Dad worked at Ford, as a sprayer.

I think growing up the son of immigrants in the East End put me in good stead for the rest of my life. Clearly you met all types of characters, from those that were really quiet to those that killed people. Do I miss there? No. But it taught me to understand how people work, how to not take people for granted, and also, don't believe their hype.

There are just so many problems on the streets now. It's not good. The backbone's going. Everything's too fast, everything's too expensive. And everything is, 'What have you got? That much? Oh this looks nice – where'd you get that from?' I'll give you an example: there's loads of people that live round here who might as well just live anywhere. It's a bit like going on an all-inclusive holiday – you turn up and you stay at this fantastic hotel, and people will look after you, and you're fed, you do all the massages and you do all of that, but you never go anywhere. Certainly *here*, in Notting Hill, there are a lot of people that live behind big old gates and they might as well live anywhere.

Around here no one cares. Everyone's all, 'There you go! Get yourself down to Portobello!' And you're down there any day of the week and you'll see four or five people you recognize from the TV or from a magazine. Nobody cares! Except if you come here and start giving it the whole 'I'm a cheese' and all of that. I expect no one's interested. You know, people come here, they got their sunglasses on, they come down here to train. It's like, 'What for, man?' 'There's so many paparazzi.' 'If you don't want the paps to take a shot, we've got a side entrance, just come through there! If you want me to pull these down, I'll pull them down.' It's not like anybody else is really that interested. [*He motions to the blinds that shade the free weights and benches of his gym, and the crosstrainer and the treadmills and Swiss balls.*]

I think that's where London's going wrong. I think everyone's started to believe their own hype. I'm just saying London in general and Notting Hill in general.

Well, you know, I have a guy that's up in the air three or four days a week. Three or four days *a week*. Now that's not good for you. You know I start work some days at 5.15 in the morning, cos someone's got to be in the office for seven. You know, these are the sort of changes. People *now* won't leave the office cos they're frightened they might lose their jobs. So instead of going, 'Look, I'm going to have a healthy heart and lifestyle so I can make sure that everyone that comes to work is healthy enough to go to work and people going to work can make the right decisions cos their minds are working.' Oh no – 'Cane them, get them in to work. Cane them; work twelve, thirteen, fourteen hours a day.' Why not have them working ten hours a day, but working properly.

The sad thing about it is that people now are actually getting used to it. They haven't got no choice. I see the effect of that on people's bodies. From not being able to sleep from rashes, old injuries coming back a lot quicker, breathing difficulties, anxiety, niggling stuff, they're never clear from any niggles – there's always something going on, there's always something that's not going right. People come in and they think they just need training. But actually, training's just a small part of it. What you really need is, you know, eight hours sleep, and to eat properly, maybe to do a little bit of meditation, or even to go and see a shrink.

I think London itself, whatever that is, I think there's a big old cog out there and it just drags you in. Staying healthy does help in the short term but it's a bit like, you come in, I realign you, we do gait assessment for your running. We strengthen your shoulders, we tell you not to sit like that, you do this, this, this and this. And you know what, for a week you're all right, but as soon as you start getting stressed your shoulders start going up, the alignment all comes out. So you're not a losing battle but you are sort of trapped. It's like a big old circle. You're not really fixing it, cos the only way you can really fix it is by taking them out from the job, putting them somewhere else, cos it's no good me fixing you and then the next day you're just back doing that. I think we all get trapped in London life.

SMARTIE

Londoner

Talk to Smartie, I'm told. Just talk to Smartie, he'll tell you about London. When I finally meet him, he bounds up to the station at Buckhurst Hill. He's short with short dark hair, energetic, up early for someone who's been driving a taxi around the city all night. You'd usually never get me up this early, he says. What is it, eleven? He inspects the day. He is wearing a special pair of shoes with Bjorn Borg's signature on the side, and he's already talking before we sit down at a table in the back of a Costa Coffee.

I was born in Islington in North London, but back then it was a poor area and my mum and dad wanted to get me out because they felt it was rough. So we moved into East London, to Leyton. I suppose my most vivid memories of childhood are being brought up in Leyton because there was lots of kids. The area then was built up with mostly Irish, Scottish, English and Italians, really, and a few West Indians. It was safe then to play on the streets and that's what we did and that's where, I suppose, I got my instinct to be streetwise. I was in a gang. We were on the streets. We never harmed anybody, but we would get up to mischief, we'd run around the streets, we'd do knock-down ginger, car alarms and we were fanatical about football. So many hours of the afternoons and the days were spent up playing football, idolizing George Best and copying what we saw in the World Cup.

In the 1970s, there wasn't any men's shops, it's not like today where you can go into Selfridges or Harvey Nichols and Harrods and buy designer clothes for men. Men then had to go to places like army surplus stores to buy clothes. There wasn't many designer boutiques. There'd be a few sort of individually run sports shops, and from that a lot of people my age have an obsession with trainers. I've got a collection of about fifty pairs of trainers, predominantly Adidas, all the trainers that we wore in the Seventies and Eighties – most of them I still wear. I mean the trainers I have on today have got Bjorn Borg's signature on them. They're approximately thirty years old. Everything that I've got on here is about thirty years old. This tracksuit's about twenty-five, thirty years old. Probably early Eighties. Back in the early Eighties this would have cost £125. That was serious money then and the retail now for something like this on eBay or in a vintage store, you'd be looking at probably £600–£800 for the tracksuit. So I have an obsession.

If we look at the late Seventies in London, there were still bombed-out warehouses from the Second World War. I remember travelling down the river at that time. Everything south of London Bridge, where Butler's Wharf is, round Tooley Street, where London Bridge Station is, that was all derelict. All around the South Bank was derelict. It looked like a bomb had hit it. They were derelict buildings and in them derelict buildings you'd get squatters, junkies, mostly heroin, because heroin was massive then. They would live in them type of buildings and it was a no-go zone. If you went over there you would probably get mugged or robbed or raped. It was like a city of delinquents, really.

There would be warehouses with big craters in them where the walls had fallen down, crumbling. If you were on a tourist boat going down there they wouldn't want to take you any further than bloody London Bridge. They didn't even want to go down to Tower Bridge. The area north of the river was built up with mostly horrible 1960s-type buildings, not very pretty to look at. But the other side was completely derelict. It was a depressing place. We wanted to strive for better.

You have to remember that England was still the poor man of Europe. We had decimalization, where the currency was put down. We had the Labour government that had brought us all the strikes and the Winter of Discontent and I think a lot of the turn came when we had the new government. The Conservative government of Margaret Thatcher, it was the start of a new era, an era of optimism really, I think, and that's where the change came. Because of Margaret Thatcher, even if you were from a working-class background or an Essex boy, you felt you could be somebody. I think that's really what drove a lot of people to become entrepreneurs, to have a go at business, to have the balls to do it. And from that, people wanted luxury a bit more. They wanted to wear some of these new fashions.

The fashion that became the fashion of London came from Liverpool. Liverpool were the most successful English football team that we had at that period and what was happening in the late Seventies and early Eighties, the fans were travelling to Europe to watch Liverpool in these European Cup – it would be called the Champions League now – matches. I think Liverpool won the European Cup three times, and its fans were basically stealing the clothes from shops in Europe: Sergio Tacchini, Fila, Adidas trainers. Adidas trainers you couldn't buy in this country, and this is where the obsession started. They were then bringing back the fashions and they were wearing them on the football terraces. Then other rival teams, say West Ham, would go to play Liverpool at Anfield. West

Ham had a lot of National Front following, they were very anti-black at that period, and they would turn up like skinheads. They would have MA1 green flying jackets, American flying jackets with the orange lining on, like sort of quilted puffa jackets. They would have red Harrington jackets on, which were skinhead jackets. If you wore a red Harrington you were seen as being National Front at that period. Their hair would be cut very short. They would wear Dr Martens lace-up boots up to here, very military, and super-tight orange tab Levis or maybe 501s, or tight Wrangler jeans.

When they came up to confront Liverpool and their hooligan element, they got there and what they were met with was a group of hooligans that were dressed like girls! They would be wearing flecked hair, would look like it had been blow-dried. Hair covering one of the eyes, like short hair with a step in the back so the hair was graduated. The casuals that they would have met on the terraces were dressed in sportswear, expensive sportswear. Jeans that were detailed, where they'd be frayed at the bottom, specially frayed, slit at the bottom so they parted over the shoe. Super-skintight, bleached Lois jeans, probably the most iconic jean from the era, worn with Adidas Samba trainers, which were black trainers with a big white bit round the front. You can still get them to this day. It's the biggest-selling Adidas trainer ever and that would be worn with either a Fila Terrinda tracksuit top or a Benetton rugby top. We followed some of the most iconic figures of this period. Bjorn Borg for style, Jimmy Connors wore Cerruti 1881 and of course the legendary John McEnroe. I mean most of us boys could relate to him because he was angry, he was confused and he just said what he thought.

The fans would be divided by the terracing, but you could clearly see what the others were wearing. And they'd never seen nothing like it. It blew them away. We want that! Don't they look cool. Because I think what it was, it was a form of modism really. It was a different form of modism where if you took a lot of these football supporters, they were probably mods beforehand so they always were into style. Fashion and style is very an English thing. Individualism, looking a part of a group, but a small group, keeping a secret, not advertising the fact you were wearing a style. You could tell somebody by what they were wearing. You could be sitting on the bus, over the other side of the bus, and I knew you were the same as me. But I wouldn't have to speak to you. Whereas now everybody looks the same. If I saw a man out there with Adidas trainers, he's just a man wearing Adidas trainers. It was different then. It was different because you had to be wearing those, you had to be a part of it to know about it, and this look went unnoticed by the powers that be for years. It was only really when *The Face* magazine did an article about football casuals in about 1983 that it became a phenomenon. It blew up. It went into the papers like the *Sun*, there's this underground look that's been brewing from say '78, '79, '80, all the way through, it took five years, this was underground and it was about labels.

Most people back when I was young would have bought their clothes from market stalls. You could be selling jeans on your stall, another man might be selling sportswear and you didn't have shops. When I say there was barely any men's shops, there was barely any men's shops. I remember driving my mum and dad mad wanting a Fred Perry polo shirt because they became the big thing and there wasn't no Fred Perry stores, you had to go to an army surplus store where you'd buy tents. An Army & Navy store they used to be called. I remember wanting Dr Martens, again, going to the Army & Navy store. As we moved from the late Seventies to the early Eighties they'd started a few little boutiques – saw the gap in the market. But these shops would have been run individually by individual people. They weren't the sort of mass stores you get now. They'd be somebody who probably thought, you know, there's a market for this. There's a need for this and, you know, I think there was a lot of continental style coming as we hit the Eighties too. Continental fashion was seen as luxurious.

Every community that's died in London, and I think this is a very important fact, has died because the market culture died. The markets were the hub. If you go to Shepherd's Bush now, they had a great street market there around Shepherd's Bush just off Goldhawk Road and once the market dies it kills real Londoners. It kills the real working-class element of London.

When I left school I left with no qualifications but it didn't mean I couldn't work in a bank because, you know what, I'd just make up the qualifications. It didn't matter because nobody checked. Do I believe I can do the job? Yes, I do believe I can do the job. I made up a CV, put as many qualifications down as I thought I'd need to get a job in a bank and off I went. I went into the insurance market, because it was all about common sense and most of these banks, even though they had graduates in the front offices, a lot of them had barrow boys because barrow boys were streetwise. They could add up very quickly because a lot of them played darts, dominoes, any games that made you add up. If you look at the trading floor where I worked, the futures market, most of the traders in the pit environment were barrow boys. They were people that came from market stalls who were rough and ready, edgy, who were streetwise, who could add numbers easily. So I went into the pit to sell an order of 100 lots for the clients – buy 20, buy 15, buy 6, I'm now down 41, buy 8, I'm now down 49, buy another 17, I've now done 66. 34 more to do on the order. They could add up quickly because a lot of them worked on market stalls and if you worked on the market stall you would take the money on a Saturday afternoon, well that's a fiver love, that's £6, that's £11, that's another £4. They were ideal to trade for these banks in the pit because they were aggressive. They weren't like somebody who went to Oxford or Cambridge or who were wrapped up in cotton wool, who were in a shell, who had never seen anybody, who had never met anyone rough, who had never met anyone black. The ones who had gone to a private school, they'd only mixed with people that were like themselves, they'd never seen, you know, people fighting or being beaten up for liking the wrong music. They weren't exposed to anything so they were in a shell. They weren't the ideal ones to be aggressive in these trading pits. So this is why a lot of these East End-type people went into the trading pit.

It's a place that people like us could work because we were fast, we were good with figures and we could release all our aggression. It was like the Manchester United or Chelsea of working in the City. I mean, if you're young you want to earn fast money. The two go hand in hand. So you ain't going to work as an accountant, are you? You want to go where the action is and this place had a thousand good-looking girls in it. There was 3,500 people in the life market under the age of 35. 2,500 men and 1,000 girls, so it was the place to work. Everyone wanted to work there. No one wanted to do anything else in the City.

The look would have been very City, but even then I was individual. All my suits were handmade. I used to get all my suits made by a tailor who used to make stuff for Paul Weller and The Jam, so all my suits were cut mod. He was a tailor in Leyton and when The Jam, before they were famous and they didn't have the money to use some of the high-class tailors of Savile Row, they used to go to this tailor to get their suits made. If you look at a lot of all the old LP covers of The Jam, especially Paul Weller who's such an icon, all those clothes were made by the tailor that I used to use.

I was meeting different people, mostly discreet Arabic customers and Russians. Anybody who had money, basically. I worked in a bank off Harley Street and they used to give me all these cheques to pay in at various bank accounts. They were probably laundering money. I was running envelopes and bank cheques all around London. I did that for approximately a year. It was great because I was always out around London, so what I used to do was just skive off. They used to give me the cheques to pay in but I used to just disappear to places like Berwick Street Market in Soho, which was a great street market, or I'd go to Camden Market to look at vintage or Kensington … I wouldn't come back. They'd say, take these cheques. We'll see you in the afternoon. So I'd do the banking in about an hour and then I'd have two or three hours to myself.

They couldn't contact me because there was no mobile phones, so I just used to disappear and come back in the afternoon after going to feed my addiction for knowledge. I just wanted to embrace and experience London in all its different forms. Being art, but mostly fashion and music. I used to just go to places to look at what people was wearing. To see what was going to be the next big thing. I would go to places which at the time people would think, that's a bit far out. Going to Camden in the early Eighties ... normal people who were from different boroughs in London, especially Essex, would think, Christ, that's way out. Them people are crazy up there. Where it's the norm now. Well, I'd go there to see what they'd be wearing. I'd see what I could take from that. You'd ape people, and you'd twist it the way you'd want to twist it. I still have things from that period hanging in my wardrobe. I don't wear them, but I can't bring myself to sell them.

It's all a part of finding your identity and it all stems back to young men, and young girls because there were soul girls too in the Seventies and Eighties, being in such a depressing place and wanting to find their own identity. I suppose you'd call it the urban decay of the 1970s, 1980s London, a city which was crumbling but had formed a root. It had got as far as it could crumble. The London of today is built on the core of that period. A film you could watch from that period is *The Long Good Friday*, about the IRA and the Docklands. It stars Bob Hoskins, he's a London gangster who wants to redevelop the Docklands. One of his men has a beef with the IRA, killed somebody who's Irish. Now if you watch that film, it's a fantastic film. It vividly shows you London in the late Seventies, early Eighties. It's all filmed along the Docklands. It shows you the burnt-out warehouses and his vision as a gangster, he wants to redevelop the Docklands. It tells you how bad it was here in London because it's nothing like how it is now. And you'll see all the Docklands in that period, all burnt-out, all derelict. Everything today is built on that.

PART II

CONTINUING YOUR JOURNEY

PETER REES

City Planning Officer, City of London

His office in the City of London is sparsely furnished. A magazine with an image of Chicago on the cover has been placed near his desk, isolated and aligned. He's dressed in a crisp white shirt.

People always say to me, 'What's London going to be like when it's finished?' I say, well, *dead* – a finished city is a dead city. The cities that come closest to being finished are places like Milton Keynes or Canberra or central Washington DC. They are the new, heavily planned, single-period cities, and they always have problems because they don't start out organic. A city like London, which is an amalgam of villages, which has just evolved, is much stronger because it can carry on evolving. Paris had no option but to build Île-de-France because they couldn't incorporate large modern buildings in central Paris, not high-rise ones, without ruining what was Paris, this planned Beaux Arts city. London is lucky in the sense it doesn't have that. We're lucky Christopher Wren wasn't allowed to replan the city after the Great Fire of 1666. If he had, it wouldn't be a world financial centre today because it would be like Paris, it would be fixed, composed, precious.

Sometimes that upsets me. I'm notorious for my tidying; friends who are visiting might move pictures to see if I notice, or open cupboards to see if they're just as tidy inside. It's very tempting to try to tidy a city. It would defeat me, of course, because the constraints and pressures are too great. When I see something that's not in the right place, something that's broken as I walk around the City, it does upset me. On the other hand, I have to tell myself that's evidence of the life and strength of the place. Things are being broken and brushed against and need to be changed.

It's difficult to see what one is doing as a very, very, very small part of a very long process and realize the impact you're having is very small in terms of the continuum of the life of the place, but a place is (a) so much more important, and (b) so much stronger than any individual, or committee or organization can be. Planning cannot create excellence in terms of building and design. We are in a position where we can sometimes make mediocrity out of awfulness – and across London, the planning system sees an awful lot of awfulness.

The problem with planning is that it teaches you to ask questions and it's much easier to come up with new questions than it is to actually come up with definitive answers, and the more you interrogate the question the less likely it is there is going to be a definitive answer, which is why I come back to saying I don't think we should be planning London, we should be managing it. Because planning does require you to come to a definitive answer, have a definitive course of action and then to implement something, whereas managing means watching it on a day-by-day basis and just nudging it and helping it. It's like being responsible for 4,000 years of history but only 2,000 have happened so far.

I always wanted to come here. I come from Swansea, which was described by Dylan Thomas as an 'ugly, lovely town'. But I'm not an outsider, I am one of the indigenous people – my Celtic forebears camped here in London on the banks of the river Walbrook, the Walbrook stream, roughly where the Mansion House is now, over two thousand years ago. We were overwhelmed by waves of immigrants, the Romans, the English and various others that have swept through. It's the amalgam of those layers of tribes that have come in and claimed citizenship of London that make it the city it is.

I see it as my role to help that fire to burn brightly, help that process to be even richer. It may sound a bit highfalutin but that's how I feel. As an indigenous British person, as a Celt, I'm very proud that people from all over the world have wanted to come to this country, and particularly this part of the country, to make London a world city as opposed to simply a Celtic one. My personal commitment is that deep and that passionate. Then that's what you'd expect from a Welshman – an English word meaning 'foreigner', which is a bit of a cheek.

Now when you come to something like the City, on the one hand it is a village. Villages thrive on gossip and gossip makes money. It doesn't matter if it's a well in the Sahara or a pub in the City, people are not just going there for refreshment, they're going there for gossip and that's their primary motivation, in terms of adding pleasure to their lives. The practical thing of getting a refreshment or getting water is very boring. It's the gossip that encourages people to go to those locations, and when it's a business location, a business village, that gossip is worth money in the sense that people can actually think up things to do, deals to do, based on the information they pick up only face to face, which they would never get done on the telephone or on the Internet. The juicy stuff. That's been going on for hundreds of years. If you walk into the little alleyways and backways of the City you'll find that to this day. The City has always thrived on its alleyways, its narrow spaces, its pubs and restaurants, and people would disappear into that rabbit warren whenever they got the chance for the sort of informal business that never happens in the office.

I'm told it's now the fashion to end a relationship by text. It certainly isn't possible to start one by text. It's the same with business. If you've heard something and you want to check it out, you probably want to talk to somebody you trust face to face. You might want to relax them first with a beer. You might want to reassure them. If it's somebody you don't know very well you'll certainly want to talk to them where you can look into their eyes before you trust them with your bit of information. You could call it chatting, discussion, but I like the word 'gossip' because it indicates there's a lot of stuff there that wouldn't be communicated in any other way. The French can't gossip properly because they're sitting at tables. They do gossip but you only hear family gossip or the gossip of your friends. The joy of the English pub is that you're standing up, often quite closely packed, and you overhear things. And in a business centre that can be very valuable.

Especially when you have a city like London where three hundred languages are spoken by schoolchildren every day. You have this great cultural mix, all these different ideas and cultures coming into central London. People standing in bars, standing in queues for a bus, or whatever it might be, being close together and overhearing each other's languages and each other's conversations and ideas ... It might simply be a pattern of words you overhear or a sentence totally out of its context which triggers a thought in your mind. It's not overhearing someone say such and such a company is going bankrupt and rushing back to your office and selling your shares. I'm not talking about anything as obvious as insider trading. I'm talking about people brushing together and someone hearing someone saying a phrase in another language or hearing a phrase in their own language that doesn't make sense, that puzzles them. Because you're so close to people you're more aware of the life around you and there's more of this friction of interaction and as a result you are more stimulated by it.

Places make the best lovers. You can trust a place more than you can trust a person as a lover. A place is more dependable and it has so much depth and stimulation and provides you with the opportunity to realize yourself. The place reflects you, provides you with stimulation, the ability to realize potential. If it's a good place it makes you feel stronger, makes you cleverer and more powerful. I did a walk with someone from the centre of the City to Soho, just taking a beeline, and on that walk ended up going into the Temple Church in the middle of the Temples so I was back in the twelfth century after already having gone into the Black Friar pub, an Arts and Crafts pub, and walking through the centre of Covent Garden and ending up in a Chinese restaurant having dim sum. Now there are not many people who can give you that much stimulation, but being with a person and having the ability to have that friend, London, as a companion throughout gives you a wonderful extra dimension to anything you do. I think of London as a partner. I'm in love with London and always have been.

London's greatest attribute is that it has the best free sex in the world. That's why the youngsters come to London. I read an article on the lively underside of Dubai, but it's all paid sex. It might be a centre for prostitution in a way that you might find in Amsterdam or the Reeperbahn in Hamburg. Any major city will provide those sorts of services, but London is full of young people from around the world looking to go to bed with other young people from all over the world. Why the hell would they pay for it? And that is, if you like, something you will only find in a city as vibrant as London and New York. There's nowhere else on the planet that can offer that range of 'opportunity'. Youngsters having gone to great lengths to come to London to work, to experience its vitality at the start of their career, will have to find a job to pay for the experience and they luckily arrive at a time when they're not just at their most sexually active but at their most intellectually active.

That's London's benefit and that, if you like, is a further acceleration of a process we've seen over the centuries where people have come to settle here. We now have a period where people aren't necessarily coming to settle here. They're coming to experience this wonderful place and move on quite rapidly. What I want to try and do is get across the way I see London as a very large, very complex organism.

You won't be surprised when I tell you that I don't believe London can be planned. It's too complicated. It's far too important to risk planning it in the way many smaller cities and communities are planned. You can't do a Milton Keynes on it. You can't pull out a sheet of paper and say how London should work. London already *does* work. It works in a way none of us understand. It's so complex, so multilayered, so interrelated with places around the world and activities within itself. You have to look at how you can *manage* London, not plan it. How you can treat it, if you like, as an exercise in gardening, look at which plants are thriving and which aren't. Weed out new plants and try new species, encourage those that are doing well. Sometimes try to corral them so they don't do a Japanese knotweed and take over the whole garden. But at the same time recognize the local climate and ecology and work with it rather than against it.

That's not something planners have done over the generations. They have laid out things like the Barbican Estate with pedestrians on one level, vehicles on another, abstract conceits that follow long-lost historical grids rather than the neighbouring street pattern, and not surprisingly they have confused people and created very arid areas. Paternoster Square is another example – all rectilinear, with the buildings laid out on abstract spaces, and it never did well. It was the first project I was faced with when I came to London in 1968 from university. We were divided into groups and the area I was given was Paternoster Square. Little did I know that over thirty years later I'd still be working away at the project. What we now have is a Paternoster Square with attractive spaces at ground level, with facilities that people use and modern office accommodation, all done in way that's harmonious to the setting of the Cathedral and fits in with the grain of the city. But it took a great deal of effort, twenty or thirty years, to unpick the bad planning.

People are earthy. We like to think we're terribly sophisticated. We commute into central London to do intricate, complex technical tasks but we're fuelled by the same desires as our ancestors were thousands of years ago. We have the same basic urges and I think we need to be aware of that when we're looking at the places we inhabit. We need to make provision for those urges and make sure London is not just a sterile working environment or worse still a mixed-use, family-friendly, nondescript boring town like so many other places on the planet.

DAVY JONES

Street photographer

London always goes on about being this financial powerhouse, which I'm sure it is – but then the City of London's rubbish, really. You know, for a financial powerhouse, it suffers from the same rubbish architecture, rubbish streets, haphazard chaos. The people you see on the streets of the City of London aren't really the very wealthy ones. You'll never see them on the streets of the City of London, because they don't go out in the street: they have flunkies to do everything for them and they travel everywhere by car or taxi. So the only people you see out on the streets are kind of careworn. The funny thing is, everybody's dressed the same in the City. Men are all in dark blue, grey or black – even brown's not really allowed – while the women are allowed a flash of colour, but there's a cheapness to a lot of the clothing. The people on the streets of the City of London look quite harassed, more than the rest of London really. They look put-upon. You occasionally see one of the rich ones and you can tell them straightaway. They have a general air of fragrance, of being freshly laundered. They smell of money because everything about them is manicured and cared-for and expensive. Whereas most of the ordinary workers are in cheap suits that don't fit them, that are a bit worn, a bit shiny in places.

He is sitting in Soho Square without a coat on, thanks to the late-morning sun. A man with a guitar strums chords nearby as we talk. When clouds block the sun, shadows move across the square and up the walls of the buildings.

At some point, London started to become a bit more boastful. It started trying to get impressive buildings in the City, and that has affected the light in the City. London is mostly low-rise, two or three storeys, whereas the City was traditionally higher. And because it is partly medieval, there are narrow streets, so it can be quite dark on the streets. With the new buildings coming on, on sunny days they act like big mirrors and reflect light into these streets that didn't really get a lot of light before. It is a kind of bluey-green light because of that tinted glass that they use. Usually it's a bit cold because there's not really many red-tinted windows. But it is a very concentrated beam, so it looks very dramatic.

As it begins to rain, we take cover under the awning of a cheap chicken restaurant on Greek Street. He stands, smoking, looking around. Sometimes, he says, a person pulling a hood over their head makes a beautiful image in London.

Sometimes I get lost in daydreams looking at people and thinking, what's their life like? What goes on with them? Do we have any similar viewpoints? Is there any common ground? Do we all live in our own little worlds? It's almost instinctive when you're shooting, and the thing is, it passes really quickly so then you've moved on. It's only when you're looking back later, when you come to the edit, that you think, *Jesus, what was going on there?* At the time you just see it as an instant. There's something that triggers juxtaposition, expression, stance. It could be an argument. Women for some reason are always quite keen to have arguments in public and you can tell that men aren't. They might want to talk about it later, privately, where a woman wants to get it out straight away. It would be quite interesting to try and do a series on it because you can tell by body language that the man's uncomfortable with discussing this in public while the woman is focused on the issue and oblivious to everything else.

You have to concentrate hard, but any five minutes in London you can find stuff going on. There are always moments of small drama. I love women and men arguing in the street, kids running away from parents and their panic, especially in the city, when kids make a dart and the parent's just lost and doesn't know if they're going to be run over or something. There's that moment of panic. Kids fighting in the street is also quite good.

But you do notice in London there's fewer and fewer children on the streets. You don't see them playing on the streets in the same way they used to. I've still seen them in Liverpool, Glasgow, Newcastle, Manchester or Belfast; in those cities you still see gangs of kids roaming, looking for amusement, either torturing themselves or torturing other people. Hitting people with sticks or something, throwing rocks at cars and all that. But in London you don't.

Shoreditch still has quite a lot of street life and of course the fashions and the clothes are different. It tends to be louder and have more distinctive outfits. It's less tightly controlled and there is less putting on a face. In a way there's more individuality. I don't want to mythologize poverty but there's more individual expression in a cheap clothing sort of way, there is a kind of individualism. Whereas West London, any wealthy area – North London as well – it's more tightly controlled. Sometimes those areas feel a bit like *Invasion of the Body Snatchers* or the *Midwich Cuckoos* or something because there's thousands of women dressing out of a Boden catalogue. It's all quite rigid and it's much more controlled and much more putting on a face to the world. That can be interesting from a photographer's point of view because there's a blankness that goes on. They display less emotion. There's less body language. In the poor areas there's a bit more flamboyance and some people might find it vulgar but there's more expression in a way. It's just more open in that sense. Street life in Brixton's always better: you get corner shops where there's some Jamaican guy running it and there's about eight of his mates in there all the time. They've got music playing and they're playing dominoes and having a drink and so they're having a kind of little party in the shop while he's working, which is a lot more interesting than going into Sainsbury's and a lot of the other chains.

You can always rely on something happening, it's just whether you can get it or not on various streets. I've done shots in New York as well, it's easier there because you can predict where things are going to go and where people are going. It's more haphazard in London, more higgledy-piggledy, so you don't get those dramatic moments that central planning can create. Obviously London has a couple of those but even when you think about it, Buckingham Palace is shit really. You know what I mean? As a spectacle it's rubbish. It's quite a boring building with a roundabout in front.

Paris is largely more planned than London, so it has a more dramatic, impressive structure inherently. I like the chaos and haphazardness of London. You can't rely on the inherent drama of a planned city in London. You have to look for other things and usually it's in the people. London is distinctively London, but at the same time it looks like a lot of other places. London, shitty storefronts everywhere. You do notice how uncared-for it is and how shitty London is. Bill Bryson has written about street cleaning, how in Paris they spend £21 per head on street cleaning whereas London spends about, I don't know, I think it's £3 or £6. It shows. There's rubbish everywhere. London is generally uncared-for, the pavements, the roads, like the way they're patched up in a really careless fashion so there's never any attempt to even them off or even make them match up. There are an incredible number of street signs in London that aren't straight. Some have been knocked in, fair enough, but nobody ever replaces them. And sometimes they don't even put them in straight. You realize that when you're photographing them because afterwards when you're looking at the photo you're aware of the vertical and you realize they're all slightly out. You think, do they not try and put them in straight? Do they just not bother?

Sometimes London reminds me of some African cities with colonial architecture that has all been knocked about a bit and nobody has cared for it. London's a bit like that, like an ex-colonial city itself, sliding into shabbiness. London looks like a place that used to be something.

JOE JOHN AVERY

Street cleaner

Pig heads, chicken livers, cigarette butts, sycamore leaves, sweet wrappers, crisp packets, coffee cups, dirty nappies, old socks, mobile-phone bills, creased photographs – he gathers it all. There's another scattering each hour, another hundred cigarettes, the street cleaners say, crushed underfoot every minute, or that's how it seems.

I know the manager from school, and he said, 'I'll give you a job.' I didn't have to go in for no interviews or anything. So I come in, I been here. It was just as I was turning 16, I come back from holiday and they said come in the next day. I said, 'No, I just want to start work,' so I started that day. I was that excited to start.

I been all over the city, since I been here. I know most of the city like the back of my hand. All the streets, some of the landmarks and all that. This firm, they do, like, the whole of the city. I'll show you my map … Yeah, this is my area here. These pink ones are the subways, the stairs to all the stations, and they'll need gritting, cleaning. It gets dusty down there. You've got the main roads here. So you do all the little ones in the morning, and you get to this by about 9.30, and then you get to the main roads by lunchtime, after everyone's been and had their lunch.

Every day I pick up, like, five, ten thousand things. Fags, rubbish, cups, everything. Chewing gum and cigarette ends. And cups, always McDonald's cups. That's all you find everywhere. That's the biggest item, McDonald's cups, chip cartons, burgers … Anything with a logo, it's the big M most of the time.

They've put in these ashtrays for chewing gum and for fags. You get some people, they'll chip it out on the ashtray and throw it on the floor. And you think, it's just mad!

It's endless. Even if it's half clean in the gulley, you might have a couple of cigarettes and you get stones and dust builds up there, cars drive past and it all winds it into there. So you still have to do that. It all adds up, man.

Starting at a young age, it was a brand-new thing to me. So it used to take me ages. But once you get used to it, know what you're doing, it becomes easier. Get there, get things done on time. Work as a team. Probably took me like a couple of months before I could relax and all that. I'd be working so hard, sweating. So now I can do it at a pace where it suits me, get it done on time.

Like I can have a sit-down now and have a drink before I go back. Before, sometimes I'd have to work through my break because I was just panicking I couldn't get it done. I should have been back here and I'm still out there working and my mate had to ring me and say 'Where are you?' and I've been like 'I'm working!'

Sundays at the market are the toughest. They don't pack up on time, so you have to wait for them. Sometimes you get the market inspectors, they go down there and they tell them they've got to hurry up, get off otherwise they get fines or something. You get a dustcart, and you get a cage-motor. One's for recycling, but if it's raining and it's wet, you can't do recycling. So, you just team up work … One goes at one end of the market, and one side of it is Tower Hamlets also, and they don't come till later, so all their stuff is blowing onto ours.

You get everything, like. Cardboard boxes, like their stock, you get cups, and you get food. Trainers, like. When people buy their new shoes they throw their old ones. They have like a stall, they do fried prawns and banana fritters, and at the end you have to disinfect it, wash it down so it's all slippery.

Sometimes I work on Saturday, like, and we go out in the electric vehicles in teams of four to do the big pavements, two of you do one side, two of you do the other. You get sick up the walls. I've seen piles, like maybe four or five, where they've just took a couple of steps and again and again. It's horrible like.

I get annoyed at the things people do. You've got to think, people have got to clean your mess. They're not really bothered like. I think they look at it as – they've got to give us a job to do.

I've had a few rats and all that, yeah. That's horrible, the rats. In the train stations, back of some shops, the alleyways. Monday we was at the salt station, and it was just big piles of salt. And you get maybe the odd brick or rock in there and you have to take it out, because when we put it into the machine, it gets stuck and it gets jammed. So one of the drivers for the tractor, he saw something in there and took it out with his hand, thought it was a brick. But it was a dead rat and it was rock hard. It was horrible.

The builders are the worst. You can't keep a building site area tidy, really. If you cleaned it, they'll throw anything on the floor. They ain't got no respect or anything for you.

I've come back to my bin before and there's a rucksack in there, and it's exactly the same rucksack as I think the bomber used. And I was like, 'Christ!' So I got my stick, and I just like lifted it to see if there was any weight on it, but it was empty. I turned it upside down and it was like the zip had ripped and it was all bust inside. We just have to check, otherwise if there's something suspicious we have to ring the police. I've seen bomb squads come down before and they've cornered off areas and all that for a suitcase and stuff. They get the buildings evacuated, and from quiet you suddenly get thousands of people all standing outside smoking, drinking coffees. You have to wait till they go in and it's just a mess. It's hard work that.

Rubbish from the city just builds up. It's mad, you could have like loads of it; just bags and bags. The most I've done before, I've got a picture of it on my phone. It's when it's leafy, you know, when all the leaves are about. You get big leaves, but you got the little leaves and they're worst because there's loads of them. Up near St Paul's they have big ones around the church, you get big leaves so they're not too bad. And when it rains they all stick to the ground. It's horrible when it's windy and there's loads of mess. The most I've done, I think there was something about like 25–28 bags there. Got to be over seven and a half stone, ten stone.

Some people come up and comment, 'Nice to see a young boy working.' Makes you feel good, it does. And last Christmas, I was working late shift, it was night-time and it was cold. I was sweeping out and they had these new flats built, and they're like one-, one-and-a-half-million-pound flats for a one-bedroom. I met this nice couple, I was talking to them, and they gave me £20 and that. I said, 'You didn't have to do that.' But it was nice of them. They said, 'Go and have something to eat, it's cold, and enjoy your Christmas.' It's nice that some people appreciate what you do.

JILL ADAMS AND GARY WILLIAMS

Bus operations managers

At the Victoria Coach Station, a queue has formed for the 08:00 to Hrubieszow, which also calls at Gdansk, Elblag, Olsztyn, Szczytno, Ostroleka, Koszalin, Slupsk, Gdynia, Lubaczow, and many others. There's not much talking at this hour amongst the assembled passengers. I hear the click of a dropped suitcase handle as it hits the bus station floor.

Housed in the same building on Buckingham Palace Road is Centre-Comm, the emergency communication centre that runs all day every day, and acts as London Buses' command and control, fielding the 1,300 calls a day that come down the line from London's 23,000 bus drivers. It's here they arrange diversions, deal with emergencies, and monitor the 1,200 or so traffic cameras that peer at London streets.

On the day I visit to speak to a Network Liaison Manager the staff are preparing for an imminent strike on the Underground. The room is calm. One monitor is stuck on Sky News, the others are fixed on street corners in London where the great red rectangles roll by. The Liaison Manager speaks to me for an hour but the whole experience becomes more interesting when one of the other employees, a duty manager named Jill, takes over when the Liaison Manager is called away to take a conference call about the impending strike. The computer system that logs all the problems, she says, is quite slow. Jill has just returned from holiday and, one of her co-workers notes, she must have missed the adrenalin of the room. After a few minutes I have to go fetch my recorder to keep up with her voice. 'We've got five people picking up calls,' she tells me as we walk down to the radio response section. We stand behind Gary, a young man monitoring a computer screen. 'We used to have one system that didn't tell us the location so we'd have to rely on our drivers,' Jill continues. 'For some of them English isn't even their second language so there were problems. We'd ask them: where are you right now? They'd say: I'm outside the Asda in North London. Thanks very much. But the interesting thing about this place is we'd have someone here who would say I used to do that route. I know exactly where he is.'

They sit in the CentreComm room like telemarketers, waiting to communicate. Their London is a colour-coded map that loads slowly onto their screens. The screen is dotted with colour and, near each problem area, is the symbol for the van called in to deal with the drunk falling down the stairwell or another selection from the list of coded problems. If nothing happens it is a bad day, a very rare day. Jill calmly waits for the computer to load.

JILL: So this is the system we use and what the information screens do is — Gary, can you just bring up an empty one and do a test for me, do you mind? Right, that's an empty screen that you'd get. It will come up, we put in the origin and we put in what the incident is. If you look on the right it's got a cause code there. It runs 1 to 99, it can be any of those.

GARY: Each number represents an incident — vandalism, security, low hit trees, general enquiries, missing persons, pickpockets, gas leaks, burst water mains, fires on or off buses ... Virtually anything that affects the movement of buses within the M25, we deal with and we report, as Jill said. We have real-time information on the spot, for police, fire or ambulance, or bus operators or any other agents, RSPCA. Anything, we cover it.

JILL: If you look under 'vandalism', we've got 74s and 77s, which are specific cause codes for things being thrown at buses. Also down the bottom, you see here, these are grid references. If we get a lot of 77s – which are vandalism, bus damage – within a certain area, it pings as a red spot into the intel unit. Somebody there will go, why are we getting a lot of rocks being thrown at buses on a Wednesday afternoon at half past five? And they might say, well there used to be an after-school club and now that's closed, so the kids have got nothing else to do. We could feed stuff through to the intel unit and it will show there's something going on in this particular area.

GARY: The most common thing is a fare dispute on the bus. That will be a code 21 for the driver, 22 for a dispute or 20 for one of our officials. So it's endless, just endless. Even new ones that are not on there. Today I had a dog boarding a bus. No owner. Stray dog, just getting on and getting off. I said, maybe he just wants to go home. That's the most unusual one I've had today. You could only put that as Other, you know. We just deal with whatever comes in and then disseminate it to the right person. The added bonus is the CCTV. As long as we've got cameras at the locations we can look and say, oh, yeah, we know that point. Piccadilly at the Regent Street junction, there's pickpockets there that work on the night shift at a certain time, so we might put a call out to the staff to say, be aware, here's what they look like, they're pickpocketing, please advise passengers.

JILL: Right now it's quiet. We've got the Peckham Rye log. So that tells us exactly what Gary's just put in, and if you click on there it will tell you who the nearest member of the forward response unit is to that incident. Have you clicked it?

GARY: Yeah, it's updating. Sometimes it's a little slow.

JILL: It's all done through their mobile phones and GPS. [*The screen updates.*] Right, there you go. See, there's the nearest person. She's 4.8 kilometres away from there. But the next person actually with a van will be the Lambeth bloke, right there – so we double click him and in a second, okay, his van will turn to purple. We still have to physically phone them. [*We wait for the screen to update.*] Ah, there you go, that's where the incident is and that's his van. So we can set him as still ongoing, or we can click on his name and put him on as meal break and it turns black so we can't use him. The screen looks like it has measles and chickenpox and any other kind of spotty sort of ailment that you can think of. That's basically how it works. That's how we manage to get people to incidents very quickly.

GARY: So *they* can deal with it.

JILL: A lot of the people in here actually have been out and done the van jobs. They've been inspectors, they've been revenue inspectors, they've been roadside officials and bus drivers. I've been a manager here for three years. But before that I was a bus station controller, a bus driver, a bus driving instructor. And I was working for the police before that as a police driver, did rapid response with them. I've literally stood in the middle of Oxford Street doing first aid on somebody whose foot was hanging off underneath a bus, and I was trying to phone here to say Oxford Street's about to shut eastbound just past Oxford Circus, can you put the diversion in via Regent Street. And while I'm phoning them, there's buses stopping the other way having a look and I'm like, naff off, and meanwhile someone comes up and says, where do I get a bus to Piccadilly Circus, my love?

GARY: Yeah, happens all the time.

JILL: They actually hate it when it's a bit quiet like this. Don't you Gary?

GARY: Oh, yeah. [*He sighs.*]

JILL: No, seriously, they prefer something to be happening because one, the day goes quickly and two, this office runs best when something's happening, they get stuck into it, you know. They actually thrive on it. They love it. You love it when it's busy, don't you, Gary?

GARY: [*Dubiously*] Oh yeah.

JILL: Yeah, you do, you liar! Don't try and bullshit me. Even if it's just a bus driver who calls up and says, someone's calling me this, that and the other and we know that, 99.9 per cent of the time, it will just blow over – this is just what the drivers need. These guys, remember, they were drivers themselves. You just speak to them in a way that you'd like to be spoken to.

GARY: We've got the radio, the CCTV cameras here.

JILL: These guys know this city better than anyone; they know where all the cameras are and everything. They know it off by heart. They're dynamite, these guys.

GARY: We just need to get out more.

PAUL AKERS

Arboriculturalist

He walks at a slower pace than his co-workers at Westminster City Hall. Most others move with purpose towards the elevators. He ambles. 'Look out there,' he says, after we exit the elevator. He's looking out the window. Across the rubble of a half-demolished building he can see a handsome plane tree. 'We planted that fifteen years ago.'

I grew up in Ruislip, big garden, backed onto a wood. I was able to roam and play freely with friends in the woods, climbing trees, falling out, landing in the river underneath and so on. Just having freedom and encouragement and deriving enjoyment from that environment really. It's changed a bit now, but the woods are still there. Ruislip Woods are still very well known for their extensive collection of oak trees. A lot of the oak trees from Ruislip Woods were felled to provide timber for the building of the Royal Albert Hall.

In those days arboriculture hadn't really emerged as a recognized profession. It was not until the 1950s and 1960s that arboriculture became more of a recognized profession to be working in. The councils then began to wake up to the need to have specialists looking after this unique and much prized and valued resource.

There are many benefits derived from trees, of course. Purer air in terms of atmospheric pollution and so on. Quality of life. And trees can increase the value of properties. The right tree in the right place: that is the practice we promote as far as is possible in terms of planting new trees in pavements and thoroughfares in the city. We assess the new planting site very carefully indeed. We take some time considering whether it's suitable or not and if it is, the best type of tree to plant in it so that those new trees are going to provide maximum effect and minimum inconvenience. Something that is compatible with the size of the buildings, the width of the road, the width of the pavement.

Some streets are very narrow, very tight, very compact and there isn't a lot of space for big trees to grow satisfactorily. So we plant something that is more upright and its branches grow more vertically than horizontally. One tree we plant a lot of are Chanticleer pears, a non-fruiting pear. They come into flower in the spring, nice clusters of single white blossom smothering the whole tree. They're like snowmen or igloos, the whole canopy is completely white for a few weeks. There's a whole load of them if you go down Oxford Street for example, from Marble Arch going right the way down to Oxford Circus.

They don't get many serious pests or diseases. They look after themselves well and don't need very much pruning. They tolerate the conditions that Oxford Street offers them, the jostle and the hustle. The problem we do get down Oxford Street is slightly unusual, people will chain their pushbikes to the trees and pedals and chains do sometimes cause abrasion of the actual trunks. But they tolerate that too. They're quite good in that respect.

When it's finished flowering its leaves will emerge in April or May. Those trees will hold on to their foliage, the same leaves, right until mid–December. They're a late-leaf-losing species. Much greener for a longer period of time than many other species of trees. All trees are good, but Chanticleer score highly.

Another good one is the London plane. London is well known for its plane trees. A lot of them were planted a hundred or so years ago because the atmosphere of London was very very smoky and the pollution was very very high and the plane tree was found to be able to cope well with that. They grow well in a smoky environment because they have a very thick, leathery leaf which stands up well to atmospheric pollution. Pieces of bark will actually fall off the outer skin of the branches and the trunk as the tree develops beyond its early years, and that's like changing an air filter on your car, you know? They get clogged up with atmospheric dust particles and so on, and when they're choked up, basically, the irregular-shaped pieces of bark just fall off onto the pavement and the tree's clever enough to actually develop new bark under that old stuff before the old stuff comes off.

You see plane trees in some of the London squares, Berkeley Square being one of the most famous, but most of them have got quite a selection of large London plane trees in them. Those in Berkeley Square are thought to have been planted in 1789, and are still growing strong. They are huge. They're in pretty good shape and they're nicely spaced out. They need lots of room in order to develop and grow properly and these particular trees have certainly got that. They are majestic. They are the Rolls-Royce amongst London's trees and they really are the cat's whiskers. They are beautiful. The Victorians and their predecessors knew what they were doing, choosing London plane and giving them space. Their branches are just beginning to converge on each other from one tree to another, rather than a sort of interlocking knitting effect which you would otherwise get.

We're taking cuttings from them at the moment, we're propagating them because the London plane is a hybrid of the American plane and the European plane. It's got blood in its system from two different plane trees. Consequently, if you try and grow them, propagate them from seed, you'll get different characteristics coming in the second generation. Whereas if you take them from cuttings, and snip little shoots off, you'll be sure to preserve the characteristics that the trees have got there at the moment in terms of the second generation. So we've got a nursery down in Hampshire doing that work for us at the moment, growing these trees on so that when they become big enough, if there's any spaces in Berkeley Square, we can pop a new tree back in so that the second-generation planes grow up and have, in 200 years' time, the same features that the plane trees have got there today.

They say there's more under London than actually above it. We have to open up trial holes and put cable detectors over the surface of streets in order to ascertain whether or not there's sufficient room, ground space, for trees to grow in harmony with gas pipes, water pipes, and so on and so forth. The two can coexist quite well. Roots are like worms, you see, they will take the line of least resistance and if they come across a pipe in the ground they will divert around it rather than going up to it and instead of finishing their life there. Or sometimes we'll insert a barrier which stops the root at a point and when it reaches that barrier the roots will turn left, turn right, go down, basically, they won't go up anyway.

The true soil of London is much much deeper than just beneath the actual surface, due to the changes and developments and alterations and formation of the city. But a lot of London is either London clay, up in St John's Wood and north Paddington, shrinkable clay, and as you come further south through Hyde Park, sand and gravels. In this area you find alluvium and black peaty sort of soil. So there are three main types, actually, which make for different challenges.

In the northern part of the city, roots of trees extract moisture and the clay will shrink. Buildings with a load of weight on the actual clay can sometimes crack and subsidence will develop. We do take that into account. People want everything to be just like a shop window basically and rightly so. They can claim off the council for damage they think a tree may have caused, undermining foundations and possibly causing damage to buildings. So we have to prune the trees quite frequently and fairly severely. We have to take these things into account when choosing new trees as well. We don't want to plant trees that are going to cause problems for the future. We want specimens which are certainly long-lived and suitable for their particular setting.

The ginkgo is also well suited here, because in London it's a few degrees warmer than outside the city. It was thought to be not completely hardy when the tree was planted at Kew, hence the position chosen alongside one of the greenhouses, but the greenhouse has now gone. It is very very hardy indeed. The ginkgo is a very old tree from China, relatives of which were thought to be grown on this land when dinosaurs were tramping around. Ginkgo biloba – some people love it, some people have less complimentary comments to make about it, but it's the oldest living tree known to man, in actual fact. There's one at Kew Gardens that's about 200 years old. It's a huge tree.

There's also the Wollemi pine from Tasmania, which was a wonderful find by some explorers in the mountains of that country. Wollemi pines have now been planted at Kew and all sorts of famous gardens. A little-known species, it's a coniferous tree which has kind of taken off. There's bound to be others in currently undiscovered parts of the world. Like the Dawn redwood from a part of Sichuan in China, a tree thought to be extinct until somebody got in after the war and found this tree growing there and sent seed back in about 1950. Now they're the greatest street trees out here.

ELISABETTA DE LUCA

Commuter

I like London, but I'm not a city person, I like being in the country-side. That's where we live and that's why I commute. My village is on an estuary about seventy-five miles from London, so my quality of life when I'm at home is beautiful. We've got an old shipbuilder's cottage and a lovely garden and we can see the stars at night and there's no planes or smog. In the mornings I walk across the park to the station and get on the 7.06 train. And then I try and get a seat.

My season ticket is £4,660 a year. My line goes from London to Norwich. It's actually one of the lines that went into administration, it's been taken back by the government, so it's in a lot of difficulty. The trains are very old and dirty and smelly. The toilets are so filthy, it's filth on another level, it's grimy ground-in dirt, like the cleaners must pretty much give up. I take toilet paper and put it on the seat, and I use it to close the lock and everything. I even hang my bag round my neck so I don't have to put it on the floor. It's such an unpleasant environment, and it's a long journey: an hour and twenty minutes.

When you commute all the time you develop relationships with these strangers and you just hate them, you really resent everything. There's this one smelly guy in particular who has got really long legs and he'll fall asleep and by the end of the journey I've had to move carriages because he's practically lying on me. There's this one woman, I call her Mrs Piss-Piss because she's always grumpy. You'd never sit next to her because she evils you out. And the seats are so narrow, it's really horrible. Somebody who reads the newspaper is immediately in your personal space. Yesterday I was putting some make-up on and dumped half a pot of shiny stuff on a man's trousers. He's probably going into a bank and suddenly he's got glitter on him, he looks like he's been having a bit of a cross-dressing weekend. He was really upset and not hiding it, whacking his leg and being really arsey about it.

The trains are always delayed. You get a 'delay repay voucher' which you can use off your next season ticket or you can spend it on the train, and so all these hardened commuters basically just get drunk every evening. They do these 2-for-£4 on cans and you get these hard-core groups from your town saying 'Oh hello, how was your day today?' And they get really drunk and noisy and annoying. So you don't want to be too near to them either.

They really pack the trains out, and people who pay for season tickets like us can't sit in reserved seats. So you're a commuter, you've had a hard day at work, you just want to sit and check your BlackBerry and do some work – and someone will come and say, I've got a reserved ticket. You're like, I've got a four-and-a-half-grand-a-year season ticket! But they can throw you out of your seat. Quite often you have to stand, especially in the evenings, while the seats in first class are practically all empty. But you can't sit down on them, you'd get fined a lot of money. Even if you're pregnant you have to have a letter. I did sit in it once and I just cried cos the ticket collector came up and he said, 'You've got to go' and I said, 'I don't feel well, I don't know what's wrong with me.' I started crying, but he ended up throwing me off the seat.

On Friday nights and especially around Christmas and Easter, people are always throwing up on the train. It's a dirty train anyway so people don't have a lot of respect for it. Recently I was sat on the train going home, probably a bit pissed as well and somebody threw up on my shoes. Some suit just goes *blueergh*, everywhere, and it's disgusting. Once I seen a pissed kid, he got some ketchup down the wall of the train and then he got his chips and he was eating the ketchup off the walls of the train. It's just so horrible.

You get kids and families when it's school holidays, they come into the mix with the commuters. Kids don't know that that guy is desperate to get down the carriage cos there's a whole stream of people trying to get that seat and knows he has to get there. They don't know that the train's gonna be really full so they shouldn't put their bags in the carriageway. I feel like a really bad person but you do end up thinking like, get out of my way you horrible stupid fucking child, I'm going to kill you! You feel really angry and you're desperate to get home and you've run to get the fast train. But they are just a family that have just come down for the day for half-term and happen to end up on the commuter train so it's not really fair to them.

It's the eating as well, and the putting on make-up and the personal conversations with friends and family that people have. I'm always reading what's on people's laptops. I'm just really nosy, so I'm always reading what people are writing. I'd say 90 per cent of people are slagging somebody off that they work with or talking about a social problem at work – they're never talking about *work*, like, 'I've really go to do that' or 'Yeah, how are you gonna do it?' It's always like, 'Well, I can't fucking believe her, she never gets anything done does she?' It's always gossip and it's always politics and I think, god, no wonder the economy's fucked! Nobody's doing any work, everybody's in some dispute with a colleague and that's the whole focus of their job.

When everybody's drunk it lubricates things, and that's when you do see the nicer side of people, like when everybody's had a few drinks or it's round Christmas, sometimes you get carriages that end up singing. There'll be some young girls who reckon themselves like *X Factor* somethings and they'll start to sing and other people will join in and there will be a bit of a drunken sing-a-long. Or the train's stuck in the station and it's come up on the board that it's been cancelled and you've been moved to another train and it's all crowded – everyone starts going 'Were you on the 6.45 last week?' 'Oh yeah, that was terrible wasn't it, I didn't get home till …' And everybody starts exchanging their stories and that's quite nice. So there's good and bad.

I think our train system is a bit of an analogy of our society, you know, there's like inequities and inconsistencies and old-fashioned divides and people being despondent and not trying to fight against issues and just going along with things and settling for second best.

When I finally get home at night, I always wonder how many mites have jumped on me on the train and then jumped off in my house. They're commuters like me. And at the weekend all the clothes that have been on the train have to be washed on a Friday. Everything has to be cleansed of London. Then I feel my weekend begins.

GLEANING ON THE MARGINS

SARAH CONSTANTINE

Skipper

We set off for Waitrose just after eleven at night. Sarah brings tools when she goes skipping in the bins around Balham, usually a metal bar and a roll of durable orange bin bags which hold the loose carrots she scavenges, and the occasional cabbage and the tiramisu that sometimes leaks through its dented packaging. The bar is particularly effective when gaining access at the Balham Waitrose.

I walk alongside her down the dark Balham streets and she continues with the stream of facts about her life, though it is hard to hold much of the torrent as it passes. She is 42. She mentions her age again and again, sometimes referring to the crack her bones make when she stretches them out thanks to her recent battle with lupus. Sometimes she mentions 42 in reference to the way she can't dance all night any longer or what her hair will or won't do. She wears her hair in a mushrooming pile that curves back over her forehead. It's held in place firmly, she says, and demonstrates by thrashing her head about as if she were on a dance floor. As we walk she delivers a loud version of part of Henry V's St Crispin's Day speech. She uses the metal bar to add weight to the words, waving it like a baton. The speech rings off the Balham houses. Immediately after, she begins the speech again in softer tones but stops as we reach Balham High Street and then she quickly, silently, crosses the road.

She doesn't need to use the metal bar this evening. It doesn't take much effort to get close to the bins. Sarah unrolls the orange bin liners and holds the flashlight. She tears through plastic bags, discards empty packages and wades through what's left. She squeals with delight when, amongst the detritus, she uncovers a cache of Walnut Whip.

There's a hospital opposite Clapham South Tube station which is now flats. It's the South London Women's Hospital, that's where I was born. Top floor, third window from the left. I asked my mother once. I think she told me just to shut me up. Rossiter Road is where we grew up. It was a pretty rough area then. Next door was a brothel – black women for black men, and they used to have big speakers on the windowsill blasting out reggae. There used to be a woman in a white bikini standing in the door. I used to go and look at her sometimes. Hey you, she said, hey little byai. Get out of here, go home byai. It was a full-on red light area, Bedford Hill, at the end. Working girls everywhere. Where the Sainsbury's car park is now was just derelict buildings. The school in Chestnut Grove used to be piles of rubble. Where the Asda car park is now was just piles of rubble from the war. There were a lot of bomb sites. It was a very rough area. A lot of alcoholics, men damaged from the war, came back and were basically drunk everywhere. Lots of shell-shocked people and it was just a run-down rough higgledy-piggledy area bisected by lots of railway lines. I remember it as lots of decay everywhere.

My mother was completely insane. She used to keep bags of rotting rubbish up to the ceiling. It was really grim. My father was about as savage as you can get. He'd been a gangster in Greece during the Second World War, he was one of the partisans and he relished killing Germans and taking their weapons. He looked like a Mexican bandit from an Italian western. Big moustache, round staring bloodshot eyes, big bags under his eyes, always cigarette smoking. Dark brown skin, always sitting on the edge of the chair like a coiled spring ready to leap. He was bloodthirsty, a fierce mad-eyed Greek who sweated adrenalin and testosterone and would explode with provocation if you even looked at him. Things got hairy for him over there. He'd killed too many people. He had to escape and that was it. He worked as a kitchen porter in 1950 in Earl's Court exhibition halls and my mother worked as a part-time waitress there.

Later he worked in a fish and chip shop in Vauxhall Bridge Road, and every Saturday he would go out and find people walking the street drunk and pick fights with them just for the hell of it. He used to come back all bloodied. He had a mouth full of gold teeth and a nose that was broken so many times.

He had loads of shotguns. He used to go out to the countryside every weekend and blast the pigeons. He came back with a mole once. I don't know how he managed to shoot a mole. And when he died, there happened to be an amnesty for weapons. I carted round a huge quantity of handguns, Smith & Wesson revolvers, automatic pistols, hand grenades. He had six hand grenades. He had a ten-bore pump-action shotgun. You're not supposed to have a ten-bore. And he had all these weapons, all these various guns he wasn't supposed to have and piles of ammunition. I think this was '95. I dragged this huge quantity of weapons. I had a car then. I went to the police and said, is there an amnesty? Yes. I opened it and he said, do you want to give your name? I said no. Goodbye. I wasn't Sarah yet. I was still George then.

I was a complete nerd growing up. I went to Tulse Hill School. It was jungle rough. Open gang warfare. Baby boom years and it was busting at the seams. And I was a pretty-faced, chubby kid who was very dysfunctional and didn't know what was going on all the time, and going home to bags of rotting rubbish. I retreated into my electronics and engineering. I used to bunk off and go to the Institute of Electrical Engineers and stroll in like I owned the place because I had the uniform, black trousers and black shoes and a tie. Go in and pretend I was a member there. It's just over Waterloo Bridge on the north bank. I would stroll in, sit down and read. After about a year they caught me.

I'd try to drag bits of machinery home, I was always dragging things back. Old televisions, old radios, mopeds, motorbikes, lawnmowers, anything electrical, mechanical, a boiler. I'd drag them into the garden and sneak them in later. It was cool.

My first job was working for my father putting food on plates in the fish restaurant. I was 15, I hated it. I worked six weeks, made three hundred quid and bought myself a second-hand moped and a helmet. I got insurance and was buzzing around on this Suzuki 50cc moped. I knew a gang of others who had Suzuki mopeds and we used to be like a swarm of angry wasps buzzing around these streets. At night, five gears, a clutch and an engine capable of five horsepower, you could do sixty miles an hour. Balham, Clapham. We used to get up to some terrible things. One baking hot summer, somewhere around Kennington, Oval area, miles of council estates and there was a house with a huge man in his string vest sitting in his chair. He had opened his front door and his back door to let the air through. We went through his house while he was sitting watching television. Rar, rar, rar. We used to go out to Box Hill and hang out with the Hell's Angels. But they're a weird bunch. Later on I got in with the Hell's Angels and I was mechanic for them. At 17 I was riding with a gang of Hell's Angels. They're not like the Americans. They mostly live with their mum and are dysfunctional people who live on baked beans and beer. They seemed to make most of their money from selling speed and as roadies and security for rock concerts, but most of the ones I met were a bunch of pussies really. They used to have axe-throwing competitions but they weren't throwing an axe at anybody. They were so excruciatingly dull. They didn't know anything about their bikes. I was really good at repairing their bikes and did many full-scale restorations of engines and gearboxes for them.

At 24, I had left engineering behind and got into electronics. I was building modular synthesizers. This is in the early to mid Eighties. I spent three years building a huge sixty-five-module synthesizer. It took up half the room. I realized I had no friends, no life, I had never had a conversation with a woman. I had never been to a pub, never been in a taxi, never eaten in a restaurant, never swum in a swimming pool, never been to the seaside. It's like, I lived in central London and didn't know anybody. All I did was my rat run, working in a factory and making industrial machinery and coming home and making more industrial machinery. That was it. I realized it was a substitute for life. I would go to sleep thinking about electronics and engineering and wake up thinking about electronics and working out circuits.

I went to work as a builder after the factory I was working in was asset-stripped. Just stumbled into building work with a guy I knew and became quite successful as a builder. Then, aged 30–31, I split with Helen after five and a half years. She was an opera singer. She was talking about marriage and children. I could do the sex. I was really good at it. I was really sensitive but I hated it because it just seemed so wrong. This intense, deep, nauseating sadness, just like nostalgia but absolutely overwhelming to the point where it's almost choking you and it's a dreadful grey misery of sadness that is all-pervasive when you try to become intimate with someone. Me being such a strong person I overrode it. But you get to a point where you think, is this how it's going to be for ever? I can't keep doing this for the rest of my life.

I was very good at dating, very good at being Prince Charming, opening doors, but that's because I had created a male persona. I could create anyone I wanted, so I created the one I wanted for myself. There was about a dozen different Georges and he was a chameleon that would match a different face to a different situation. When I was with Hell's Angels it would be like, Souf London geezah. Ya mate, I'll sort that out for you. But there wasn't one George. It was just a series of pastiches. It got to the point when you realize everything is fake. Everyone only sees a mask that has been stuck on. You're constantly paranoid you're going to be found out. It's the nausea. The nausea of misery, having the wrong hormones. I just started taking hormones out of curiosity to see what it did to me.

I saved £23,000 in two and a half years from rickshawing, paid for my surgery, paid for my laser, paid for my hormones, paid for the psychiatrist, the recovery period, everything. I don't claim benefits or anything.

When I transitioned, one of the things I found out was that about

80 per cent of male-to-female transsexuals have a background in electronics and engineering. I'm not kidding. It's so freaky. One day at the psychiatrist – you have to see a psychiatrist for two years – there was a notice on the board in the waiting room. A self-help group had started up in someone's living room. I phoned up.

'Oh yes, if you do want to come around. You are trans—'

'Yes, I am.'

So I went around. There are about eight sheepish-looking, ropy-looking transsexuals. And we're all sitting there in someone's living room. Things were a bit awkward. We didn't know what to talk about. Someone mentioned in passing they were into electronics. I said I was into electronics. Someone said, 'I started with this Ladybird book. It was called build your own transistor radio with a plank of wood.' I said, 'I remember that book. Use the OC71 transistor.' Someone else said, 'Oh yes and the OC45 for the radio frequency.' All of a sudden everyone in the room was fighting – the same numbers like a trainspotters' convention. It was like … It dawned on me. I mentioned modular synths and someone said, 'What chip did you use for your Rodgers-controlled oscillator?'

'I used the LM13700.'

'That's the preceding?'

'That's right because it had linearizing diodes in the input and non-dedicated diodes.'

'That's right. It can with an 11 fuel pin.'

All of a sudden it's like [*hums the theme from* The Twilight Zone]. What's happening? They all know the same code numbers as I do! I looked at them, they were all looking back and I realized they're all really nerdy. Subsequently I went to so many transsexual clubs and I realized they're all trainspotters. It's not what I would have thought at all. Top ten most common characteristics – right at the top, electronics. Restoring old radios, old motorcycles, old cars. I used to go out with a transsexual woman. She's the engineer who maintains Crystal Palace television transmitter. She also restores old cars and she also is a trainspotter and we went to Brighton one day. We pulled into the station and she said, 'You see that train? It should have a little plaque on the side that said it's the first train through the Channel Tunnel.'

And it did. And she's a big Yorkshire bloke with a wig, heavy make-up, you know, dressing like someone's mum.

I used to take these trans women out shopping and on trips and things because they just wanted someone to hold their hand really, especially when you take hormones you go through a female puberty which lasts quite a few years and is extremely violent. My goodness. That's when I had the beard. I hadn't had the laser yet. The laser takes three years. Months and months of extreme pain and violence of burning with a laser to get rid of the beard. I'm half-Greek. I had a dense, dark beard, really thick. And so, you know, I was in a queue going to a club. I was talking to this rather nice lady I'd met in the queue, just chatting about the New Romantic era. I had been a full-on New Romantic with baggy velvet suit, full make-up and everything. I remember telling her about this time. We were talking and a group of Essex boys came up. This is a hard-core electroclash club and what these Essex boys were doing with their fin haircuts is beyond me. This is about 2–3 years back. I'm in full dress, corset, suspenders, fishnets and heels. I don't wear these now but I went through a period of experimenting with it, with ideas, like any teenager. I had all the make-up and everything, all the jewellery, fingernails, all the stuff. Goth. I'm standing there. You always get one who plays to the gallery and he's like, he comes up, all with their alcopops and says, 'All right, doll.' And he goes to me, 'All right, geezer.'

I'm already fifteen moves ahead. I say to him, 'No, it's doll.'

'Nah, nah, nah, you're a geezah.'

I pulled my breast out and squirted him full in the face with milk. He recoiled about fifteen feet.

'Fackin hell, fackin hell!'

Because it really used to squirt a lot. I used to have pads and everything. His mates were all falling about pissing with laughter and I turned to talk to this woman again. My gypsy antenna is twitching.

I can hear the heavy clog wheels of his brain moving. Baby-milk-titty. He couldn't figure it out. He came up to me and said, 'Aw, my mistake, doll. No hard feelings.' He puts his hand out. So I go like this. Slap it away. I give him my hand. He kissed it.

I'm back in the front room of the Balham squat with its ivy-green walls, painted that way to cover the graffiti left by a bunch of roving Spaniards. The floorboards are white and scuffed thanks to all the bikes. Most of the current tenants of the squat are couriers. A Taxi Driver poster is affixed to the wall.

She stands near the fireplace reading out expiry dates of the evening's haul — May 2nd for the Muller Lite is too late, May 6th is too late for the vegetarian lasagne. It is the final hours of May 9th and most of the stash is on the knife-edge, good or bad. The bog roll is fine. The cheese? Well, says Sarah, some cheese gets better, doesn't it? She holds out some quiche. I remember the moment she uncovered it at the bin. It paled in comparison to the shrieks of joy that accompanied the discovery of the upscale puddings that hadn't made it too far past expiry. I ask if we should heat the quiche. 'You don't eat quiche hot,' she replies. 'You have to appreciate its fine subtleties, the sautéed mushroom taste.'

Her memories, she says later, have become feminized since her change. She views the world in a feminine way, even films from her past.

'How would you have viewed Star Wars*?' I ask her.*

'Before, I would have had a crippling fascination with the technology.'

'And now?'

'My memories of Star Wars *now are to do with the love story in the middle. Princess Leia and whoever that guy was.'*

'And London?'

'London was about systems, about circuits, connections, roads. It was an emotionless place where things simply operated. They moved from place to place and did their job.'

'And now?'

'After the change,' she said, 'London is an emotional place. I feel the flows of emotion. I see the sadness of buildings, the sad gorgeousness of light on the streets.'

JOHN ANDREWS

Angler

Fish have been swimming in the canals and rivers and ponds in London since before Roman times. And when you catch a fish, it's not radically different from then. Broadly speaking, the types of fish you catch are the same that the Georgians would have caught, that the Victorians would have caught. Chubb and dace you're only going to get in a river, not in still water. Roach, pike, bream you'll get in both, carp you'll get in both, gudgeon you'll get in both. Barbel you'll get in the rivers, bleak you'll only get in the rivers, on the tidal stretches you'll get flounder coming in, eels. Bass you'll get coming in on the tidal stretch. If they've got ponds in Buckingham Palace – which I'm sure they have – they'll have carp in them. There's carp in the Serpentine. All through the Thames, all through the Thames tributaries.

Everywhere is alive with fish. You could fish down at Rotherhithe, you could fish opposite the Houses of Parliament today and catch fish. So why go fishing? Well, if I gave you the chance to walk down a London street and go through the door of a house and suddenly be transported to a different era and a different time, wouldn't you do it? I think for a lot of anglers, it's that mystery that draws you in.

There's always been a massive angling culture in London. If you had to choose a golden age, it was 1820 to 1960, 150 years or so. When leisure time was created. Before that you would have gone off and fished for an hour here or there to catch your supper, or you would have poached a bit, but it was the creation of leisure really that allowed people to fish. People got money, because of the development of industry. So they would go fishing on Sunday or after work on a Saturday. Trains arrived, took them to places they didn't used to be able to get to. So a lot of these guides sprung up because you had gentlemen who had made money out of industry who could afford to buy subscriptions to fish the really posh places.

And then workers would go and spend their wages in the little time they had off, on the trains or the paddle steamers and get a day ticket at those places and a subscription to the waters, and fish. What you've got to remember is that people then kept fish to eat, so as well as the sport, they were eating fish.

In the late 1800s there were probably about 200 tackle makers/shops just in the square mile of London. The tackle industry fed that need and then it grew and grew and formalized itself into the growth of clubs. And they formed associations, so they had some form of political power and leverage. If you go to the British Library and you get a paper out from 1880–1890, it will have four or five pages with just the notes from each angling club's meeting. Somewhere like Kentish Town would have had five or six clubs between here and Camden all based in public houses. So you know where Angler's Lane is, there's a Nando's restaurant? There used to be the Angler's Arms pub there, with a club. And in Stoke Newington they had something like eight clubs. Because everyone had their local pub, and fishing was a mass recreation.

It kind of mirrored the changes in society, so you had a big working population in the Victorian era. A lot of people angling on their half a day off. They might fish on a Sunday but a lot of people go to church on a Sunday. There were a lot of people who were no longer working age who fished, and a lot of kids who fished.

And then everything that happened in the twentieth century killed it. The two world wars, social changes that they brought about, the arrival of the car, the arrival of television, massive pollution on the Thames, people taking water out for building houses and agriculture. The volume of water in the rivers was reduced by half. Less water, less fish. And what has the last fifty years been about except individualism, really? People didn't need to be in clubs any more, where it used to be a sociable activity, much in the same way as you'd go to the dog races or watch the football. The decline in angling in London mirrors that in dog racing. We used to have a dozen if not more dog-racing tracks and now we've got one or two. Fishing is the same. We used to have twelve good rivers or more going into the Thames, but a lot of them have been built over, polluted, ruined. All those little places, havens where you could have fished, completely over-populated and polluted. And then angling just went out of vogue, really.

Carp were brought by the monks in the twelfth and thirteenth century from continental Europe, bred in stew ponds, then introduced to the wild. They were wily old fish, hard to catch. They were very big and powerful so even if you caught one they would break your tackle, even if you had them on the bank. In the 1950s and 1960s you had this growing body of anglers who just fished for carp. By the Eighties and Nineties, the people who were happy fishing for small species like roach and dace and perch started being overtaken by people who wanted to catch bigger fish, mostly carp. That grew into a massive industry. In London you had a lot of waters that were neglected, the municipal ponds like Highgate Ponds, Hampstead Ponds, stretches of the Thames, Bushy Park, Victoria Park. All of these waters held carp. They were in there from medieval times. The locals would put them in there and they'd breed and then they'd take them out and eat them. Some of those fish bred on, they lived to a very old age, they got very big. People went back to fish for them.

So now if you go and walk round Highgate Ponds when the fishing season's on, nine times out of ten they are fishing for carp. That's a massive movement within angling, and it has destroyed the old culture of angling where you just fish for lots of different species. It's an obsession with size, speed, power, modernity, synthetic baits, imported fish. It's angling gone mad, really. So a young kid coming into fishing now, is he going to want to float-fish for a smaller roach or a small perch? No, he's not, because he can buy a cheap bit of kit and go carp fishing with a synthetically produced bait and probably catch one first time he goes out. It's like saying, do you want to ride a bicycle or do you want to drive a Formula One car? Most kids will say, I'll go for the Formula One car. And then what happens is most kids do it for a few years and then they get bored of it and give up.

Against that you've got a renaissance movement where people are going back into the older forms of angling and fishing the waters that were neglected by the carp brigade. They are returning to old ponds and bits of river where there aren't any carp, and fishing for the other species. So the modern angling landscape now is totally different to what it was a hundred years ago. A hundred years ago I'd say that less than 1 or 2 per cent of London's anglers fished for carp. Make that the reverse now.

If you want to make a correlation, carp fishing is a bit like satellite television. It's very similar. You've got all the basic analogue form of media – television that exists quite happily alongside radio and print and all the other things – and everybody dips in and out of each one and then satellite television comes along and says, I'll give you everything bigger, brighter, cheaper, instant, it's a full-on experience and you can have it on your own. Modern carp fishing has brought the experience of catching a carp. It's like instant coffee. I would say that there is a struggle for the soul of angling that exists between carp anglers and everybody else. Everybody else is desperate to keep all the other forms of fishing alive, recognized, available. The carp angler would say, 'I only want to fish for carp, I'm not interested in other forms of fish,' which they call nuisance fish. So they might catch a fish that a normal angler would be quite happy to catch, like an 8-pound tench, they'd be like, 'Shit, I don't want a tench.' That's the modern landscape.

There's still a real passion for fishing and angling in London. You're connecting with what lies beneath as it were, a whole different world which is completely untouched by human life. A stretch of water is as tangible as a building. It's as constant as a building. It's always been there. It's a body of water, it's like a building but it's just in a different form. It's got its features. It might have gravel baths or deep holes or weed beds or patches of lily pads. A lot of these places nature just replenishes them so they keep going. And because it's water they don't necessarily get built on, so they don't get destroyed. I mean, you can't touch the Thames. And because of the law that Henry VIII passed it's free for any Englishman to fish on the Thames as far as Staines. You need your rod licence, but no club or individual can control a stretch as far as Staines. So you can go and fish it.

Logically there shouldn't be any fish in there, if you think of all the changes that have gone on in London since industrialization – the face of London, the landscape, everything. You go down to Waterloo Bridge and look over when the tide comes out. There's gonna be fish on that side and you just wouldn't believe it, but there are. The water's so filthy and muddy and dirty and everywhere you look there are barges and traffic fumes and there's oil on the roads and every time it rains all that gets washed into the river. You know, it's a dirty place isn't it, any city. But to be honest, there's always something – pollution, cormorants, over-fishing, natural diseases – there's always something that the fish population has to battle against. And I like to think that nature will always come through, see it out as it were. I think most anglers will have faith in nature. I'm fairly optimistic. I think that's the nature of the angler, to be optimistic.

MIKEY THOMPKINS

Beekeeper

We are standing on the roof of the Royal Festival Hall, not far from a small beehive tucked away from the wind curling off the river. It's called the Royal Festival Hive and is shaped like the building.

People say to me, how can they have anything to forage on, we're in the middle of the South Bank? And you say, if you look quite closely there's Temple Gardens and there's lots of houses with green areas, and then you start to notice lots of undeveloped areas which are quite overgrown and you start to see how you might make connections across the green sites but also how a bee might be able to make those connections as well. If you look at it on a map and you think from the bees' point of view, there's quite a lot of productive spaces. Green Park, St James's Park, it's quite nice for them on the Embankment. There's loads of greenery for them. Trees are very good for bees because their surface area's enormous. Fan it out, it's huge. An area of a tree is probably as big as this rooftop in terms of forage for a bee, so a flowering tree is pretty important. And there's lots and lots of flowering trees. I don't know what London planes are like. But there's lime trees, there's all kinds of trees around that are productive at different times of the year.

There's also a big question about what do we do with all this rooftop space? There is a huge resource up there. Where I am in East London, there's not a lot of ground space. There's less ground space for me, but suddenly, you know, you start to see lots and lots of productive spaces. [*He points across the Thames.*]

But I also think that we shouldn't see cities as just a space in which things come into. It's a space in which we can be productive and quite creative. I have beehives in the shape of the Royal Festival Hall, a scale model. There's all types of creativity in there, but I don't think it's just bees, generally producing things in the city is a really important thing. Anything that helps the ecosystem is really really important and bees are one of the best things we've got for the ecosystem. They're also a good indicator of how well an ecosystem is performing. If you can put a beehive in the middle of the South Bank and you can get lots of honey off it, that means that around here there are lots of things that the bees can forage on, so it's a good indicator of what's happening in a city as well. I also think that it's good to educate people about the interconnections between food and cities and spaces and the environment.

I suppose because you make connections between where this food comes from and the environment around you, you make a direct connection between the way that this city's put together and its potential productive ability. And you start to think, okay, you watch park-keepers going round with lawnmowers cutting down dandelions and you go, no, stop, stop! There is a big thing with beekeepers about saying, you know we need some wild areas in big cities where bees can forage. We need a different relationship. A city's very much about the controlled, the designed, and the stuff that bees like is the messy stuff at the edge. The stuff that grows out of walls perhaps or the stuff that we just leave alone, so you start to have a different relationship to the stuff that grows around you.

CHRISTINA OAKLEY HARRINGTON

Wiccan priestess

My dad's from Kent and my grandmother is from Edinburgh. I spent a fair bit of time in London as a child, but my father, who had a PhD in geology and was a geochemist, decided in about 1965 that he wanted to join the United Nations third-world development programme. He was posted first to Korea, and then to Japan, and then for a three-year stint to Liberia. So my idea of what religion is was shaped by the religion I experienced, which is tribal religion. I didn't go to church.

In my late teens we repatriated to the West and I was sent to upstate New York to go to high school. God save us, it was a little town outside Albany, a massive culture shock for me. I couldn't play the game, couldn't do it; it was as if I was a different species somehow. It didn't work very well. Then someone gave me a book on paganism and it was like, oh, this is it! He was this short, half-Jewish, half-Irish guy who had been adopted as a small orphan by some Native American Indians and he'd just come off the reservation. And I thought *I* had a weird upbringing: his parents had been killed in a car crash, he'd hitchhiked at 12 across the country, been adopted by the poor folks on the reservation, and just returned to where his birth parents were from. I was very normal compared to him. He said, you should look up this thing called Wicca, and gave me a book called *Drawing Down the Moon* by Margot Adler. I read it, read it all night long.

She sips from a Diet Coke as we sit in her shop in Covent Garden sur-rounded by books on spirituality, esotericism, anthropology and religion. Occasionally customers come in to browse but the shop is nearly closed, as an amateur dramatics society is holding auditions in the basement. A version of the Heinrich Heine quote at the front of the shop reads: 'Wherever they burn books, they also end up burning people.'

I moved to London in 1989 and never looked back. The minute I got off the airplane I thought, oh, it's going to be okay. I was looking for a coven of witches to take me in to adopt me, and that took about four or five months. How does one do that? You pray, basically. You talk to the nature spirits of the place and say please help me find them, because it's all word of mouth, it's never ever written down. You want people who are in the old initiatory tradition instead of just what I call spam books, you know, like *101 Spells for Teenagers Today*, that kind of thing. These were the days of fanzines, little pagan magazines, and there were small adverts in the back of them. You would chase them and follow them and then go to something called 'pub moots' and you'd quietly be identified. You'd go a few times and say quietly you're looking for a coven, looking for initiation. You wouldn't know who they were but they'd be looking at you. If they liked you they might invite you for tea and you'd have to work out that that's what they were.

Then you have to ask for initiation. It can never be offered. You need to be sincere, you need to be discreet, you need to be persistent but not too pushy. They're looking for people who want a vocation and it's a mystery tradition, a secret society. You have to have a calling for it. They're looking for people who are going to be doing this in their seventies if they're in their twenties, thirties, forties now. You also have to think, if you're going to train someone in witchcraft, and they're going to be in a coven with you, you may be spending up to twenty years with them.

With me it went really fast – four months to find a coven. I met someone who said, 'You've got the mark of Cain on you.' [*Laughs.*] 'You've got the calling.' And I did. The night I read that book, I knew what I was. *This* is what I am. This is what I'll be till the day I die. This is what I've always been. I just have a name for it now.

Witches in the city, I suppose like in most things, are more likely to be single, more likely to be a bit bohemian. There are more gay witches in the cities than in the suburbs but that's just because people of alternate sexualities tend to feel more at home in cities. And witches who live in cities, I think they love people more. It sounds funny. That's the thing about living in London. You just have to like the excitement of lots of people. That's why you're here. Those in the countryside or suburbs tend to be more introspective as people.

It would be terrible to be a pagan and not be within walking distance of the British Museum. I mean, how do people do that? A lot of the witches in London are research-inclined, so a lot of them wangle tickets to the British Library. That's a great magical act – wangling your British Library ticket. [*Whispers*] You get some people who should never have them. I don't know how they manage it. Fake letterhead? There's the reason there's a three-hour queue for books.

There's a connection between magic and people researching magic, whether it's Greek or Roman or magical grimoires or ancient manuscripts of magical or angelic texts. In Victorian England that was done and in Edwardian England that was done, so there was this long tradition of consulting the books at the British Library. Joe Bloggs lives in his mum's bedsit in Brick Lane, left school at 16, but he wants his British Library ticket because he wants to sit in the reading room and have magical books delivered to his desk just like MacGregor Mathers, the founder of the Order of the Golden Dawn, used to do.

Waterloo Bridge is also fabulous for witches. The view is beautiful: you get Westminster and the City, and all those Celtic bent swords and offerings that had been thrown in there from Romano-Celtic times and then the pilgrim badges thrown in off the bridges and the remains of spells that we throw over the edge. Let's say you make something on a wax talisman, you do something on wax or you do a bundle of herbs and burn a candle or do something. Usually at the end of a spell, which will be at the end of the lunar month, you'll have the bits left over. The work is done but you've got the physical remains and they have to be got rid of. The craft of the witches has always been to bury it or put it into running water. You don't want to see something that was powerful get covered in dust or have your earrings left on the corner of it or spill tea over it and you don't really want to put it in the rubbish either. It's a bit too special for the rubbish.

So I just do it on Waterloo Bridge on the way to work, just chuck it over the edge. Of course there are commuters going by, there are the buses behind you, and there's the traffic warden, yeah. You just have to have a quiet moment, lean over the edge, say thank you to the river, and let it go. It's a lovely and precious moment.

FEEDING THE CITY

ADAM BYATT

Chef

*It's warm in the restaurant he runs, Trinity, where the late-afternoon crowd is
thinning to the sound of small spoons on saucers. Outside, the wind whips
across Clapham Common. The cooks are busy cutting pork belly and rattling
cutlery. The copper-bottomed saucepans glow under the fluorescents. He has
close-cropped hair and tattoos on the pads of his hands, below the pinkies,
a J on his right for his son Jack and an R for his daughter Rosie on the
left. He drinks coffee with plenty of sugar lowered into each cup. As we talk
he is approached throughout the afternoon – an employee taking home two
pheasants; his lawyer with post-lunch congratulations; a cook with news of
the gnocchi – and like chopping vegetables, he deals with each before sliding
the results to the side. He moves his hands about – the tattoos flash, J and R,
R and J.*

In the Nineties, apprenticeships were a big thing and I went to a jobs
open day with my mum. They were all in this hall, the Ford Motor
Company and Barclays Bank and queues of these students lining up,
and there was the Savoy Education Trust in the corner with no one.
So I dragged my mum there and I said, I want to be a cook. They
said, okay, we've got an apprenticeship at Claridge's or at the Savoy.
And my mum said to me, the Queen eats at Claridge's, Adam. So I
said, okay, I want to work at Claridge's. That was it. On Monday, I
turned up at Claridge's and I had the very worst day of my whole life.

I was streetwise, cocky, not off the rails but close to it. So I walked
into the chef's office and he said to me, okay, you need to go and get
changed. Go into the changing room at the end there, ask for a guy

called John – he will give you a jacket. Unbeknownst to me there were eighty-seven cooks at Claridge's on that day, in that brigade, I was number eighty-eight, yeah, and I walked into the changing room and said, hello, mate, you've got a jacket for me. And he said, okay, number one, I'm not your fucking mate and number two, if I don't get that jacket back tomorrow morning pressed and ironed, I'll kill you. And my day just deteriorated from thereon in. I was taken into the back room, given six boxes of spinach, told to pick the stems off of it, then shown how to blanch it in boiling water, refresh it in ice, and then blend it in a machine to make a creamed spinach dish for a banquet. By the time I'd blended it and passed all the fibres out through a fine sieve I was absolutely covered in green spinach on this guy's jacket which said his name and Senior Sous Chef, Claridge's. So everybody, all day long, had this little five foot two, cocky little Essex boy and they were just ripping into him about being the senior sous chef at Claridge's. Ripping me to pieces. I finished that job at 5.30 and they told me to clean up, which took me another hour and a half.

I'd started at 9.30, and by then I was like a wreck. I'd never stood on my feet that long in my life. They let me go eventually at eight o'clock and I got home at nine o'clock and just burst into tears. I laid on the sofa and I said to my dad, I can't do that. It's horrible. I hate it. I didn't like the Tube journey. I travelled in from Essex, I was living with my parents. And my dad said, well, you must do what makes you happy, but this is an opportunity and if you don't go back tomorrow you will never go back and that's something you need to make a thought of. I didn't know what to do. I set my alarm for the next day and I woke up and I thought, I'm going back. There are junctions in your life and that was one of those junctions for me. I went back and I stayed at Claridge's for the next four and a half years.

That was twenty years ago, and I've cooked ever since.

Growing up in Essex, going up West was for Christmas lights and to see a play with your nan every five years. Going Up West was a really special thing. But suddenly there I was every single day of my working life. When I'd come home, everybody would ask, what's it like? Like it's this land that's fucking ten miles across the road! Go and have a look. They were frightened to go there. There's too many people there. It's too crazy. You get stabbed, you get killed, come on! And they become very insular in that world, they get very insular. My wife and I were really against that. She worked in the City and I worked in Mayfair and we were just like, this is stupid. We were being exposed to fantastic bars, great clubs, new fashion, we can be individuals here. Where we'd come from, it was very you will buy a Ford Mondeo, you will live in a two-bedroom terrace, you will have two kids, maybe six, and a dog, you know, you will claim benefit if you can, and all that. We just thought, no, that's not right.

But the fact is, I never saw much of the West End. I saw the cars and walked past the shops but to be honest I didn't really notice that. I would walk down Bond Street simply to get from A to B, but I wasn't looking in the shop windows, I was looking out for my sandwich guy to make my sandwich and not trip me up. I guess you walk past all the Bentleys but I didn't really care about that. It was just all about my egg sandwich. It was the only thing that was going to get me through the day. Later, when I worked at The Square, lunch was a double espresso and a mini Mars Bar. That was my lunch for the first year and a half of my life there, and dinner was a meat pie and baked beans. Every single day. So if you worked four days in a row, what you ate was: four double espressos, four mini Mars Bars, four meat pies and a tin of baked beans. You're serving truffles and lobster and foie gras and John Dory and turbot, you know. It's warped. It's properly warped. And that's why my guys sit down and have dinner together. Proper dinner, every single day.

I've seen food in London go through three or four different stages. When I first started twenty-one years ago, it was classic, classic, classic, classic food all the way down the road. Remember I've only ever dealt with haute cuisine, as it were, or the higher end of it. I've never really dealt in the middle market or part-bought brasserie food. I've never really done it. But it started out as very classic: sole veronique and beef wellington, these things that everybody would know as really posh food. Certainly not food I grew up on. Then it became a newer version of classic food: less preparations, less techniques, more simplicity on the plate and more influence directly bought in from the likes of Italy, Spain, Portugal, yeah? People like Simon Hopkinson took that classic food and pared it down and made it viable for a restaurant by removing the unwanted cream, by introducing lightness and interest and intrigue from other countries. And then there were the innovators that pushed it forward a little bit and put a saffron vinaigrette with it and did something more interesting with it, and that era is what I loved. I loved that era.

That was The Square really, the beginning of The Square. '96, '98. Where a classic fish soup would be the sauce for a piece of roasted John Dory. That's clever at the time. Now, of course, that fish sauce is turned into a foam and it's frozen-dried and pre-boiled and it's air-dried into a crumb and it's rehydrated into some kind of … it's just gone mad. People have gone mad. But that's the food right there that I started to fall most in love with. That's when I fell in love with food and that first love affair has never gone away.

After that it got all a bit weird because then people took that food and started to do really artistic and creative things with it, and things started to be crispy and standing up and lots of angles and lots of big piles in the middle of the plate and stacking things up and presentation became much more important. Some stupid fucker put presentation at the forefront of importance in restaurant food, and all of a sudden food just looked like some kind of art display and it was awful really. And that lasted for a while until some clever guy started putting food in a water bath and all that stuff, and molecular gastronomy was born and here we are in a new era where molecular gastronomy is very prominent in the upper echelons of fine-dining food. And I think, you know what, those people that have got half a brain, take where they were from, stick to what they were from, cherry-pick some of this presentation thing because it's quite nice, cherry-pick some of the molecular, cherry-pick some of X, Y and Z, keep it real to themselves, put it on the plate and send it – and those are the restaurants right now that are stormingly busy. That's how it works.

I had a conversation with a young chef two days ago. I took him for a drink because he was a bit off. He had worked for somebody extremely high profile for a long time and he said to me, I went with that chef to do a little television thing recently. We had to eat the food that he'd put on for this show, all of his own food – and he didn't want to eat any of it. He said, I don't cook for that, I just cook it. But you can't stop eating your own food!

I couldn't believe it. It's not a product – it's dinner! You're not creating some innovative washing-up thing, it's someone's dinner. Thankfully I think we're moving back into a time where it's actually becoming a bit more honest. In France, the guests are stuck in their ways. In England, they don't know what their ways are, so they can't get stuck in them. The roots for the English are toad-in-the-hole and shepherd's pie – doing anything slightly more innovative than that is the road to laughter.

DAVID SMITH

Director of Markets, City of London

There are six wholesale markets in London, of which I'm responsible for three. The big ones – Billingsgate for fish, Smithfield for meat, and Spitalfields for fruit and vegetables – tend to be unseen, because two of them are slightly tucked away. Smithfield, of course, everyone knows about because it's right in the middle of the city and it's got two major thoroughfares running through it. And there is also this

whole raft of street markets and retail markets around the capital, 180
of them still around London.

His office is in the City of London – he refused to be stationed at any of the
three markets he oversees, lest it suggest favouritism. There's evidence of fruit
in the office: two bananas browning in the corner. His is not an old market
trading family; he was alerted to the job while reading the classifields in The
Times.

These wholesale markets have been here for ever. Billingsgate is now
down at Canary Wharf, it's been there for the last twenty-six years,
but that is just a little flash in history. It used to be in very impressive cast-iron-and-glass buildings right on the Thames, down near
London Bridge, and it had been there since mid-Victorian times. But
everyone knows that there has been fish sold on that site since long
before that. When the market moved, the archaeologists came and
started digging. They found a lot of fish debris there from the pre-
Roman days – which implies there was some sort of trading in fish
going on there 2,000 years ago.

We sell 150 different types of fish down in Billingsgate. During
the course of the year you will see parrot fish, tilapia, different types
of bream. Barramundi farmed in Australia, prawns out of Thailand,
there's a huge fishing industry in Oman and that gets flown in. In
fact I can barely think of a country that has a coastline that doesn't
send product into Billingsgate. Huge lumps of tuna, whole swordfish.
You know, these things which weigh 100 kilos, these are big lumps of
fish. If there's a market for it, a merchant will supply it. There's a guy
who sells live eels. He has them in racking with water going through
the whole time and he opens the drawer up and these eels poke their
heads out to come and talk to you. In the olden days if one escaped it
was just allowed to go off into the dock and good luck to you. These
days they're so expensive they go and catch them – come back!

Smithfield, there's been a market there since the early part of the
Middle Ages. They had a live cattle market there until the middle

of the Victorian age, by which time it moved a mile or so up the road, to Islington Fields, and that's when they built those magnificent buildings, still operational. They are breathtakingly beautiful buildings of their type. And they make a very fine meat market. We spent £70 million on it a decade or so ago, upgrading it so that it now meets all the EU standards of hygiene. Those who were used to the market fifty years ago say, of course, it's no fun and it hasn't got any character; that may be true, but it's clean and it's sanitized. I can remember when they had wooden floors covered with sawdust and everything was open and you had these porters carrying half carcasses over their shoulder and a cigarette hanging out of their mouth. There was no refrigeration as we know it today, but nobody got food poisoning or anything like that. It may not have been as clean and as sanitized as things are today, but it was still healthy.

Smithfield today is a bit old-fashioned in its ways of doing business, but it has a buzz about it. It sells first-rate quality meat, so long as you want to buy a decent quantity of it. You wouldn't get away with buying less than a box of chickens late in the day and they wouldn't want to sell you one leg of lamb or something like that. On the other hand, you can go down on a Friday about seven o'clock in the morning and they would be more than happy to deal with you for a bit of cash. It helps their cashflow and they would be able to get rid of some of the stock before the weekend. These guys who work there all work in white coats and overalls and white wellies and hard hats. When they start, they are absolutely immaculate, that's an absolute rule. But if you're a meat cutter you're going to get blood on your clothes, and even the proprietors of the businesses have got pretty bloody outfits by the time it tails off about eight in the morning.

Spitalfields has been operating under Royal Charter since 1682. It moved from just outside the City of London to new buildings in East London in 1991. We've got 115 stands in the main hall at Spitalfields, of which more than half are foreigners of one sort. The tenants are under no obligation to tell us how much they're selling, but based on the number of forty-ton trucks that come into the market every day, we reckon we sell not far short of 700,000 tons of fruit and vegetables out of Spitalfields every year. That's a hell of a lot of fruit and vegetables. (By comparison, we sell 120,000 tons of meat in Smithfield, and in Billingsgate about 22,000 tons of fish.)

The majority of people who come to Spitalfields are either running restaurants or cafes or catering companies, and there is an enormous colour spectrum that you wouldn't have had in London a hundred years ago. But the spirit, the humour, the doggedness of the traders – that hasn't changed. The knowledge that they are merely here for a small period of time but the market has been here for hundreds of years, that you are a custodian of a tradition. That remains.

You must really get down to one of the markets.

PETER THOMAS ET AL.

New Spitalfields Market traders

New Spitalfields Market sits on a 31-acre site in Leyton, East London. Inside its great shed are those 115 units for wholesaler traders to sell vegetables, fruits and flowers, the largest such market in the United Kingdom. In the early morning hours it's full of stock and alive with the sound of beeping forklifts. Here in the far east of the city, the rest of London is a distant wash of orange in the sky. There is no pedestrian traffic, no late-night wanderers cut through this part of town. If you are out on this patch of concrete, at these unsociable hours, it's to buy fruit and veg in bulk.

The first couple of times I visited the market, I was a danger to myself. Stand for too long in a delivery lane and you'll feel the strong arm of someone guiding you out of the path of a forklift. They move quickly, buzzing past the stacks of cucumbers, squashing errant tomatoes, the drivers peering over their shoulder, sometimes gumming bits of pineapple. On one occasion I left with a box of lychees; another time I came back with a box of spring onions, because the white bulbs of the Spitalfields onion looked like they were made from ivory. Sometimes I'd get fixated on one particular vegetable and the whole mad din of the covered market — the reversing forklifts, the shouted exchanges between buyer and seller, the twittering birds and occasionally the wash of rain outside and the loud, tinny radios playing Heart FM — faded out. Usually I stayed for just an hour or two.

During one visit, I noticed a buyer who moved up and down the aisles with particular speed, wandering, looking, negotiating and ticking off his checklist. He walked up and down for hours. He never came to rest. I sought him out and tried to ask him a question; he waved me off. I persisted and he told me he'd been in this industry since he was 16. 'You have to be the greatest actor in the world,' he said. 'You have to say exactly the right thing. And you have to say it at exactly the right time.' He told me his name was Peter Thomas and when I asked if I could accompany him through the market sometime, he said, 'Sure. If you can keep up.'

1.00 a.m.

JOHN: What, you've got a bouncer now, Pete?

PETER: Yeah, a bouncer, yeah. But I look after *him*.

We are standing on the cold storage floor, where the sorting and food prep takes place. His operation takes up two floors and sits across the parking lot from the market.

PETER: What happens all night long, Craig, we put them orders together in these boxes. They load each lorry up and they all go out to different areas.

CT: How many lorries are there?

PETER: Fifty-five.

CT: So every different area in the city has a different ...?

PETER: It's bigger than the city. It's really the entire M25. Tonight, most are used. On a Tuesday and a Thursday, not all the trucks are used. Come in here, come on.

★

He wears brown cords, a brown jumper over a dress shirt, thick glasses, black dress shoes. He has no belt this morning so he keeps pulling up his trousers, tucking in his shirt. He walks across the cold storage floor towards the milk floats he uses to move back and forth from the market to his office.

This is what we do in the early hours of the morning. Upstairs, we get what we call a song sheet out the computer. It's a long sheet of paper, which tells us every single item that's been sold. We then take our stock sheet out. Our stock sheet is a physical stock that my boys take at nine o'clock of the morning. Okay? Ian, who comes in at midnight, sits down with the stock sheet and the song sheet and compares what's been sold against what the stock is. Now, we're only human beings and we haven't got a crystal ball, so sometimes we run out of certain items, which is the way I want to run the business anyway because it keeps it nice and fresh and turned over. Another employee, Tommy, makes up what you call the shortfall. So for instance we might have a hundred boxes of broccoli on stock and we might have sold 120, which means we're going to be short of twenty boxes of broccoli. That's what Tommy does. So that's where we're going now, to meet Tommy. [*He tucks in his shirt as we jump onto the float.*] We've got another one of these floats. Mind your head on that … That's it. [*He drives the milk float drives across the parking lot. The early morning air stings. Up ahead I can see noise and hustle of the market and the constant mechanical ballet of the forklifts.*]

CT: So where will these trucks be heading to?

PETER: Hospitals, schools, colleges, restaurants, clubs, care homes. All within the M25.

1.20 a.m.

[*Out of the milk float, he walks past the stalls. He is endlessly moving, calling out to the different guvnors, most of whom stand consulting their accounts behind podiums that sit on pallets.*]

PETER: All right, Mark. You owe me a turn as it happens.

MARK: What?

PETER: Yeah, you fucking do and all …

MARK: 10p.

PETER: All right. [*He takes my arm, leads me away.*] See, I said, you owe me a turn. He didn't know whether he did or not. Anyway, he thought about it, but even at this time of the morning you can't let them have an inch. Okay, now we'll just wait here for Tommy.

CT: Do you have a route that you stick to every night?

PETER: What I do, I go down every aisle. [*He points to the lanes.*] I look at every firm. People don't know it, but I'm using my eyes all the time to see if someone's got a lot of something. If they've got a lot of something I know how to bet, do you see what I mean? Hello, Tommy. This is Craig, he's going to spend the day with us and see what happens. [*Tommy nods.*]

TOMMY: Mixed peppers come in from Montgomery. Strawberries, jamming strawberries, they're in.

PETER: Yeah, I want another 20p though.

TOMMY: They're 70. I've got all this top stuff, real cream gear. And I want to put 10 French beans.

PETER: Go on.

[*Peter wanders over towards some asparagus. Tommy rattles his printout at me.*]

TOMMY: This is a short sheet, yeah? This is what I do. The drivers might be waiting for a box of this or a box of that, so I run around to make sure we've got it all so the lorries can get out. The first lorry's going out at two o'clock, so you need to be on your toes. After the lorries go you get a main buying list and then you start again.

PETER: Come on then. Here you are, Craig. [*He deposits a box in my hands and points towards the milk float.*] Just put that asparagus on there. Nice and dry underneath. Smells okay. Got that crispness. Hear that? That squeak. This is Peruvian. This time of year it all comes from South America. English has just finished. You have your seasons, you see. [*He turns to the guvnor, perched behind a podium.*] Ain't bad, John, is it. What's the ecrip?

JOHN: Tom Mix?

PETER: Okay, come and talk to you in a minute.

JOHN: All right.

[*The guvnor, John, wanders away. Peter looks over some courgette flowers and says quietly, mischievously:*]

PETER: Now then, what I want to do, Craig ... we might have some fresh coming in in a minute, see? But he's only got three here now. So that I'll get this, I've got to hide the courgette flowers somewhere.

CT: You're going to hide the courgette flowers?

PETER: Now at least I've got that, you know what I mean? Now when the fresh comes in, I'll change it over.

[*He hides the veg out of sight, straightens up, tucks in his shirt, and starts to walk.*]

PETER: Keep up. Now over there I spoke to them in rhyming slang. I said, 'What's the ecrip?'

CT: The what?

PETER: The ecrip. Did you hear me say, how's the ecrip? That's 'price' backwards, so that you didn't know what I was talking about. And he said to me, Tom Mix, which is rhyming slang. What's Tom Mix?

CT: Six.

PETER: Yeah. This was why the language was designed, so that I could talk to him and no one knew what we was talking about. 'Carpet' means three. That one goes back to years and years ago, when people was given a prison sentence, and if what they got it was either three months or three years, they got a carpet in the cell and that's what they used to say. How d'you get on? Oh, I got a carpet. Oh, fuck me, did ya? And that's what it was. It was either three months or three years, but I know a carpet is three. 'Ben neves' is 'seven' backwards. 'Thgiet' is 'eight' backwards. 'Flo's line' is nine, 'cockle' is ten. 'Bottle of blue' is two and then I'll sling one at an Aristotle. An Aristotle is a bottle. Double rhyming slang. All veg has got different ones. Celery is 'horn root', because years ago they thought that celery was an aphrodisiac. And they said it give you the horn. So they called it horn root. 'Self starters' is tomatoes. 'Navigators' is taters. 'Boy scouts' are sprouts. 'Tom and Jerry' is cherries.

CT: Do you have different banter with people who aren't English? Like the Turks?

PETER: Yes, it's no good talking rhyming slang to them, is it? They just about understand proper English. One of the young Pakistani fellows learned the rhyming slang just so he'd know what was going on. [*He gestures around the market.*] Now these people are all salesmen and they're all here to earn as much money as they possibly can. They will try to get as much money out of me and I will try to get as much money out of them. There's no friends in business. We'll be talking about football and all of a sudden the business side comes to it, and that's it. All the time we're talking, we know that any minute now, any second, it's going to be, 'How much is that?' Then we go back to talking like friends again. You can't drop your card.

Now then, because we're short of produce we have to take it in the middle of the night. We can't buy as we normally would buy. We're at their mercy, slightly. Take for instance we've had to buy strawberries first thing. We're short on strawberries. We've had to take them before the market has got going. Danny, who sells them, said they're 15.50. Normally I would wait and go back there later on and say, Danny, what you going to do about them strawberries? But we're short, so I've got to buy them now. He's got me by the old thingybobs. But I can assure you I'll get it all back later on, one way or another.

1.50 a.m.

PETER: Craig, come on. Look sharp! You okay? Now, what you're going to do now, Craig, you're going to sit there, right, you'll take the handbrake off. *The handbrake* … That one there. [*The milk float springs to life.*] Come on, let's go and see Tommy. All right, Dave? [*He calls out as the float moves past.*] All right, Mark? [*He yells as the milk float slows down.*] There are tricks, you see. Sometimes I've done my old phone trick, but I've been caught out before when I used that one. The old phantom phone trick is when I tell a guvnor, hold on, I'm just going to call Tommy and I put my phone to my ear and say, all right, Tommy? What kind of price on the broccoli? Now, it usually works a charm but one time I had it up to my ear and it started ringing. The phone started ringing! [*He notices some rocket.*] Now, I've just realized something. This is rocket, this is. It's very short and I'm going to put it on now, because in another hour there won't be none in. I want to get hold of Tommy because I want to pick it up now, see?

CT: So do you ever come into contact with the supermarket people?

PETER: Sometimes. The ironical thing about it is, sometimes when they have these promotions they're cheaper than this market – how about that?

CT: So you can buy from them?

PETER: Well, I do sometimes. Only little things, because otherwise what happens is my customers say to me, how come you're charging this, that and the other? And Tesco is only like 50p or something like that? And it's because they've got this great big buying power and they can just source it, you know? [*He notices some raspberries.*] Okay, English raspberries. Dewdrop English raspberries. Here you go, mate. [*He hands me a punnet overflowing with the freshest raspberries I've ever seen.*] That's all the stuff. Got your raspberries? They're lovely first thing. There ain't many people eating raspberries at two o'clock in the morning, Craig.

[*He stops walking for a moment. We eat raspberries.*]

PETER: So when you see your mates having breakfast at eight o'clock, say I had mine at two o'clock this morning, on a bit of rocket, I had some nice English raspberries. I tell you what you do, Craig. Eat your raspberries for two minutes. I'll shoot upstairs and see Ian and ask him if there's another list.

[*The forklifts move past. The smell of crushed onion and coriander mingles with exhaust in the air. I lift up my boot and pick cherry pits from the treads. The market is both inside and outside. It's hot tea and heaters in the Portakabins and fingerless gloves out by the stacks of fruit.*]

2.05 a.m.

PETER: See all these people here? [*He points to some of the customers looking at stacks of fruit.*] They're all shopholders, see, they've all got shops, but they're all Turkish. Not many Englishmen in the industry now. The Englishmen come a little bit later. The stallholders from the market. And you'll see them come in.

CT: So which markets would those be?

PETER: People from Surrey Street in Croydon, Berwick Street in the West End. There's markets in North End Road, but they would normally go to Covent Garden. There's a street market in Stratford that's still got a few stalls there. [*I start the milk float.*] Be careful. Okay, your driving is okay.

CT: Beginner's luck.

PETER: Just think, if ever you're not a success as a writer, you can always drive one of these. Though because you're a stranger in the market, everyone's looking at you. They think you're a policeman. Let's go and see if those courgette vans have turned up. Come on. We'll see Kevin. He's one of the most experienced men in the market, Craig. There ain't much he doesn't know. Anything you want to know about the business, that's your man. [*We approach a large stall.*] Kevin, have you got any fresh courgette flowers to arrive?

KEVIN: No.

PETER: No! Fibber.

KEVIN: No, I forgot to order them! As soon as those words come out your mouth I thought to myself, oh fuck! I've got no memory.

PETER: Okay, Kev, I'll see you later. Don't forget to order them for tomorrow, eh?

KEVIN: Yeah, that's right.

PETER: He forgot to order them. [*We're away.*] He forgot to order them. Now there's a lot of winding up goes on in this market. One of the worst things is for a seller to come over and see what you're up to. If a salesman knows you're rushing about for something and you need it, then they get you at it. Now I've gone in there for courgette flowers and there ain't none in and I need them for a customer, an important customer, so I go to Kevin just now and I said, Kev, courgette flowers? You just missed them, Pete, I had them. That's what he said, been and gone. I said, got any fresh, I see you're out of them. He said, I forgot to order them. See what I mean, it winds you up. That's why I put those courgette flowers to one side earlier. See what I mean? Because at the other stall he only had three left and if he had none fresh come in I'll bet them other two there are gone now. And I'd have gone back there and he'd have said, I did have them, Pete, but I sold them.

CT: How do you know how to do all this? Is it like an instinct every morning?

PETER: I don't know. You've just got to be on your toes. The minute I get out of bed I start thinking all the time.

2.30 a.m.

[*He tosses an apricot pit in the air and kicks it. He eats another apricot.*]

PETER: I have a permanent stomach ache, Craig. What can you do? It's fruit. You can't change the fact it's fruit.

2.45 a.m.

PETER: See them girls over there? From Poland? They'd rather come over here and start work at eleven o'clock at night, working in the caff, delivering cups of teas round this market. All from Eastern Europe. Afghanistan. Romania. Czechoslovakia. All parts of Russia. They all come from there. All lovely girls, nice-looking girls. I think a few of them might have been prostitutes, but I'm not going to go there.

CT: Are there more countries represented in this market than thirty years ago?

PETER: Yeah, and I've got to be honest with you, Craig: it's the salvation of this market. Thank the Lord for the Chinese and the Turks and the Asians. Because there's not enough Englishmen here now. All the talking, the work that goes on – you see what I mean? You wouldn't know it was nearly three o'clock in the morning. And all the business that goes on, people don't realize. The millions of pounds that's traded. All right, John? He's one of my drivers. [*He wears a fluorescent vest.*]

JOHN: Did I tell you when I got escorted out of Tesco's one day? I said their fruit was a load of shit. Which it was. Absolute rubbish.

PETER: They'll sell you what they want to sell you.

JOHN: The worst thing in a supermarket is bananas. They'd be about grade 4, I should think. Personally, I go through everything. I go through every box.

CT: So what are you looking for?

JOHN: It has to be top quality, if it's not good enough it doesn't go on the pallet. You don't just pick a box up and send it. That ain't how it works. Take this one: I've opened this box to make sure the fruit is okay. Like they used to years ago, people should come to the main market to buy their own food. Back then you could turn around and say, there's pride over there. See the way they lay the stuff out. There's pride in the stuff.

CT: So who's this pallet going out to?

JOHN: Lord's Cricket Ground. We supply the King of Dubai. He'll come over every summer for the racing. Yeah, it's only a small order today. The other day it was over £2,000. Most people don't realize good from the bad. They'll just take what comes. They'll eat category one, two and three without knowing the difference. We're category one. That's what we are. If I think it's bad, I'll tell Peter and Peter sends it back and gets me new stuff.

CT: Is there someone at, say, Lord's who inspects the pallet?

JOHN: Yeah, they won't take it unless they see it.

PETER: You can come with me today. I want to go out because I want to see the man. I'll take you out to Lord's today. Did you bring your cricket bat?

3.30 a.m.
Sometimes he answers the phone by saying, 'Courgette.' Sometimes when he handles new potatoes he says, 'Are these already parboiled?' A stallholder tries to dissuade him: 'It's too rich for you today, Pete. It's Fortnum and Mason around here today.'

3.40 a.m.

PETER: See, I'll slow down. I slow my pace down when I'm on the market because if I'm rushing about for something they think, oh, hello, Pete, what you looking for? So I take my time, I walk on, I stand. Make out you're not interested, know what I mean? But really I've seen something – cor, I like that – but the worst thing to do is make out you're interested, you know what I mean? So I walk in the market, casually, not really interested, like this. 'All right, Peter? Lots of salad here,' someone will say. 'Yeah, I don't know if I want it today. How much is it anyway?' You can't show you're interested. The minute you're going somewhere a little bit lively, the minute you ask for cherry tomatoes a little too quickly – they know.

CT: This is when the acting starts? This is like the curtain rising on the Second Act.

PETER: If you like, yeah.

4.00 a.m.

PETER: I'm going to tell you something now: I want to meet up with him, Boris. What's his name?

CT: Boris Johnson – the mayor of London?

PETER: Yeah, Boris. I want to talk to him because I'll tell you something, you can't imagine how much I have to pay in Congestion Charge. Every lorry I have to pay Congestion Charge. Colossal. The red routes, there's parking fines. I'm the biggest hospital supplier in London. We must serve thirty hospitals. As far as I'm concerned, I'm providing a service. I'm like one of the fourth emergency services. I'm supplying. So I want to say to Boris: Listen, Mr Boris, Peter Thomas. Why should I have to pay Congestion Charge? All I'm doing is trying to get a living delivering. It isn't like I'm going into London, parking up and having a cup of tea. So, am I an integral part of London? Yes, I fucking am!

4.10 a.m.

[*He leans in, adjusts his shirt, tucks it in. He and the guvnor speak under the roar of the market. He walks away. He walks back. We walk on.*]

CT: What just happened?

PETER: I asked him how much it was. He asked me a Tom Mix. I said a bit of a Flynn. I said, I'll meet you in the middle, which is what?

CT: What's a Flynn?

PETER: Flynn is a fiver.

CT: Meet you in the middle, at £5.50?

PETER: Yeah, and I've said no. I was going to walk on and he called me back.

CT: For what?

PETER: Down to a fiver. So I've saved myself £20 there. Just like that. Right. I've got to buy all these items today, right. We only want twenty boxes of celery, but I might want 200 of tomatoes. So if I save myself 20 or 30 pence on 200 tomatoes, it all adds up at the end of the day, six days a week. My money, see, that's the difference, it's my money.

4.20 a.m.

PETER: We've been in the game all our life and we know. It's like a watchmaker, like anyone who used to make things years ago. Once that industry has finished, the artist has died with it. There was artists in this industry, but we're a dying breed because of the supermarkets. They've nearly killed us off. And once we've gone, that's it.

CT: So what is the artistry?

PETER: To know your produce. To know a tomato and to taste it and to know that's a lovely eating tomato. A lot of people come in the industry now, they don't know that a nice small tomato this time of year from Spain is a lovely eating tomato. They go for Dutch, which ain't a great flavour tomato, you know? It's just knowing. My son's in the business. You'll see him later on. I show him, but where do you go from there? I don't know. Every year more people drop off the edge, it's yet another stallholder that's gone out of business. You hear it all the time. I might say, I ain't seen Fred for some time? He's packed up, retired. What's happened to his stall? Well, no, there's no more stalls. What about his son? No, he didn't want to do it. He was in another game, you know. That's it.

That's another family business gone.

5.00 a.m.

PETER: See, now, these tomatoes are nice, but I want a little bit more backward. Backward, green. If you want something to last, you've got to buy it backwards, see? If they're too coloured by tomorrow they'll be a bit more coloured and I don't want them, so what I want is a bit of backwards.

5.40 a.m.

PETER: I just want to do a check on my list here now, Craig. And then we'll have a quick cup of tea and then we'll shoot out to Lord's.

CT: Is there anyone you don't get along with, in here?

PETER: We all need each other. You have the odd discrepancies but you've got to make up for it because my grandfather said to me, son, a proud man will starve to death, you can't afford to be too proud. Especially when you're buying and selling. We spend a lifetime together, all of us. You might call someone a c–u–n–t but you'll still buy £1,000 from him. The language round here gets interesting. Everybody in here – Chinese, Pakistani, Turkish – knows a few of the more international words. I've come from one lorry to fifty-five. I ain't done bad, have I? And when I retire, I'll be able to walk out with my head held high and these boys saying he fucking supported us all through his life. See what I mean? Keep moving. Butternut squash. Let's go down. This way, Craig. A couple more places, then we can go and have a cup of tea.

6.00 a.m.

[*He examines a squash.*]

PETER: Butternuts. There ain't a rhyming slang for that. I fuck about sometimes. Nutterbut? Oh blimey.

★

6.20 a.m.

[*The birds arrive. The noise of forklifts gives way to chirping. The skies are brighter as the morning light seeps in.*]

PETER: What would happen years ago, Craig, all the buyers here in the market would buy all their stuff, buy all their bargains and there'd be a competition who'd bought the best. And you'd hear them. What you done? I bought some tomatoes, they're out of this fucking world. I only give £2 for 'em. I bought some cucumbers – as long as that, green as grass and he was only charging half a quid, and it was all lies, know what I mean?

CT: Like being round a bunch of fishermen.

PETER: Yeah, exactly right, yeah.

CT: Do people ever come up with new tricks? I mean you guys have known each other for so long. You must know everyone's tricks and they must know all of yours.

PETER: It's all different. If I was buying lemons I'd find a bad lemon and put it in my pocket and when I go across there, I'd put a bad one in the box. And then I'd call him over and say, look at the state of these lemons? Fucking hell! I'd say, I might be able to have a go, but the money's got to be right, if I'm buying them you've got to do something for me. My boy, look. [*A young man approaches.*]

CT: Is that him?

PETER: Craig, this is Ben, my boy. Ben, this is Craig. He's going to write a book about me.

BEN: Yeah, right.

PETER: He's been here since one o'clock this morning.

BEN: Have ya? You done well.

PETER: He did do well, didn't he?

BEN: Did you have any Red Bull or anything? You feel all right?

CT: No, I'm fine. Why didn't I have any Red Bull?

BEN: Do you want a Red Bull?

CT: No, not now. God, no.

PETER: Ben was in the building game, doing all right and all of a sudden it fell away. Building trade just fell away, so he's come here. There's a fellow who had some rounds selling to cafes and restaurants and he's retiring, so he was selling his business, so I bought it off him and give it to my boy. All I've done is bought him a set of tools, the rest is up to him. He's done fantastic.

CT: And you know what happens when you start with one van.

PETER: Absolutely right, but I won't let him go to two. I forbid it.

CT: Why?

PETER: Because he's doing fantastic. He's got a nice lifestyle now. Fantastic. I don't want him to have the stress and the worries that I have. Worrying about drivers turning up and people not turning up, people not paying you. Too many worries. The way he is at the moment is the best way. Let's go out to Lord's Cricket Ground. We'll go out there and when I come back I have to run the business, don't I, lots of paperwork, all that's got to be done. I get home about four o'clock each day, do a bit of gardening.

   I've enjoyed working here very much but it's not been easy. It's got to be harder now than what it's ever been. Yeah, what you have to put in to make it pay. But that's what you have to do, to be successful, it's what you have to do, whether you're in this game or any game. You've seen the whole operation from one o'clock. This afternoon, all my office staff will be taking orders. Then from six o'clock my night staff come in up the office. It's like a conveyor belt, know what I mean? And then it starts again.

6.40 a.m.
[*The morning shimmers in front of me. More birds have gathered in the girders and they swoop down towards the spills of the day. Peter gets into the van.*]

CT: So which hospital is that? Which one did you just mention?

PETER: The Edward VII.

CT: The Edward VII and the Royal Dubai, the Dubai Royal Family.

PETER: The Dubai Royal Family. They got properties all over the country and we do one out at Newmarket which is a stud farm because they love their horses. You feel all right? It'll start creeping up on you now.

CT: That's all right.

PETER: Well listen, I'll tell you what to do. It'll take us about half-hour, why don't you close your eyes for about half-hour and I'll wake you up when we get there? Little ten minutes, quarter of an hour will do you the world of good.

CLIMBING THE LADDER

ASHLEY THOMAS

Estate agent

He strides across Upper Street in Islington to greet me, well groomed in a T.M. Lewin suit. Inside his agency, the waiting room is dominated by a few curved, space-age chairs. There is a drinks refrigerator behind reception. The receptionist sits in front of flat screens showing houses that slowly disintegrate into pixels, replaced by more houses. A young couple sits with an estate agent nearby providing details of their life together. The young man slowly peels the neck label of his beer and his partner lists their dreams, plans and expectations while a double-decker 38 bus moves slowly past the large glass windows.

My trade is full of dishonest people, I'm afraid. We are hated just as much as traffic wardens. It's known. In the hate tables we are right down there. Sometimes we advise people that an area is changing, and they won't believe you because estate agents aren't to be believed. A friend of mine that used to work for the same company as me used to have a big pink cushion in the back of his car, with sequins on it that said: TRUST ME, I'M AN ESTATE AGENT. It was just for comic effect.

In my industry generally people are not mature – they're usually in their early twenties, a little bit spotty and they don't really know what they're doing. I do know what I'm doing, and I think people buy into that confidence. Sales is all about confidence. If they don't have confidence in you they won't have confidence in your product. You need to look smart. You need to have a bit of energy. You need to have fantastic communication skills; I'm daily speaking to bankers, lawyers, magistrates, musicians, artists and you need to be able to converse with all of them. I think frankness and honesty are two really important traits to have.

So people come to the office and they wait for me to arrive and they're expecting somebody in their twenties, who doesn't know anything about property, who's going to lie to them, who's going to not show up for viewings, who's going to get the wrong keys. And then I walk in.

The London market's really really strong; zones 1 and 2 of the central area, we've got loads of people flocking to London. One out of three buyers is a cash buyer, which is immense when you think of the amount of transactions in the London market. One out of four buyers is foreign. We're getting buyers from Asia, Australasia, North America, Europe and they're flocking here to buy London property. It might be for themselves, it might be for their siblings; the demand is incredibly high for London property.

Everybody wants to be in London. It is perceived as being a great city in the world and everybody wants a part of it, so there's always going to be heaps of demand. That's why property prices double every six years. We haven't got limitless land in central London. The only land you can build on is brownfield, which is old industrial. That's it. Or knock another house down. Everything's going up now because we've run out of land.

I think in England, the importance of property is ingrained into you. 'An Englishman's home is his castle,' you know. You need to get on the ladder as quick as possible. Basically, you need to be on the ladder in order to engage with the ladder. Property prices are always going up and if you're not on the ladder with that asset climbing in value, the more time you're away off it, the more difficult it is to get on. Typically you'll need a deposit of between 10 and 20 per cent to get on the ladder, so when you buy a property for £300,000 you need between £30,000 and £60,000 just as a deposit to get on it. Now that's a lot of money to save up, it's a lot of money. If you haven't got parents who are going to give it to you or you haven't inherited the money, you know … let's say property prices go up by a third, by 33 per cent in two years. If you haven't got on the ladder in two years, then that property now is going to be £400,000 so then you've got to get between £40,000 and £80,000 to get on there. So that's why it's vitally important to get on the ladder with whatever property it is as quick as possible because then your equity is going up in the property as the property market starts appreciating. As time goes by, your salary will go up, your equity is going up in your property. So then it's time to sell and then move to the next size property. Because generally you should always want a bigger property because you're single to start with, then you get into a couple, then you have children, so you always need a bigger property. But what a lot of Londoners have been doing in the last ten years is they have their one-bed property and then they think, hold on a minute, I need a new pension vehicle, so they keep their first property, rent it out, release the money from it and buy their second property. And that's how you get portfolios of like three, four, five or, like me, ten properties.

When I bought my first property, I rolled on the carpet. It was in Bromley, in zone 5, and for the first six months I had bailiffs knocking on my door every other week because I was defaulting on bills. But I knew I had a property. I said to myself, this is *my* carpet. Well, actually it wasn't mine, it was the bank's carpet. I didn't own any of it really. But I always do that – you know, touch the walls, roll around, say out loud: it's mine. Even with the new ones that I buy now, I get very excited because it's a chunk of London that's mine.

It's never too late to get on the ladder. We try and make them realize that if they use their brain and use the right connections with regard to finance then they actually can afford something. Whatever they *can* afford we'll show them their best option and try and convince them to buy it. We are salesmen at the end of the day and we do earn a fee from selling something, but we are right in saying you must get on the ladder or it just flies away. I think the average age four years ago of first-time buyers was 31. That's probably increased now. And so generally people can only get on the ladder if their parents are going to give them a wad of money and not everybody has rich parents who can give them £30,000 or £50,000, so you know there are people in our offices on decent salaries trying to save a deposit, they're in their late twenties and would love to get on the ladder. And the first property they'll buy will be in an ex-council block and people hate the thought of having to live in a council block when they're used to renting a nice apartment. But you've got to get on, you know? That council block will be full of professionals because everybody's doing the same thing, so there'll be half council tenants and some of them may be rough, some may be very nice, but the other half will be young professionals just trying to get a foot on the ladder.

I see it all the time because I'm always dealing with clients that have to move. They're a couple in a two-bed flat, just about to have a baby, so they *have* to get somewhere with a bit of outside space or a third bedroom. They have a budget that's higher than what they're selling at, and you usually organize the finance for it so the step is there all the time. You're always seeing the ladder. It's like steps, really, going up into this very big house in a great big cloud. Never ending.

And then you see it on the downside when the economy's not good, you see people losing their jobs and forced sales and downsizing. We're seeing a lot of downsizing right now, but there's always somebody who's on the up who will buy that house. Something will always sell in London because there are so many weird, quirky, unusual people. For instance, most people want an old property either to do up or to move straight into and a lot of people don't like new-builds. But the Chinese and Japanese, they love new-builds, they won't even touch an old property. So there's a market for everything, you know. That dark and dingy basement that nobody wants to buy – well, some people love dark and dingy basements. I've just been out with a guy that wants a big basement. Great, I've got some for you because nobody else wants them. Yeah, you'll always sell.

We've sold houses in the past where there's been murders. There was one house where a whole family was murdered. I think it was a mother and three children, and we were selling the house. You don't mention things like that. If they want to do their research, then of course they can do their research. It's not lying to them. It's just not presenting them with all the facts. If they ask a question we will answer it, frankly and honestly. But if they haven't asked … At the end of the day we work for our client and they want to sell a house, so you're not going to tell everybody there was an awful murder in the house. It's not going to sell it, is it?

On a single day I go out on six hours of viewings and I may be showing stock at £400,000 one-beds to a £3 million house, and it's lovely dealing with that variety of people. The variety of perceptions that they bring to us range from ultra-negative to ultra-positive. You watch body language, you watch whether they smile or not. If they're smiling in a property you know that something's igniting their p-spot, as I call it. Their property spot, instead of a g-spot. Some of your buyers, you can get on with them so well that when it comes to the business part of things, the offering, it can be a bit awkward because you really like them but you've got to squeeze another £50,000 out of them, so you have to switch from 'I really like you, you're lovely,' to 'This is business.' There's no point being there if you're just going to not sell.

I'm the second-best performer in the whole of Foxtons. The only person that beats me is someone in Notting Hill and we cannot compete with their ticket price in Notting Hill. For *the* biggest company. It's good to know you're in that top position. But the overriding emotion for me is somebody comes to me, they're looking for a home and I find them a home. It's a very exciting moment when they see that home, then it's the hard work of getting it to be legally theirs. That's very difficult in this country. It's not easy at all. But when you hand over the keys, it's a very special moment because you know that they're going to go to their property – they probably won't roll around on the carpet like I do – but they'll do something that will be symbolic and, you know, sometimes when you give them the keys tears come to your eyes because you know what it means to them. They're finally in that beautiful property, whether it's small or big, whether it's ugly or needs doing up or is absolutely sensational inside, it really is a great feeling.

ROBERT GUERINI

Property owner

Margaret Thatcher came in as prime minister in 1979, and she realized soon after that to get the votes and to be politically in the ascendancy she could offer council tenants the opportunity to buy their houses or flats. This was a social disaster – why? In the city centre, we need people to maintain the city, guys to do the gas, the electricity, the water and so on, and people to run the transport system. We can't have these people come miles. What's happened now, the council flats in the city were all sold to the incumbent for a very low figure because they were sitting tenants or they'd been there for so many years. So a guy and his family, he's a man of 60, he's able to buy his flat for £20,000 and he's able to sell it within a year, I think they had to wait a year, they could sell it for £180,000. Of course he sold it, packed up his stuff down to Bournemouth where he bought a lovely flat overlooking the sea. Well you can't blame him. But, having said that, the person that got that flat then was often a buy-to-letter who rented it on to somebody else, but not at £50 a week. It was £100 a week. Now slowly but surely cheap accommodation for working people in the city contracted. It was a real tragedy in my opinion.

In the front room of his house, just off the King's Road in Chelsea, there are photos of his family on the walls and drawings by his grandchildren on the door. He wears a light yellow shirt and tinted glasses and speaks in a slight Irish lilt.

★

I've got people from every part of the world in the flats I own. I've got Mexicans, Somalis, Spaniards, Germans, Algerians, Lebanese. I've just taken a man from … where is he from? A Kosovan. The first Kosovan I've hired a place to. I hired to him last week. When I think about it now, I just think: are there any English people? In the suburbs you tend to get English people. I've got flats down in Sidcup, I've got English people there.

I've never had to sell cheaper than I bought. Ever. Even now, because so many people come into London. The minute there's unemployment over the country, there's always work in London. Why? Because of the need to service those million people a week that are visitors. They come in and they need service. They need to be fed and watered and housed and so on. So that's a huge crowd of people who need that service and therefore when people are out of work they come into the city and get a job as a barman. You go into any restaurant in the city, it's all young foreign people. I went to a restaurant, a very smart restaurant yesterday for my wife's anniversary, we went to a restaurant down near Mayfair, and all the servers there, including the manager, were foreign. There were no English people. Quite incredible.

I like all the ethnic groups that are here. It makes the city more cultural. Go up the Edgware Road and see the hubble-bubble pipes and stuff like that. I can be in Arabia or I could be in Edgware Road. I can be in St Lucia by going to Brixton Market. I enjoy that. I go to Brixton Market a lot. I've got flats there and I go down there and buy some fish. Go into the fish shop in Brixton and you will get ten black women telling you how to cook a bit of fish. 'No man, you don't wanna do that …'

I've never been able to understand race or prejudice, really. I find it very difficult. It's like going to a library and saying to the librarian, I'm sorry, I only read books with red covers.

The other night I went to a dinner with a young man who had just come down from university and was living in London with a young woman. They both were decrying the fact that it was very difficult to make a living, very difficult to find accommodation, very difficult to buy and to live, and so on. And I said, there is a resolution to your problem. They said, what's that? Well, you could get a job that wasn't too taxing during the day, and every evening get a job serving tables in a restaurant where the tips are good. Don't go into a classier restaurant because it'll all be on the bill, 12½ per cent and you won't get cash. Go to a little cafe that does good business, near a railway station or something, be there on time, be immaculate, be glamorous, you, young man, dress yourself up. The guvnor will only pay £5 an hour for six hours, which would be £30, but you'll get £20 in tips. You'll pick up £50 a night, five days a week, that's £250 in addition to your salary. I said, the two of you making another £250 a week. That's £500 a week, that's maybe £15,000 a year with which you'll be able to buy a place. And you know what they said? We wouldn't be prepared to do that because we wouldn't have a social life. I said, but you've got no money. You've got no social life! But they couldn't see it. They weren't willing to put that sort of effort in.

If you're not willing to put in the effort in this city, don't come here. This city is about effort. Effort is rewarded, no question. I know some fine young people here work night and day and they collect that bread; all right, so they spend a year all over the world with it, but at least they've achieved that. They were capable of working sixteen, eighteen hours a day. They were capable of saving £10,000 a year. They were capable of doing it. But I don't find any problem with that. Social life, hang around pubs drinking beer? Forget it. As my father says, it takes not the wits of a donkey to drink five pints of Guinness and fall down. Right?

STEPHANIE WALSH

Property seeker

I grew up outside of Cambridge and was desperate to get away from home. Not because I didn't like it. I was just excited by London and thought it would be a good adventure. Being 18, I was kind of naive, like, 'Oh yeah, it could be amazing and easy and brilliant!'

I came for art school, and at first I was really awed by London. Once, we were given a sculpture project to make a self-portrait. I made a life-size sculpture, a weird abstract thing with a frame out of bamboo sticks and tissue paper, and thought that I could take it on a London bus. It was enormous. I had no idea that London was so busy, that people weren't interested in things like that and that they wouldn't make space for you. If I'd done that on our school bus in the village everyone would have been like, 'Oh wow, you can have a whole seat to yourself.' In London, everyone's just like, 'Stupid art student.'

I lived in Brixton for about two years after college and then a really good friend had a flat in Old Street with a room going, so I moved up there. We lived in an ex-council flat just behind the fire station in Old Street, and it was really good fun. That was quite a hedonistic time. The job I had, it was demanding but it was also pretty sociable, and suddenly there were a lot of gallery events to go to, and Old Street was convenient for bars. I spent loads of time going out.

The whole flat was grotty, though. It was really cheap, but it had concrete floors and no curtains and was freezing cold in the winter. The friend that I was living with was working at a magazine and I was working at a gallery and our lives weren't crossing over that much, so we were both using the flat as a bit of a dumping ground. There was a three-seater sofa that had obviously been there for years. All the cushions had flopped in the middle, and none of us wanted to spend any money to sort it out. One weekend her parents were coming to stay and she bought a new throw for the sofa and a plant for the living room and it transformed the whole place. It was like, 'Why didn't we do that before, you know?' We were all so tied up with going out and doing work things that we just weren't spending any time there. We couldn't really be bothered.

I was probably around 30 and had been with my boyfriend Tom for seven or eight years by that point. We'd been spending a lot of time thinking about careers, and you begin to wonder what else there is. And I guess being a girl and hitting 30 you start thinking about children. We talked about families and the long-term future, and I think we realized that maybe London wasn't going to work, because we couldn't afford to buy somewhere big enough for us to have the lifestyle we wanted for our children. Both of us grew up in very traditional, stable families in nice houses, and I think we both aspired to that for our children. That was going to be really difficult in London, working in the arts. I don't think we could have done it unless we'd inherited loads of money.

We happened upon Broadway Market by accident. I was writing an article for an art magazine about an organization that opens studios up across the East End, and quite a lot of artists had studios in Broadway Market. We ended up going there one Saturday, which is when the farmers' market is on, and thought, this is quite nice. It didn't feel like it was trendy in the same way that Old Street was. We'd been looking to buy a flat in Chalk Farm or further north, and realized that we couldn't afford it. We ended up buying a flat near Broadway Market, overlooking the canal and really loved it at that time.

But I think there was an epiphany moment when I had Sarah two and a half years ago. She was born about a month early and it was all a bit of a shock. I was in complete denial about having a baby and I'd just finished working on the Festival of Architecture. There were five hundred events and I was doing all the press for it and it was a really manic job. I had to stop working just before the Festival because I was up on maternity leave. I had this morning where it was like, oh my god, I've gone into labour. We rushed into hospital and it was all quite full-on. I ended up spending five days in Homerton Hospital. I felt a bit institutionalized by the whole thing. I walked out of the hospital with Sarah, who was tiny, and Tom, and we went to get a taxi. There was some pissed guy outside the hospital ranting and raving, and I remember thinking: what am I doing here? Why aren't I at nice, middle-class Addenbrooke's Hospital in Cambridge? And just thinking, I really don't want to have to deal with this now, I can't get my head around having to look out for myself in the same way that I could before.

The sun plays across the wall behind her. She's waiting for a delivery. Her free mornings are freighted with errands as well as periods of the kind of deep relaxation young mothers must plan because, as she says, they're not going to be handed out free.

We spent a day at home, and then I went out for a walk in Broadway Market, because I needed to get out of the house. I noticed all the graffiti everywhere and the gangs of kids with their fighting pitbull-type dogs. It suddenly felt like I had to really look out for this little baby and I couldn't be relaxed about being in this quite edgy area. It became a bit of a hassle rather than something that was exciting or interesting.

For the first time I noticed the air quality. I don't know why but I was walking over the little canal bridge by Broadway Market and it seemed really smelly. It was probably because I'd been indoors for five days in the hospital and was just noticing the litter. I was having to find my own feet again in a different way, because none of my other friends had children and I was trying to discover places like playgroups or other groups of parents and it was just quite hard. Previously, all my friends had been working in the arts or creative industries and suddenly I was hanging out with people who were solicitors or doctors or social workers. It was a real mixture of people, which was quite interesting, but at the time I didn't really want to deal with that because I had this new baby. I just wanted to be in a bit of a secure environment and be able to adjust to being a mum, and not have to think so much about the environment I was in.

Previously I'd been the sort of person who pushes myself all the time. I'd be like, oh yeah, I can just nip off to Shepherd's Bush for the evening and then go to Brixton on the way home and then back to Old Street. I thought nothing of jumping on the Tube and sitting there for an hour quite happily, and forgetting to take a drink with me and things like that. And then suddenly it was just a bit like: right, if I'm going to leave the house I'm going to have to pack up a bag with nappies in, and then walk to the Tube and it's a bit of a hassle because if I walk *this* way there are loads of things to watch out for, and if I go *that* way it's really noisy and smelly and I don't want Sarah to be exposed to that. And then I can't go on the Tube because the steps there are really annoying, so I'll go on the bus instead. Oh no, actually I can't go on the bus because they get really irritated by pushchairs and that's the wrong time of day to do that. I guess when you have children you just want to stay a bit more local because you have to do things quicker, because you have to fit around sleeps or eating and things like that, and spontaneity goes a bit. So suddenly London started to feel like a hassle and a bit more isolated.

I was amazed when I moved back to Cambridge, because in the street people move to one side if they see you coming with a buggy, and people are just polite and say hello to you if you're walking in the park. Whereas in London, it just makes no difference, they're just rude, you know. You say 'Excuse me' on a bus and they're like, 'What? What do you want? Mind yourself.' They don't make any allowances.

You don't want to go through a social experiment. You just want what's best, to give them lots of space to play. But it feels like you need to have a lot of money in London to make those kinds of choices. And even then, people that I know who have got lots of money, and send their children to private schools or invest a lot of time in after-school activities, it still feels quite pressured and competitive.

Their child goes to ballet one evening, then swimming another, it's all organized activities and children have very little time away from parental supervision in London. Whereas if you're somewhere suburban, or somewhere a bit less edgy I guess, you can give your child a bit more freedom.

I was getting grumpier and grumpier the more I was there. I was feeling more claustrophobic. Moving up to Cambridge I've kind of rediscovered that thing when you're an art student and you're being asked to look at the world in different ways, or try and express how you're looking at it. I think I was forgetting to do that while I was living in London. I was forgetting to look at the good things and I was forgetting to use the good things, so I was getting more and more frustrated with it because it just felt like it was becoming more and more of an inconvenience. Whereas, moving up here I can spend more time in the garden and that's a bit of a creative outlet. I've learnt how to play a bit more again. London was beginning to take that out of me, and I was feeling tired by it. If I was still there I'd just be feeling really wiped out.

NICK STEPHENS

Squatter

His current squat is above a NatWest bank on Leicester Square. The windows look down on the bust of Hogarth, Tom Cruise's handprints, tourists attempting to picnic and hydraulic cranes preparing for another premiere at the Odeon. The walls of his squat are newly beige with paint taken from a nearby B&Q skip. There are a few candles, sleeping bags, an orange couch, a Mac, a printer, a George Orwell paperback. He had recently found an electrical junction box below the lift, snuck out of the flat – always a risk – and turned on the electricity.

★

When you're opening a property, it's a monumentally stressful activity. You're always at risk of being caught. You have to keep your wits about you and you have to make split-second judgements. First, you find a place that's empty. I know a couple of people who have tried to squat places that haven't been empty and they ended up being chased down the road at two o'clock in the morning by a guy with a bathrobe round his waist and a great big baseball bat. So you find a place that's empty, you get your crew together and then you acquire access to the building. Then you whack up a Section 6 notice on the front door and you house-sit until the police or the council or the neighbours turn up. Then you deal with them.

The first place we squatted was a derelict council estate in Brixton. Most of the residents had been evacuated, removed and replaced some place else and the only tenants left were roving hordes of teenagers. A community of about ten of us lasted there for three months. We left due to the hostility of the remaining tenants. Our doors would be kicked in, friends of ours would be mugged, bicycles stolen, there was a lot of violence within the estate during the time of our occupancy. Early one morning someone was shot to death. Police cars and ambulances visited the place frequently. In fact, when we were squatting the place, we were changing the locks on one of the houses and the police turned up at our front door. They asked us what we were doing and we said we were squatting the place. Instead of arresting us, they looked us up and down and said that we were very brave and that if we heard or saw anything out of order we should contact them immediately. So that was our first squat and then we progressed elsewhere.

With each squat that I inhabited, I ended up with a large community of Polish ex-pats. Each of them had a degree of some description and each of them had abilities in some form of home maintenance, be it plumbing or electrical rewiring or something of that fashion, so it was hugely beneficial for us as a community to be able to repair the things that weren't working properly in our squat. We had about twenty-two Polish people who basically took care of all the maintenance works. They were a feisty lot. They didn't take any shit. They were committed to saving money and to reinvesting that money in their communities back home.

The last time I actually rented a flat was in Kilburn with my ex-girlfriend, where we cohabited a tiny room measuring about 8 metres by 5 metres. We were paying £120 a week and it drove us mad. It was the size of a large cupboard. There was barely any room to move. The bed doubled as a sofa. We had a tiny stove on which to prepare our meals and a tiny compartment which hosted a shower unit. It was horrendously small, horrendously overpriced and it drove myself and my girlfriend apart.

Before that I lived in Chelsea and I had a job in IT, and I remember just how extraordinary it was at the time I was shifting jobs and shifting apartments, the stress involved. I think finding a place to rent in London is probably one of the most stressful activities you can partake of in this city. But squatting opened up a lot of doors. You don't pay rent. You rarely pay council tax or bills. It affords you a lifestyle that you would otherwise not be able to afford, especially if you are a low-income earner. The minimum wage here is just over £5.75 an hour. The average rent per week, on the bottom bracket, is £70 per week. £70 a week gets you a room in a bedsit on the outskirts of London, a room in a hostel, or a roomshare with three other people in Zone 2. £70 a week doesn't get you very much at all. Squatting, however, gives you a lot of freedom. You choose the people that you live with. You can always choose the area that you live in, because there is always an abundance of empty properties. And the lifestyle, while it lasts, is good. You can save money. You can do your thing.

The downsides to squatting are that you are continually on the move. You have to travel with a limited amount of possessions. You can be left homeless. If you are evicted without due notice you can find yourself in rather unpleasant circumstances.

One time we were squatting a house in Peckham. The house was terrible. There was only one working tap. I was dying to get out of there anyway. We were evicted prematurely on an old eviction notice and we had to leave within a week; we'd been there for about four months. Suddenly, more than twenty of us found ourselves homeless. We had no place to go. Luckily it was the summertime, so we slept on park benches in St James's. And in the park in Westminster, near Embankment station. So we slept there and for two weeks we went roaming around London, we tried about fifteen places and for some reason each one was either too derelict to inhabit or the police came or there was some other complication. There was a lot of camaraderie. When you're working together in such a situation, you have to be able to get along. You don't have time to bicker, you're too stressed really.

We spent about two weeks being homeless before we landed upon a series of arches underneath the London Bridge railway line. We managed to acquire access to those, each one individually, and we settled in there reasonably well. There were no domestic facilities so it made life rather uncomfortable. There was one tiny kitchen, no bathroom, no shower, nothing like that, so we settled in and were in the process of making the third arch into a magnificent night cafe. We were going to have a spot of gambling. We were in the process of building the bar when we were stormed by the anti-terrorism police. I remember the exact time because I was sawing up the bar in my underwear. I was dripping with sweat and wielding a great big handsaw when the door burst open and all the local constabulary burst in: I found myself confronted with about two dozen anti-terrorist police and local councilmen. That was rather a startling experience. They evicted all of us under new anti-terrorism laws. Railways were particular targets, and railway security had been tightened. So I wouldn't recommend squatting in arches underneath a railway track.

MIKE BENNISON AND GEOFF BILLS

Residents of Surrey

The sign on the quiet private road of the Oxshott Way Estate in Cobham, Surrey reads: VEHICULAR ACCESS WITH PERMISSION ONLY. *A great English oak towers over the entrance. White vans pass through the white gates and dutifully lower their speed to twenty. Not too far away is the Councillor's large, well-kept house. He is an ex-pilot, a Conservative who grew up in Elmbridge and Long Ditton, never far from the spreading borders of London. He drives into Claygate to the home of one of his constituents, Geoff Bills. Bills' mother readies herself for an appointment in Claygate while I talk with the two men.*

MIKE BENNISON: People round here will go bananas if you even talk about putting a house on the green belt. But people in London, I don't think they even think about it. It's like they think milk comes from bottles, not from cows.

GEOFF BILLS: They're trying to make the M25 the borders of London one way or another. So everybody regards everyone inside the M25 as you're a Londoner now. You think to yourself, where the hell did that come from? It's only because they've built a motorway out here what should have been put through London in the first place ... I mean, if they'd have widened the North Circular and took all the traffic lights out and all the rest of it and put plenty of underpasses in and just carried that through it could have done the same job.

MIKE BENNISON: We are right on the edge. We're two minutes from the M25, and two minutes from the country. We are twenty-five minutes on the train from central London. But this is what feels like Surrey. Well it is Surrey, it was Surrey, it always will be Surrey, I don't care what they say, personally. We want to keep all this green. We are the greenest area around. We don't want any of that to go.

GEOFF BILLS: It's just this insidious, creeping urbanization. They come down, tear up nice farm fields, put fences on it, put rubble on it and spread general rubbish and just make it look an unsightly mess. Suddenly it's turned into an industrial brownfield site, you know, overnight. You look at it and you think, that could be anywhere in Essex near the river. Somebody comes down with a load of crunched-up rubble with a few tippers and chucks it all over the fields. It's always going on.

MIKE BENNISON: That's right. If you go along this road on the other side, the parallel road to this, and then go all the way round, until you hit the borders of London, right the way out, it's all green. It's just grass.

GEOFF BILLS: You can see the difference within a matter of about two miles. Claygate is about the last bastion, or Chessington. And Claygate's on its way now. They're infilling it. I went down there the other day, I looked and thought, what's going on here? Tippers, developers. I thought, Christ. The reason for it, it's pretty obvious, it's because they want to meet the demand. It's for Londoners to move in as well. So you put one up front and they want two next to it as well.

MIKE BENNISON: We don't seem to be able to control anything that goes in.

GEOFF BILLS: You can knock a house down and put flats up. The reason it's happening is because the developers know they can sell everything they build. For everything they build there's ten Londoners out there who want to get out of the stinking hole they've created of their own. They've turned their own place into something that's untenable to live in. They want to get out of there. I mean, we've seen it ourselves.

MIKE BENNISON: And they can afford to buy a house and knock it down, full market value or more, just knock it down and put a brand-new one up and it gets a premium. People want a brand-new house. And then they want to turn it into London. I've got a letter at home I could show you. Some woman's moved into my division, and said, 'I've moved into this new house, the pavement's in a state, the trees all need cropping, all the hedges are overgrowing the footpaths which are in a terrible state, and everybody's speeding around in their cars and I think the place is dreadful – what are you going to do about it?' I think you'd better go off back where you came from. You knew it when you bought the damn place. We don't want to change. My attitude is, just leave us alone. We do not want to know. We're dead happy.

GEOFF BILLS: It's a nightmare. But the planning is all done to meet the pressure. The pressure's there from London. Londoners say, jump! And Surrey County Council say, how high? If you want it, we'll do it. Rather than going back to them and saying, no, we won't. They keep shouting up there. They keep saying, we must have more houses to meet the demand. They keep bringing more and more people into their rotten city all the time. They keep saying, let's bring more people in, they keep wanting it, they want everything up there. Then when they've got it they can't handle it, so the next thing they do is shout at all the neighbours and start saying to all the neighbouring counties, will you meet some of the demand for our housing?

MIKE BENNISON: One of the words is 'infrastructure'. There is no rules or regulations that puts the infrastructure in: the schools, the drains, the parking and everything else that you need – there is nothing like that. They come along and they just keep building, don't they? And the schools are jammed. It's terrible.

GEOFF BILLS: It will come, the infrastructure does come, it does, they do the buildings, like they did in Chessington that was a nice little rural village. Within living memory, you're talking about up there. That went within a matter of probably fifteen years. I lived in Chessington after it had been developed. There was no sense of community because all the people who you've grown up with, they all moved out and Londoners moved in. They've just got a totally different outlook on life. The way they go on. Hooliganism, trouble, police, violence. It's just a bloody nightmare. It goes from ordinary living out in the suburbs to living in the inner city. It's all been done by development, population moving, shifts in the population.

It's untenable to live under their way of life. The inner-city way of life is totally different to the country way of life. We know people that have come from London. You talk to them and the first thing they'll say: wherever we go we take London with us. It doesn't matter where they live, they'll take the way they think with them and they'll want to turn that environment into where they are. It's like an invading army. See what I mean? So you can get a Londoner who can move into

Surrey but he still regards himself as a Londoner and what he'll do, the insidious thing is, he'll put pressure on the council for development, they'll get that place turned into London one way or the other. They'll develop it into London. They'll bring their people in. All of a sudden you'll find that's another part of the county gone. That's how it happens, all the time. It's just a rolling bleeding expansion.

PUTTING ON A SHOW

HENRY HUDSON

Artist

*He walks into a room in the Hoxton Square gallery where his work of art,
Crapula, stands by itself, surrounded by a few empty plinths. The gallery
is preparing for the annual Frieze Art Fair. He can't find a light source to
stick into the sculpture, so he picks up the sculpted head – which has his
nose – and walks into the office where a few rays of mid-afternoon light shine
through the window. He holds up the sculpture so that the resin is illuminated
and the strands of human hair appear, criss-crossing in the resin. Out the
window, across the square, the White Cube gallery looks grey. A group of what
look to be Japanese tourists walk around the square, cameras in hand.*

I was trying to think about London; about how you could take
and unify everybody. I liked the idea that I could have a little bit of
everybody in London in something, you know. So I was naturally
drawn to the Underground, and I was down in the Tube at King's
Cross, and I felt these gusts of wind and then there it was: the
tumbleweed. It was just sort of rolling at the bottom of the stairs,
that's where it catches, the hair. I didn't necessarily want to touch it
and there was only tiny amounts. I ended up spending seven months
picking up hair and having people look at me in a really dodgy way.
I didn't know if it was full of diseases and I didn't really want to be
taking it back home. I'd heard about these fluffer trains, which are
sent down at night after all the trains have stopped and clean the
tracks. All that waste, they have to get rid of it. I called the Northern
Line, but they didn't want anything to do with me. So I was left to
basically pick it up myself, this human hair.

I knew that there were a lot of tunnels meeting at King's Cross, so I knew there'd be a lot of this stuff ending up there and sure enough there was. The best places were King's Cross from the Hammersmith & City Line, the Metropolitan and the Circle Lines, mostly at the bottom of staircases. My studio at the time was in the Barbican, so I'd stop off and put my Marigolds on and pick it up. Or I'd just have a plastic bag, like a Tesco's bag, and I'd have that tied inside over my hands and then I could just pick up like that and tie it into balls and stuff it into my dinner jacket. You know, you could go out to these really fancy dinners in London with Lord and Lady whatever and inside your breast pocket was a sort of dreadlock of everybody's hair in London. It was quite romantic and disgusting at the same time, and that's what I really liked about the whole thing.

The other place that was really good is the Central Line. Going through the Central Line at Oxford Circus to the Victoria Line. There's quite a deep tunnel there. That's really windy and you can get a lot there but that was really embarrassing because that tunnel's really small and if you stop, people think you're quite strange. I just ignored them. I mean, the irony is, once I'd got over the initial embarrassment, I didn't really think about it. People obviously take notice of you but if you just get on and do it, nobody cares. So I'd be very quick about it. I wouldn't mess about. Most of the time it was at the bottom of steps because that's where it accumulated.

What was weird was that, for the amount of blonde people and probably peroxide people there are, you can't actually differentiate some of the blonde hairs. It is mostly brown or black. Maybe because they are so caught up with one another, they don't stand out. The hair itself tends to be dreadlocky and blacky, dark blue. With bits of cloth, bits of paper. Tiny bits of, I don't know what it could have been, from people's pockets. You know if you leave a card in and you put it in the wash, that sort of stuff. Initially I'd try and pick it out but it's all part of the identity of whoever that person was. It's clumps, basically.

So I collected a bit of this hair, like a handful, which took, I don't know, about two weeks, and I had that in a plastic bag that was just in my studio for a while. That was it. I didn't know what to do with it. It was there for ages. It was impossible, horrible. You can't pull it apart. It's knotted itself so much. You could probably stretch it apart and weave it if you knew what you were doing, but no, it's impossible. It is a dreadlock made of all these different people's hair. It's fascinating in a way.

I tried putting a comb through it. Impossible. There's no way. I bought lots of hair waxes to try and see if I could get it to stand up straight, but of course it didn't. I knew I wanted this idea of unification somehow. I knew it was disgusting, and I wanted to somehow turn it into something hopeful or beautiful. It was just about this romantic idea that I could be holding a little piece of everybody in London.

I decided in this show I was going to make a sculpture about me in London. So I thought, well, what better way than cast a head of myself and put this hair into my mind, because that's where it had been for such a long time, you know, almost playing with my mind because I didn't know what to do with it. Also I thought it would be a nice way of keeping it in my head. I wanted the head to be looking up into the sky. I wanted it to be bathing in some kind of hot sun in some hopeful way and the light, specifically the amber light, was definitely a hopeful one. I've often been hungover or coming home late from a party. I might be walking down the street and look up. If you're cold outside on a winter's day in London and you look in someone's house and you might see a fire. I like the sort of colour that comes out. It's very beautiful. So I wanted that to be illuminating from my head.

I called it *Crapula*, which means hangover. It ended up with that name because it's about that melancholy blue in the morning when you're walking home and you feel a bit disgusted with yourself. Like four in the morning, and you've been to a nightclub and you've got the bus home or you're walking home. I've always called it melancholic blue, melancholy blue. I've always preferred that blue to the evening blue.

I'm not really a sculptor, so it was all very experimental and the head that you see now is actually warped. That's not how my neck is, for example. The resin's quite dangerous. It can set quite quickly, so we did it in different stages. Then we laid the hair in around the top of the head, poured a bit of resin in and then manoeuvred it and let it set.

It's strange because hair is dead cells. When it's on you, we all want to touch it, but as soon as it's off you, in your bed or your shower, it's suddenly, oooh, horrible. So hair's a really weird thing. But I think it's sort of beautiful.

MARTINS IMHANGBE

Actor

When I got to secondary school I got involved in little drama things. I was pushed to be involved, because everyone was saying, oh you're quite funny, you're quite this, you're quite that. So I got involved in a youth art centre in Deptford. And that's when I really thought, boom, this is what I want to do. This is what I want to do for the rest of my life.

I've got friends that look for quick fixes, that would rather get a job now than go on to university or something bigger. And they went on to get jobs and they were getting their cars, they had the money and you're thinking, okay, you've got money now, but there's nothing to fall back on. No education, no training, no nothing. I'd rather go the long way than take a short cut. But three years in drama school – and I can't do any professional work. I've got friends that have already got agents that are auditioning for stuff, so you kind of think, three whole years! You can't audition, you can't do nothing. But I try not to think about that at all. I'm going to do this training and at the end of it I'm going to get what I wanted to get out of it.

So it's a personal thing, really. It's about finding your own focus, your own drive.

In my youth arts centre I done a workshop with the police. I played a police officer and the police officers played young people, so we put ourselves in a police officer's shoes and vice versa. We had a whole discussion about how it felt being a police officer and a young person. A lot of conflict was happening between police and young people, and young people always thought that the police are against them, because the police can stop and search anyone, for any reason. So young people feel that the police are picking on them. They don't know what the procedures are, so they don't know what to say to a police officer if they get stopped and searched. I've been stopped and searched before. They said I looked suspicious and that this is a drug hotspot. [*He gestures around at the Subway restaurant, where we're eating 6-inch sandwiches. The gesture continues, gets bigger, to suggest Lewisham in general.*]

So they stopped and searched me and because I really know the procedures and understand why they do some things, I was cool about it. I've done nothing, so what can they say. They gave you a record of why they stopped and searched you and that was it. But other people don't know that. They'll be like, why are you touching me for? Why are you trying to stop me? What have I done? Don't touch me. And that causes conflict and it makes it a bigger affair. It's frustrating. But it happens a lot. You could be in a group with your friends going home and they just stop you, saying, why are you in a group? They can stop you for any apparent reason.

Nowadays you can get into a conflict for the dumbest reasons. By looking at someone wrongly. Bumping someone by accident. Stepping on someone's trainers. There's been fights over that. And it spreads from one generation to another. The older lot recruit youngers and give them their name. So say, for example, you're called Killer and you recruit someone who's younger than you. You give them the name Younger Killer. And they do most of the things that you don't want to do. For example, say you're selling drugs and you don't want to do that. You would give it to your younger to do it and then your younger will do it because he wants to keep up with your name. He sees you as a big boss, so he'll do it just to keep up the name.

[*His demeanour changes when another black kid walks into the Subway. He looks up, acknowledges him. It's quick, respectful, automatic; then back down to the sandwich. He's an Arsenal fan, missing the match to be here while the rain pounds down on the Lewisham streets. 'How old do you think I am?' he says at one point. 'I don't look nineteen, do I?'*]

You know about postcode wars? If you live in SE13 and I live in SE14 then we might not get along with each other. Or you live on that street and I live on this street and there might be conflicts because we don't like each other. A lot of people don't know what they're fighting for because there's this old thing about Peckham and Lewisham. But the people in this generation don't really know why they're still doing it. It's just one of them things that has been passed down and they don't know why they hate each other.

If you ask a lot of young people in Lewisham, why don't you like Peckham? They will say, oh, because I don't like them, innit. That's the reason. There's no deeper thing. They're not like us and we don't like them. But why? They don't know. There was a gang fight the other day, in Lewisham. There were these young schoolgirls and this group of boys were insulting them. The schoolgirls called some other boys, probably their older brothers or something, and then they all came down and there was this whole conflict near the town centre, by the police station. This is the biggest police station in Europe and they want to be having a big old conflict over there. It's like they don't care about the aftermath. When they've been arrested and get sentenced, that's when they start worrying about things. They're living for the now.

At first, when I started Lewisham College, we done physical fitness and I wasn't too keen on that. In my mind I thought acting was *acting*. I didn't know there was all these different elements to it. There's all this movement, you have to be good with your posture, your voice and all of that. I didn't really appreciate it much when I started, but I grew into it. Having a physical workshop and then going into a script and going into acting, I felt that I was more free. I felt I was more free and open, yeah, now I'm more open to it. I'm excited to do it. Like in my auditions, they played with the text, so with my monologue, they asked me to do it as if I'm a paracetamol tablet. Do your monologue as if you're a paracetamol, they said. At first, I was like, what? It was hard, but then I thought about pain and the flow of it going in. So my movement was all … I tried to embody the paracetamol going into me and stuff like that. That's the first thing that came into my head.

Then they said, do your monologue as if you're a wet pond in the middle of nowhere. A wet pond in the middle of nowhere! I had to imagine it. It's all about how quick your imagination is. I pictured it being cold and lifeless and so I just started my monologue in a still voice in a still way.

They also asked me to be a dog, because my character, Angelo, he was a duke and his personality was kind of doggish-like and he was a snob and so, yeah, they were saying what animal can you relate to your character? So I said, a dog. And they were like, become 90 per cent dog and 10 per cent human. I swear. And this was an audition. So I had to embody it and she was like, she'll do it with me if it makes me feel embarrassed. But I was like, no, it's okay. I'm all right with it, and then I started behaving like a dog. I was on the floor breathing like a dog, barking and stuff like that and then she was like, okay, okay, now 60 per cent dog, 40 per cent human. So it's like evolution. You have to have the dog qualities but slowly come out of it. And then 50 per cent dog and 50 per cent … down to 10 per cent dog and 90 per cent human.

This year my tutor entered me for a UK-wide schools competition. She chose me out of the whole year group to represent Lewisham College. I sat with my drama teach and we were trying to look for a monologue that I can relate to and people can look at me and believe. A character that's my age and that I can relate to. We were going through a monologue book and we came across the Stephen Lawrence monologue. It happened in Eltham, which is quite up the road and yeah, it was just a perfect monologue. Because I know the story of Stephen Lawrence. There was a racial attack in 1993. Basically, he went to Blackheath Bluecoat School and he left school with his friend Duwayne Brooks and these guys was running towards them shouting abusive stuff, they were saying, 'Come here, you niggers,' blah, blah, blah. One of them caught up to Stephen Lawrence and hit him with an axe. Duwayne Brooks carried on running but then he realized that Stephen Lawrence wasn't with him no more. So he went back and saw his friend laying on the floor with blood pouring from him and he didn't know what to do and he was in shock, so he ran across to the phone box and he dialled 999. But when the police came they treated Duwayne Brooks as a suspect. He was saying, that's my friend, and they're asking him questions like are you sure they called you 'niggers'? Are you sure they done this? And he was saying that if they had asked for descriptions of the boys' details, the other boys, they would have been sensible questions. They were making him feel like a suspect, and his friend's just been murdered … so that's what actually happened. Sad story and they still haven't found the people who did it.

So I went to the first heat in Nottingham. There was sixteen people, we all done our monologues one by one, and then they picked first, second and third. I came second out of sixteen people in the heat. They really thought I connected with the piece. It's emotional and it sends out a message as well, it makes people aware to the fact that this stuff happens. I feel very passionate about wrongful acts, about people getting caught for no reason, so I just felt good that I could tap into it. I went on to the final in Manchester, in which I came runner-up. It was an honour to be put up for that competition. The murder happened in Eltham and I took it all the way to Manchester. I don't think they would have heard of the Stephen Lawrence story. I don't even know if they know that it's a real story.

LAETITIA SADIER

Singer

On Regent Street, on our way to a coffee shop, she stops briefly and admires the clothes in the Barbour shop. She is wearing a scarf, a vestigial piece of Frenchness. Inside, we can still hear a road crew drilling outside, a droning, repetitive rhythm. She walks to the windows and closes them carefully. A lifetime spent in recording studios means a lifetime of minimizing sound.

I first came to London as an au pair in 1988. But, okay, my intention was to find musicians. I knew music was happening in London and not in Paris, where people's egos are much too big to allow for action. There it's all about talking and judging but no action. I'm sorry, but if you want to do an artistic endeavour, you have to do it and get the amps and get the practice in. Here it seemed part of the reality was doing it rather than just talking about it. So I was very attracted to London.

I wanted to do music and that's it. It was music, music, music, music. Music was my only friend, my only *raison d'être*. I ended up going to the Bay 63 a lot, which is somewhere like Notting Hill, Ladbroke Grove, and I went on Saturday nights so it was kind of reggae, rocksteady evenings. I knew I was looking for something, I just didn't know exactly what. I found it really hard to make friends because I'm French and the French are rude, you know? They just tell it like it is and they don't use little nice words, you know. I had absolutely no refinement and I know it shocked the hell out of everybody. So I had to learn how to have the right words and be much more polite than I was. And also here it's very coded. You don't say straight what you think. You say the contrary for the same effect, you know? But finally I found this man from the Sperm Whales and we went out for a while and that was kind of my introduction into this world. There were little clubs, little indie clubs – indie in the sense of not indie music, necessarily, but the DIY mentality was out there. It was kicking and it was vibrant, alive and visible. It was just not some super underground thing.

I met Tim at a concert in France and basically said, okay, wait for a year. I don't want to go back to London to be an au pair. I earned money temping in France for six months, then I moved in at his parents in Barking for three months and then we came to South London, to Brixton, and I've lived ever since around that area: Camberwell, Peckham, Brixton. London was kind of hostile, you know. It wasn't the romantic London any more. It was like, this is where I live and this is what I have to deal with. And, you know, we were starting Stereolab. We signed on the dole, and it was the beginning of the adventure. Practically every night we went to gigs. Our number one venue was the White Horse in Hampstead, Belsize Park, because they had the Sausage Machine there. The Sausage Machine brought bands over and it was £2 or £3 to get in. I remember seeing Gumball. Every week Th' Faith Healers would play. Lots of American bands came through. Bikini Kill came and the girls who played, what were they called? They had a record called *To Mother* and they had a blonde girl and she was kind of a really strange person. Do you remember them at all?

But that whole scene, you know, around the time of Nirvana, you had all these kind of, not subgroups, because they were very very excellent groups for the most part, but from this movement, from the early Nineties and throughout the Nineties. We used to go to The Venue in New Cross, or The Falcon in Camden. The Falcon was a big pub, you know, pub music with the pub on one side and the venue on the other side. My Bloody Valentine played around then and where else did we go a lot? Then places in Camden like The Underworld opened, but it's not the same, it was more like a professional venue. It was not the pub atmosphere. But yeah, we went to Kentish Town, Town & Country, at the time when it was the Town & Country, to see bigger bands. We were always going to gigs.

And at the same time we were starting our band slowly, recording, you know, and although we didn't have any money somehow things just started happening. We grew from being a really tiny little thing and had some reviews and single of the week in the *NME* or *Melody Maker*, I can't remember which. We supported Wedding Present. That was our first gig and that was a thousand people there.

We used to go to a studio near Borough, it was in a church called All Hallows Church. It was called Black Queen Studios and we were there at some point, six months a year, recording. When I'd get cabin fever I would borrow a bicycle and cycle around and up on that strip of the river, around Waterloo Bridge, the South Bank complex. That part of the South Bank, you know. There was no Tate Modern at the time, it was just kind of invisible, a phantomatic building.

At the time you could not see it somehow. It was just a shadow of itself. Now it's illuminated. It's Tate Modern. You really see that because it's busy. You didn't really notice it before, but I got to notice the building one night. I had stopped in front of it and I was looking at the water and I felt a presence in my back, and I thought, that's strange? What's that in my back? And I turned round and I'd never noticed that building before and it really sent shivers down my spine. I was nearly in tears. It's you, I thought. Getting that from a building is kind of bizarre. But it really hit me. I really liked all that area, which at the time had nothing to do with what it's become now. It's much more commercialized, but still I like the energy there and the culture that comes out of that place is pretty amazing.

There is a freedom here. I can be myself much more than in France. I've had people tell me that to them I am an embodiment of what it is to be French. I'm a kind of ambassadorisse of France. Little do they know that I am almost in exile here – voluntary exile.

RINSE

Rapper

In North London when I was coming up, a lot of the MCs were really technical. It was all scientific, with really developed flows and everything. But in East London they were actually talking about what was happening around them. I suppose there was more happening in East London.

Everybody was just packing their lyrics full of slang and there was no content that way. Like 'ming', which meant wicked. Like, oh that's ming or nang, that's nang or whatever. They faded out really quickly because people wanted to get new words to put in lyrics, they changed and changed and changed. I think a lot of it was taken from Jamaican and then they'd just put a little bit of a twinge on it, change it around. Or old words even, really old words that haven't been used before, like 'swag'. Swag is a swag bag, isn't it? To steal or something like that, but people would use that as a word for crap. So you're swag. You're crap. They'd just completely change the context of the words and the meaning of words. Using 'bad' as a good thing. Eventually people got better and started introducing actual vocabulary into the lyrics, which developed into grime. It's hiphop but we have our own way of delivering, rather than sounding like Americans. There's no denying, grime has evolved into a form of rap. It's just I think it had to start from scratch in order for us to evolve it to a stage where it was our own and it wouldn't sound uncomfy.

Myself, it took me ages to even think about finding something to say. At the time I was into comics and animation and sci-fi books and things like that, so I would kick all these lyrics … I mean, I wasn't talking about guns and things like that. I was talking about crazy ways to metaphorically speak about murdering someone on a beat and all this sort of stuff. It was cool, and people used to always be impressed by it, the flow and everything, but that can only take it so far. I didn't have anything to say and everyone else had something to say, like, they were living a hard life and all this stuff. I didn't really feel like doing that. I just decided to use the nerd thing. I thought, I'm into this stuff, so why not just go with it completely?

There was actually a real phase when everyone was like, I'm from London where this happens or that happens. People would start to glorify, you know the way they do in America. You're starting to say London and take pride in it. It developed here first, the whole grime thing, and it's like we've got to stay ahead and we've got to let them know this is ours. Like Manchester guys, Birmingham guys, also quite skilled, but it was here where it was happening, so it was like London, London, London. East London, North London and South London. As far as I'm concerned they're the same, just some areas are worse than others.

So I would just kind of draw it in, like one song called 'Main Road'. Down here, 'road' is the word for gangster. It's like, I'm road, innit. It means I'm streetwise. So I've got one where I've taken every cliché of that life and flipped it over. I am a snitch, I will snitch on you. If I see a knife I will run a hundred miles. Completely opposite to it. Find the funny side of it. But it's the truth, because if you see a guy with a knife, you're not going to want to hang around. Throw your ego away, let's be honest. Your average guy who goes to work 9–5 every day, he doesn't want to come across drugs. He doesn't want to come across prostitution. He doesn't want to come across violent crime. He just wants to get from A to B. I've just taken that and inserted it into my music. It's just humour.

Of course, you have guys who want to glorify the postcode where they're from. Or the street name where they're from. Or the estate where they're from. It makes them feel safe, and it's only natural that people will pick on people they don't know. And people make themselves feel safe by coming into gangs. It's human nature, isn't it? Bring yourselves together and make yourself feel safe, you belong to a sect which means if other people know you belong to a sect they know that you have people who represent you and will back you up or whatever. Indirectly, it's not just that we're a gang, but you know

I'm from this area. This is an area where this guy shot this person or this is an area where these guys sell drugs which adds credibility. People want to take pride in that area.

It just depends on where you're at in your life. A lot of people grew out of it. I mean, I remember there was some guy from Tottenham, he used to be into his stuff. I was performing a poem in the new Louis Vuitton store the other day and he was security there. I was talking to him and he was like, yeah, you know, this one's gone to prison and that one's gone to prison. No one wants to get involved in that, he was smart and doing his thing. He just wants to work and get on with his life. As people get older they start to realize it's a short road. You end up in prison. You end up seriously hurt or someone you love gets hurt and then that just leads to a cycle, doesn't it? Sometimes it's quite hard to get out of it.

The music at one point, it did glorify this whole London life. Like, you know, when you have other MCs who are saying, it's bad, it's bad, my area's this bad. If you come to my area, if you walk around my manor you'll get stabbed up. If you walk round my manor you'll get shot. So it's a big competition who can glorify their area the most. What happened is you'd have people who weren't saying these lyrics, people who weren't spitting these lyrics, they were just listening to them and it was someone from his area who was doing this, so he's representing our area, so we're going to do the same. So they'd see someone else they've heard of from another area representing their area and it'd be like, these guys have nothing to do with each other, you know, but basically he's the competition of the person who's representing our area so they'll probably rush him. So you can just be spitting lyrics, walking through some area to meet a girl, as you do, and these guys would see you and hate on you straightaway. It'd just be like, there's that guy who said he's from this area and he's in our area.

Sometimes it will literally be a street versus a street. My lot have gone into another estate and someone's got beaten up and stabbed, and then someone's come into our estate and stabbed and beaten someone up. So you do something else and then it just cycles. There's a whole lot of people getting pissed off. There's family members, close friends, family of those close friends and that's when it all gets crazy. And then it literally doesn't stop for years. It's almost like *Romeo and Juliet.* Even if there's not a girl involved.

I just like to say I'm from London, I don't have any specific area I represent. I'm not representing for a small group of people. I'd like everybody to be able to relate to a nerd, because everybody's a bit nerdy. I'm more interested in that than where they're from. I'm more interested in what people do.

DARREN FLOOK

Art gallerist

I was born in 1971, in the industrial countryside outside of New-castle, a coalmining area. So I grew up at a time when youth culture magazines were suddenly everywhere, youth TV was everywhere, and everyone talked about London the entire time. It was like you'd go to a crappy newsagent's in your mining village and flick through *The Face* and *ID*, and then you'd watch the burgeoning Channel 4, and it was all telling you about London. It was sending out a signal to the entire country saying: leave your shitty villages and come and live here in wonderful media-land and you'll have a life of never-ending clubbing and glamour and wonderfulness.

We sit in the back of Hotel, the gallery he runs in Whitechapel with his partner and which started in their home and relocated to the shop space beneath the flat in Bethnal Green, before migrating here. They are between shows and occasionally he pushes his long hair away from his eyes to survey the newly painted walls.

★

In the Eighties, the village I grew up in just ceased to exist. I don't want to paint too rosy a picture, but it went from a place where people would scrub their doorsteps and leave their front doors unlocked, to a place that had 75 per cent unemployment and houses with no value. I remember my grandfather took me down a mine when I was little to tell me that if you don't work hard at school this is where you'll be going. There's nothing more fucking terrifying than going down a mine. In the Eighties that all ended. I guess people with my background now work in call centres or whatever.

If you grow up in a small town like that you very quickly work out whether you're the type of person who stays or you're the kind of person who leaves. And if you decide you're the kind of person who leaves it's like, right, okay, how do I get out of here? I can't play a musical instrument. I'm useless at football. Art was a thing that I liked from the youngest age and I knew it happened elsewhere. It happened in Paris, it happened in New York, it happened in London, which were almost interchangeable in my mind. They were all places where Gene Kelly lived and there would be a Gershwin soundtrack and people would chatter and girls would be beautiful and people seemed to be drinking wine all the time without ever picking up a bar bill. The art world is out there. The art world doesn't happen in villages.

Be as snobbish about it as you like, but as an art gallerist what you sell is not very cheap and you don't sell a lot of it, you're not selling cars, you're not selling 100,000 units, you're selling two or even just one. I still find it amazing that people would love something enough, that is not necessarily pretty, not useful, not easy to look after, stuff that falls apart, stuff that you're going to have to take the windows out to get it into your apartment, stuff that you might actually never be able to show in your actual apartment because you're going to have to store it for the next twenty years and you're willing to spend lots of money on it. It's an incredible thing that people have that love – or if it's not love, they have a belief that it's going to be worth more money, a belief in its multicultural value or a belief that they're helping.

Happily, the art galleries in London are run by people who are closer to the artists than they are to the collectors. The accountants haven't taken over, thank god. We've got the world's biggest auction houses in town, they can deal with that bit. When you go to the openings, they're full of artists and art students, and to see a collector, especially in East London, is a rare thing. It's very much in that vein rather than the gallery as a salesroom. The galleries here are also very collegiate. It's an amazing thing but if you walk into The Approach or Maureen Paley or Sadie Coles and ask what good shows are on in town, the person behind the desk wouldn't think twice about telling you how the other commercial gallery down the street has a really good show on that you shouldn't miss. In New York, it's hilarious. You can go to a gallery that's as shit as hell that's next door to a brilliant gallery that's got an amazing show on and you say to them, what is good in town? They'll look at you and say, you should go to the Museum of Modern Art. They will never tell you to go and look at another commercial gallery. I think it's because it's a business, in the same way that a stockbroker wouldn't say, well, you know what, Merrill Lynch also have some amazing investments that you should check out. It's like you'd be fired on the spot! I think if in an American gallery you're found telling a potential punter that one of your so-called competitors has an amazing show on then you'll be hung, drawn and quartered and shipped off back to New Jersey or wherever it is you came from.

When I was first going to galleries in East London it felt that London must end here. It cannot go on any further, surely? I've been on the Tube for fucking ages and I'm at a bit where I think, where am I? Is this part of the UK or what is it? I remember going to the Blue Nightclub in Hoxton Square when that was running and Hoxton Square felt like, you know, 'beyond here there be dragons'. The English Channel must be just over the next street. It felt like you were right on the edge and now it's, god, those multimillion-pound property areas with free wi-fi and everything.

We used to have a gallery in Bethnal Green and we were looking for somewhere to move and I wanted a big space. Everywhere seemed to have been chopped up into live/work units and had hideous sunken lights in the ceiling and fake floorboards on the ground, it's just disgusting, and not my idea of the gallery I wanted. I wanted a disused industrial space that had an urban feel to it, which oddly now is very difficult to get, an urban environment, it's like having a fake Tudor house. But then we found this place.

I don't know originally what the building was. The whole area was the garment industry, first Jewish and then slowly but surely Asian. We're the only non-Muslim business on our street. The neighbours come in and they're quite friendly but I think they just think we're nuts. They'll tell you, they'll see things coming off the truck like a head wearing an old man's jacket and they'll ask, so people buy this? And I say, yeah, sometimes. And they look at you as though you're mad. You never dare tell them how much you sell it for. They think you've managed to pull off an amazing con trick. When we moved there were certain people saying, you'll have problems about what kinds of work you show and because you'll have people drinking on the street. We're right next to the biggest mosque in London, after all. So I went and asked some people next door, what's the religious calendar, what days would be a disaster to have people drinking on the street? Then you ask people, please don't drink on the street outside. You know, in the same way there's certain things you wouldn't do outside of a church in Italy. It's the same deal. Like don't go out in your bikini. Don't drink on the street outside on a major religious festival. It's not very nice. It will annoy them. But the thing about what we show – they don't come in. My neighbours downstairs have never been in and my neighbours upstairs have never been in. They come into the office and stand there and chat to you but they don't go in, in the same way I wouldn't go through their inventory, you know what I mean? I don't look to see what they've been selling. It's of no interest.

As soon as you do something like this, other galleries come round. People think, right … And you can suddenly spot the white people in skinny jeans wandering up and down the street holding estate agent leaflets. I'm really sorry, I think I might have fucked up the neighbourhood.

Berlin is now in the moment that London was in when I moved here. There's a lot of people moving in from everywhere, you can still get studios, there's a new gallery opening every weekend. But does Berlin become London? I don't think so. It'll become something else. It'll become whatever Berlin is in the same way that London won't become New York.

London is established now. It's got roots now. I think what has happened is a mixture of the Turner Prize ... well, I guess the Turner Prize, Saatchi and Tate Modern and a few famous individuals like the Damiens and the Tracys and all those kind of things. They grow in the sophistication of London. Now everyone drinks cappuccinos and knows a bit about art, whether you hate it or you love it. Tate Modern gets four million visitors a year. That's phenomenal. Most of them are school kids dragged there and are not interested in the slightest, but it's still four million people a year.

I think now art is in a place, not just in London but in the UK in general, where people *do* have an opinion: they care to hate and they care to love. No matter what your background now, you can probably name a living artist, or even two or three. You might be able to name a couple of galleries. You might know who's won the Turner Prize. If you're from Newcastle you might be proud of the *Angel of the North* or, if you're from London, you might think that Tate Modern is a pain in the arse and has wrecked the South Bank of the river, or you might think it's amazing and it's brought people from all over the world here. Whatever your thoughts, art is here and it's got roots now and it won't blow away.

In a way it's different to a literary boom or even a pop music boom because art needs buildings and permanent things. Once you have a flourish it tends to hang around for quite a long time. Unlike, say, music and stuff like that which may have a few venues and can close very quickly, sadly, or record labels that shut up shop, once art has found its roots in a place and once those places have been developed, they are always going to need stuff in them and they're always going to need ways of getting people to come and visit them. Like it or not, you've now got an art scene in this city.

GOING OUT

DAN SIMON

Rickshaw-rider

Rickshaw-riding brought me into contact with a great deal of people, people that you would never normally meet. It gave me an insight into London which I think few people ever get. It was a very romantic time of my life. My relationship with the city was quite intimate. It was very satisfying to see people that you normally would hold a barrier up to in the street and being able to converse with them, they were just like anybody else, not just the down-and-outs but people of all calibres from all walks of life. Rickshaw-riding was an amazing medium whereby you could communicate with just about anybody on any level. I found myself speaking as candidly to celebrities as I would to people that genuinely fascinated me. Distilling from them their life stories and experiences. It built me up as a whole and those years were the most memorable of my life, I can honestly say. They were definitely my best years in London.

Soho has got an enormous amount to offer in terms of sights, sounds and smells. It tends to operate on a shift rota. In the early afternoon you've got the smell of frying fish that emanates from the kitchens. Further down you've got the faint smell of bread and coffee that comes from all the local coffee shops. Soho's quite alive at that time, there's a lot of people toing and froing about the streets, it's busy, it's always loud with tourists, Londoners, commuters. Later on into the night it changes a little. There's a lot more beer, a lot more alcohol going up and down the streets.

You get a lot of bravado. Men who are desperately needing to be perceived as men, for some reason. It's funny because a lot of the

263

men that we take as rickshaw passengers, the ones who are the most full of bravado are, for some reason, the ones who are most eager to sit on their friends' laps when we have to squeeze three of them into the back seat. They love it. In fact not only do they love it, they plead to be the ones that are doing the sitting-on-the-knees thing. It's incredible to watch. You get three great big beefed-up guys who are trying to manifest their heterosexuality in every conceivable way and they end up contesting with each other as to who's going to sit on each other's laps.

My very first fare were two guys I picked up in Covent Garden. They were a couple of drunken guys wearing suits and they wanted to go to Liverpool Street Station. I equated Liverpool Street Station, for some reason, with St Paul's and I charged them £7 each and ended up on an excruciating journey which lasted over an hour and a half because I got lost and ended up going via Angel, Islington, up Pentonville Road. The hill up to the Angel was so extraordinary. The pain I was suffering was immense and it was pissing down with rain. It was an all-over ache that started at the bottom of my feet and worked its way all the way up to the bottom of my neck. It was pouring down with rain and I was pouring with sweat and I ended up pulling the rickshaw over to the side of the street where a bus stop full of people were jeering at me. They were just going, come on mate, you can do it, get up the hill. And I looked back at the two guys and they were just slouching over each other with cigarettes and I said, guys, look, I'm going to have to leave you here, I don't know where the hell I'm going. And they said, well man, listen, you've got to go back down the hill. I said, what do you mean, I've got to go back down the hill? I've just taken you up the hill. They said, no, no, you're going the wrong way. I said, why the fuck didn't you tell me that before? So I ended up taking them to Liverpool Street Station in the end, an hour and a half later. They paid me my miserable fucking £14 and then I went and ate like I've never eaten before in my life. I had two burgers, two portions of chips, two bottles of Lucozade and a chocolate bar. I ate like a pig. I've never been so hungry in my life.

It was an all-night cafe, twenty-four hours, populated by cab drivers and night owls, and I just sat there and hogged myself. The rickshaw was just a sight. It was parked, two wheels up in the air on the side of the kerb, abandoned in my wild haste for food.

I got not even a quarter of the money I was owed for that ride, but I felt that I was doing something that I was enjoying, not some bullshit that had been driving me insane the year before. It was tiring, it was exhausting, but I felt every bone in my body. I felt my muscles like I never had before and I felt alive.

After three months of rickshaw-riding I had legs like rocks. They were so big that when I tightened my muscles I could see every contour. It was quite nice actually, having these big, powerful legs. You have to develop very quickly an awareness of yourself and the vehicle that you're riding. You get a fairly instantaneous idea of the proportions of the rickshaw and you really need that if you're navigating through traffic. A good rickshaw-rider will be able to navigate successfully through congested traffic, you know, deftly negotiating his or her way through a pile-up without scratching the rickshaw or a car. Through tiny spaces. That's very important. It's part of rickshaw-riding. And you develop an eye for people. You're always on the lookout for people, much like a vulture is, I guess. And you get an awareness of what people want.

Great big hordes of men really late night in Soho want a brothel or they want a strip club, they rarely want anything else. They are all fairly young, from the ages of, say, 22 to 32. They all dress with white shirts, or chequered shirts with running lines of blue, and they usually wear navy blue trousers and they've all got short spiky hairdos, they're predominantly white and they always look lost.

Guys who want strip clubs will huddle together in a group on the corner of a street looking in every direction. Guys who want brothels will be pretty much the same, except a tad more desperate, they'll walk up and down the street looking in each direction. It's a feeling that you pick up. I don't know if I get it right or not, but nine times out of ten, if I pull up to a group of guys and they fit this description, they're going to want a strip club. Guys who want brothels tend to walk in fast small batches, usually only two of them. Then you get nightclub-goers. Nightclub-goers always dress a bit more funkily and they're both men and women, so if you see a group, say there's about eight of them, half girls half guys, that are dressed like they want to party, they want to party. So you ride up to them and you take them somewhere nice. And then you get people that just want to eat out, they want a restaurant, they want a late-opening bar, they want a late-opening place to eat, they want falafel and chips; if they don't want falafel and chips they want kebab and chips, they want a place they can buy cigarettes, they want a place they can buy cocaine, they want a place they can buy you name it.

Where can we buy late-night alcohol? Where can we buy cigarettes? Where can we do this? Where can we do that? Where can we get a minicab? Where can we get a taxicab? I know all these places. As a rickshaw-rider you have to if you want to make money. So we take people that want minicabs to a minicab office, we take people who want taxicabs to a taxicab if they're available. We know where they come in at night empty.

And there's always a lot of people that are desperate to get something off their chest. You get people that want to confess their sexual deviances to you. You get people that want you to participate in their sexual deviances. You get all kinds of people with all kinds of fetishes. I've been propositioned numerous times by an enormous amount of people. People that want me to participate in group orgies: come back with us to our hotel, we'll make it worth your while. You know, women and men. I took three gay guys to their apartment over Chelsea Bridge. They said, come up, come up, we'll give you champagne, you can snort as much coke as you want. I said, no thank you. I saw them again – it was incredible, the same three guys one year later, the same ride to their apartment over Chelsea Bridge: come up, come up, come up, we'll give you champagne, give you cocaine, anything you want. No thank you, gentlemen. I had a ride with a good-looking black girl, halfway round the trip she told me I was kind of cute, she ruffled my hair, said, why don't we pull up in a nice quiet place.

I mean, god, people with foot fetishes. A friend of mine called Andrzej, he's a good-looking chap, a big hunky Pole, right, he takes this American tourist to Waterloo for £20. All the way over to Waterloo this American chap has got this disposable camera and he's taking photographs of Andrzej's feet. So they get to Waterloo, the guy gets off, the guy pays Andrzej £20. The guy says to Andrzej, you know, I think you've got beautiful feet, I want to buy your socks. I'll give you £100. Andrzej, he's a workaholic, he says, no man, I'm going to need these socks. I'm going to be working through the night. And the guy says to Andrzej, give me one sock, I'll give you £100. So Andrzej agrees. Andrzej gives the guy a sock and the guy gives Andrzej £100. The guy's really grateful, he takes a photograph of Andrzej and he says, I'll be back in two weeks' time to buy your other sock. Andrzej says, right, okay. So anyway, Andrzej comes back and tells us all about it. Two weeks later he has the same trip again, picks up the American guy, takes him to Waterloo, fare is £20, the American guy pays him £20, then he buys the other sock for £100. So Andrzej made £240 off this motherfucker and we all hate Andrzej afterwards. A couple months after this incident happened, I got an email from a rickshaw-riding friend who is working in New York. He goes, 'Dan, you're never going to believe what happened. I took this big fat American guy for a ride and he bought my socks for $100. And then he showed me this photograph he had in his wallet of Andrzej!'

There are a lot of lonely people and a lot of them do confide in rickshaw-riders. I've had a lot of passengers like that myself. There was this Indian man who always used to take a ride with me. He'd pay me £5 to ride him round and he would sit in the back completely disinterested in anything else happening around him and we'd pull up, we'd stop, he'd nod and then leave. I think he just did it for company. One time it was awful. I picked the guy up on Shaftesbury Avenue. He gave me £5, looked at me with these sad, sad eyes. The guy was a mess. Obviously he didn't take good care of himself. I get the guy into my rickshaw and he gave me £5 to drive around. So I drive around and the guy never says a thing. He's so quiet you can forget he's there. Unfortunately, I did! I was riding around and riding around and I got completely lost in myself and I started thinking and I went into a bit of a daydream. And I went on this massive excursion around looking for fares and just completely forgot he was in the back. I was going, hey miss, where you going? Would you like a lift? And she was going no, no, no. And I was wondering what was going on, so I decided to give up and I decided to pull in to a cafe near to Frith Street to have a coffee. So I pull up, get off my rickshaw, go into the shop, grab a chocolate bar and the guy is still sitting in the rickshaw. Just sitting there as he always sits, not interested in anything going on around him, just slumped with his shoulders slouched forward, looking ahead, looking completely and utterly miserable.

On the weekends riders tend to finish around five o'clock in the morning. In the summertime it's beautiful. You see the sun rise over Soho as the filth is swept off the street by roaming bands of little caterpillar machines and the street sweepers. There's the odd pool of vomit here and there, the odd debauched-looking prostitute, the odd drug dealer. Nice and quiet, very few people about. You return to the base via the bridge if your base is in South London and it's very nice. I've always enjoyed riding over Waterloo Bridge, especially at night, because looking out across the Thames from Waterloo Bridge is like looking at a gemstone that's been sawn in half and displayed. All the lights sparkle like gems. It's like seeing London cut open and exhibiting its gems, riding across that bridge. You feel exhausted, but satisfied. Relieved to be going home. Happy that you've endured the night and looking forward to some bagel on Brick Lane, some beer at the base. Watching the sun rise over the Millennium Bridge if it hasn't already risen. And then off by cycle to Brick Lane for the Sunday morning coffee and bagel and maybe a kip in the local park.

DANIEL SERRANO

Cruiser

Basically, the thing with being gay in London is everyone's had sex with everyone. They say it's a city of like eleven million, but it's a tiny village. The whole point of me having no-strings-attached sex was that I could possibly never meet any of these people ever again, and to an extent that really worked. The majority of people I haven't seen ever again.

I think what perhaps started as a voyage of sexual discovery became a habit and then I kind of lost a sense of what one normally does with one's time. If I was bored and waiting for a train I'd perhaps go looking for sex. I'd be looking for sex seven days a week and often have sex with four men a night. I've been late for social engagements, I've kept friends waiting cold outside cinemas, all because I've been in some bush with someone. Lots of people, actually.

You have no standards when you cruise. If you were to go into bed with someone, they have to be attractive to a degree, they have to smell good and be of a certain age. All of those things go out the window in terms of cruising.

I'd finish work, I would walk down to a well-known public toilet, and I would loiter. The place would be humming, buzzy with other men who were there for exactly the same thing. At some points it would be just like a brothel. It's not very pleasant if you think about it. I would stand next to someone and would eventually make some eye contact and then take it to an alleyway which was close by. And then I'd do the same thing again.

I never really did parks and overgrounds as much as I did confined spaces. I had less chance of being murdered in a toilet than I would in a park, and although I'd have more chance of being arrested, someone would hear my screams. I was cautious. I did some night-time cruising in Hyde Park once and just got terrified. It's pitch black and people are hanging around, walking about, wandering.

The whole thing involves no conversation whatsoever, that's the weird thing about cruising, actually. I've had whole episodes where no conversation, not a single word is passed.

Once I met a guy in the Liverpool Street toilets, that's a well-known cruising ground. We gave each other the nudge-nudge-wink-wink and then we moved across to a graveyard. I've had so much sex there. I remember one guy showed me a mobile photo of his daughter afterwards.

Marks & Spencer's in Canary Wharf is another well-known cruising ground. Very conveniently, there's a toilet next to Marks & Spencer's, it says, THESE TOILETS WILL BE CHECKED IN THE NEXT ... and it has a countdown, every hour. Until it's got like two minutes remaining, you know no one's going to walk in, so it's really ridiculous. As the person who's been cleaning leaves, it goes back to: THESE TOILETS WILL BE CHECKED IN THE NEXT 45 MINUTES, and you've got almost 45 minutes to get up to no good.

I was obsessed at one point with finding disused toilets in London. There's a book called *For Whose Convenience?* It was written during the 1920s and it was a discreet gay guide to London for cruisers, under the guise of being a guide to where public toilets are in London. What do you do if you've had ten cups of tea on Mortimer Street and you're stranded? For a whole summer in London I made it my mission to visit these disused toilets. Some of them were concreted up but still had the GENTLEMEN sign outside. Others were completely obliterated. There was one by Holborn, an original Victorian pissoir which is no longer in use but is still on street level. There's another one by Foley Street, behind Oxford Circus. They're almost certainly all of them gay pick-up joints. Whenever I pass I think about what used to go on in there.

There's a cottage in Piccadilly Circus that's been closed down. There was this public toilet there but it's no longer in existence. They shut it down. That was about five years ago. It was too rough. It was dark. Oh my god, there's a public toilet by Petticoat Lane market. A friend of mine said he went down there once and he almost had his dick ripped off, so I thought I'd give it a miss.

I used to wear a dark blue, navy pinstripe suit with a handkerchief. One evening it had been raining, so I had my umbrella with me and I'm not sure why but I ended up in Mayfair of all places. I think I'd just decided to go for a stroll. It was a bit too early to go home and it was such a nice day as it had just finished raining. I went to a small verge, triangle, to cross over the road, and he caught me up and he said, are you lost? I said no, I'm fine, thank you and smiled and nodded and carried on. Then he turned a corner and I thought actually, I'm just going to follow him. I followed him out of Mayfair and down to Hyde Park and he entered the park. He walked along and then sat down by a bench and I kept on walking, but I thought, okay, he's sat down, maybe I should reverse. So I went back again and walked towards the bench and sat down next to him. I saw he had a copy of the *Irish Times* and he was writing a birthday card with a fountain pen and he was formally dressed with those shoes that have tassels and was in a grey kind of pinstriped number.

I sat there next to him and it transpired that he was actually Welsh. Anyway, he asked me if I worked round there and I said yes, and we had a quick chat about superficial things and he said he worked for a wealthy Irish family in Mayfair, he was a valet and he looked after them. He said the family were very wealthy, he travels with them to France and they had a fine collection of art, they had furniture by Robert Adams in the house, and were very well-to-do. And then I said, can I entertain you? And he said, yes, but where? And I said, maybe over there ... and he said, no, no, it's too exposed. I said, well I only do open spaces and then he said, why don't you come back to my club and I said, okay. So we walked together to this club in Mayfair. For some reason we went to the car park. Because he knew the people who worked in the car park. And we had sex in the stairs. That was the first time round. I said goodbye, and he said, don't go and talk to any strangers, and I left.

Two weeks passed and then I thought I'd go walking again, why not, and I heard this name: Daniel! I turned around and it was the valet. He'd been to Paris and he was feeling a bit depressed about work. He was quite tired, quite run-down. We were having a chat and we exchanged telephone numbers and I thought to myself, why don't I just sleep with him. So I texted him and said: are you around for sex? Then he said, come to this hotel in Mayfair. Say you're going to the Morning Suite and go to room 551. So I walked up to this huge, impressive Mayfair hotel and I was head-to-toe in my suit, so I thought I'd have no problems. I swanked in and I was asking all these people where the Morning Suite was. I went through in these black Barca loafers, brogue-type things, walking through, very gentlemanly and then saw where all the rooms were and made a dart down a side exit and went up to the fifth floor. And I knocked on the door and he opened it and he was in a bathrobe, a white towelling bathrobe. I walked in and was like, great, where's the bed? And I looked at the bed and realized that there was this black rubber mattress with a talcum-powdered gimp mask on it.

The room was quite nasty, it was quite sordid. The bed was basically the width of the room. It was a very small room. I said, one moment please. I walked back and tried the door and thankfully it wasn't locked. I don't know what would have happened if that door had actually been locked. I opened the door and then ran so fast down this corridor. I ran so fast that I turned down the staff staircase instead of the public one and it was only very narrow and it could've only fitted one person at a time, and I started pulling myself forward on both of the handrails all the way down and I ran so fast that I ended up in the basement. I'd gone too far down the staircase. I started climbing back up and I started hearing footsteps on the stairs. Then I made it to the ground floor and left the building. All I could hear was the traffic on the street. I had this text message: 'Are you okay? What's going on?' I didn't go back to Mayfair for a long time after that.

★

I sometimes think I'm only doing in real life what people are doing on the Internet. I'm only doing on the streets what people are doing behind closed doors. I don't want to look back on my life and be like, it was a big, jaded life. It just involved a lot of sex and no love. That's a bit sad. It's not really that cool past the age of 30 to be doing this. I'm 28 now.

EMMAJO READ

Nightclub door attendant

London isn't as 24-hour a city as it likes to think it is, but in Farringdon there are three 24-hour caffs, a 24-hour diner and a pub that opens at 7 a.m. for the guys in the meat market. Sometimes I'll be pissed off after a really horrible night on the door and I go to get a coffee and there'll be like an Eastern European woman behind the counter who can barely speak English and these guys covered in blood from the meat market and some cabby slagging off whatever … I love that. You know, that's Farringdon.

Up until recently, I've done the guest list at a club in Farringdon. Fridays it's 10 till 6 in the morning, Saturdays is 11 till 7. People queue up and my job is to see if their names are there. If their names aren't there I maybe say to them, whose list are you meant to be on? And I see if I know the name of the person, if I maybe find they're a friend of a friend or something like that. Or if they drop the right names then I might let them in but make them pay. But you can only get on the guest list if you know somebody who works there or one of the artists or you're music industry. So obviously people get quite pissed off. Sometimes there'd be two of us and one of us would do guest list and the other one would walk up and down the queue deciding who could and couldn't come in. That's really awful.

You can tell a blagger a mile off. It's all in their comportment.

You'd know they're not on the guest list. They always open with a story: 'Right, the thing is ...' The blagger is generally, I don't want to say aggressive, but there's something quite determined about them. They might say, 'I'm on the manager's list.' Nobody who's really on the guest list says that to you. Different music attracts different types of people and different crowds, right? So if it's a drum-and-bass night and somebody says 'Y'all right? My name's this.' You know they're not going to be on the guest list. Somebody who's down there for a drum-and-bass night would have a bit more swagger. They'd definitely call you a pet name like sweetheart, darlin', babe, love, all those. I once got called – what was it? Babygirl. That's one of the guys who generally goes to drum-and-bass night, babygirl.

I've also been called fats, ugly, bitch, whore, slag. Somebody called me an Arab whore once; I had on a big snood. They thought I was wearing a religious accoutrement which was actually a piece of knitwear. I've been spat on. Someone threatened to rape me. I've had things thrown at me. You just have to ignore it. Or you judge it on your instincts. To some people you'll be like, shut up, do you know what I mean? And they'll just walk away with their tail between their legs. Other people you say that to and they'll be in your face and screaming at you.

Generally, from half twelve till half two is peak time for people coming to the club. The East–West divide is really obvious. A West Londoner will have really good skin, be really healthy looking, a bit too presentable and a bit too clean. What they're wearing is trendy, but it's not expressed with the same kind of conviction or originality as somebody from East London would wear. Everything will just be in place and clean and sharp and new. Whereas somebody from East London will have red lipstick on and it's halfway across their face and it's fine, whatever. Nobody from West London would do that.

They're quite strict on the Eastern European men getting in. Because most of the pickpockets in the club tend to be Eastern Europeans, like a lone Eastern European male wearing baggy trousers. Generally all the pickpockets will wear two pairs of trousers, like baggy trousers on the outside and tight trousers on the inside so they can stuff things in the pockets of their inside trousers. Also a lot of the gropers, the people who sexually harass girls inside the club, tend to be Eastern Europeans. This is based on having worked here for years and having seen the people who get thrown out for which offences, etc.

The music can be quite race-specific. So on a Saturday you get a lot of Europeans for the house, for the techno. The Italians and Spanish love it. It's like all these really rowdy young Italian kids and they go mental. So it's quite white and European, whereas on a Friday it's a lot more mixed.

There's also a clear distinction between the drugtakers and the drinkers. You have people who have come for a night out, hear some music, get a bit drunk, dance; they're out of there by four, because they can't sustain it – financially or physically. Drugtakers, however, perhaps because the club's open late, it might be their second or third port of call. That's where they're going to end their night, you know, so they're the people who might come at half two, three, the later end of the night. For someone who might have come from Essex or Kent, it's a bit of a big night. The girls are really done up, perfect tans, heels, they look immaculate, not a hair out of place. They're generally drinkers. They want to have champagne and cocktails. Whereas the drugtakers are a mixture of boys and girls, people who look a bit cool.

When people come up to you in the queue, you can tell if somebody's drunk, if they've had a line or they've had a pill or amphetamine. If somebody's had a drink they're quite unsteady on their feet, a bit slurry, and they try to hide it. You can see them struggling to look you straight in the eye. It's a real struggle for them not to give themselves away and yet they always do. And when you say, have you had a few drinks? No, I'm not drunk. You're definitely drunk if you say you're not drunk. Their attempt to conceal it makes it worse. Also you've got to look out if somebody's friend has got their arm round them a bit or they're having words with them at the bottom of the queue. Because there's always one friend who's more drunk than the others. Somebody who's had a pill, they're really wide-eyed, the jaw's going a bit, a lot of energy, but also very sweet and nice and they're quite apologetic, yeah, just really friendly and really nice, sort of self-aware actually. There's something quite tense about somebody who's had a line. They're anxious that they're not going to be on the guest list, they're looking over you and saying, I am there, I am!

You get people who try and get in when they are absolutely out of their minds. They don't have their eyes open. They can't talk. They can't stand. It's quite disturbing. They can't even talk, can't even form sentences. That's ketamine. At what point do you give up? That's what we always say about these people. You've just pulled your pants down and you're sat on the kerb, what are you going to tell your mates your Saturday night was like? You're sat here waiting to get in. You think we're going to let you in?

Obviously the amount of male attention you get is just bloody through the roof. Sometimes I'll wear a skirt or something that would slightly draw more attention to me. My face could look like an I-don't-know-what, but as long as there's something a bit clingy, you're fine. One night I had some baggy, low-cut boys' jeans and some army boots and a leather jacket and a big scarf and I had my hair tied back. A massive group of Australian girls, dressed up to the nines and really drunk, turned up in a limo. If somebody comes in a limo she's not getting in. I knew they were going to be trouble. I said, look, I don't think this is going to be the right place for you. You all look really nice. It's not that kind of place in here. Maybe go down to the West End. I was really nice to them. They got ushered out the barrier and yelled, you fucking lesbian, you're just fucking jealous.

No matter how much you try and gloss it over, you are ultimately saying to people, you're not good enough for here. And that's when people kick off the most. They'll be like, you don't know how much fucking money I've got. My dad could buy this place in a second. They don't understand how they could possibly not be getting in there. Men and women. How can they possibly be getting it so wrong? I do think that is something to do with the whole topography of London. It's a bit gnarly and you never know where you're going to be when you turn the next corner, do you? You can't know the rules everywhere. You can't always know what stands for what.

From about half two, it's absolute mayhem and all you can do is stand back and think, what the fuck, because it's really surreal. It's a door person in-joke. You get the casualty hour, when everyone is a complete mess and everything just goes nuts for about twenty minutes to an hour and a half. You've got new people trying to get in, you've got people who've got thrown out from the club trying to get back in, you've got people having fights or discussions about how terrible the club is. You've got people being sick, people going to the toilet in the street. It just descends.

There's always somebody who's got a really strange story. Honestly, every week there's somebody who's trying to negotiate with you as to why they need to get into the club or why they're loitering outside. Like they've lost their friends or their phone or their cloakroom ticket or they've been thrown out but it wasn't fair. These stories never ring true. It's like, you've been in a fight, you've been bottled and you're trying to get back in?

There's something about that hour when you don't encounter a single lucid, sane person. People who are absolutely off their face and have been taken out of the club because it's dangerous for them to be there, they will just sway. They will hold on to the barrier and they'll sway and they'll be in their own world, talking to themselves. It's bizarre. It's quite gross as well.

They're really flummoxed, and they'll be trying to strike up conversations with passers-by, trying to be normal. But they won't be aware of the dire state that they're in and that they need to go home. They will hang out for hours. And then you see really pervy guys. They'll go up to groups of girls and they'll try and have conversations with them. They'll offer them lights. Offer to take them into the club and buy them drinks. Some of them are clearly quite deranged but they wouldn't behave like this nine to five. And if they could see themselves they would see that it's totally unacceptable behaviour. But all the boundaries and rules that apply in the daytime are gone. And you can't reason with people like that. People's worst qualities come out at night.

When she reaches across for her drink I can see the three-inch taffoo on her lower left arm. She doesn't knows the font; it was taken from the label of one of her dresses. It's a single word: London.

At the end of the night I love getting my coffee or a Kit Kat and being really sober and clearheaded, like the cabbies and the guys who work in the meat market. I get in a black cab on Clerkenwell Road and the guy says, how was your night, love? Well, I was working. Oh really? I thought you'd been out. And then I bitch about my night. I love having a different perspective to everybody else he's spoken to, or she's spoken to.

What I especially love is in summer when it's about half three, four in the morning, and you get this kind of purple-pinky hue to the sky. It's one of the very few places I've known in London where you can see stars. When I've been at my most pissed off, my most offended and just felt really despairing, I look up to the Barbican Tower and I see the top of Smithfield Market and that sky, and it's like I'm just *in it*.

SMARTIE

Stockbroker/DJ

It's past noon at the Costa Coffee in Buckhurst Hill, on the western edge of Essex. I've been speaking with Smartie for hours — and I've hardly asked a question. The mothers at a nearby table have stopped speaking to each other and are now listening in, listening to Smartie, while rocking their sleeping children in their prams, pushing them with their feet.

The City life came to an end, I think, when it became an American environment. The City changed in the Eighties and Nineties to a new type of work regime where people didn't lunch any more, you worked through your lunch, you worked at your desk. It was a sandwich culture. The English sort of London-type living, boozy lunches, that had gone out the window. That killed the character, the culture and the framework of what it was all about for me, and I got disillusioned with it.

I was still looking for new fashions. By the early Nineties, all my suits had different colour linings, they weren't just your normal City stockbroker. I used to have paisley linings. Always cut differently. Instead of maybe having a slit here, I'd have a flap pocket. Flaps here. Higher lapels. Cloth buttons, so you didn't have just like plastic buttons. The buttons were covered in the cloth of the suit. Lapels that opened up. I mean this is way before anyone else was doing anything like this. The trousers would be cut very very tapered. Some of them would be jacked up. They'd be cut maybe two inches above the heel, so I'd show my socks off. No one was doing that then.

Armani suits really was the defining look for most City boys. I'd be wearing tailored. But then I'd come from an insurance background, which was always very tailored anyway.

They'd be wearing three-piece mostly, with a pocket watch with a chain. Even in the Nineties, there would be not many in the bowler hats. I suppose the bowler hats went in the late Seventies, early Eighties, that era, but it would be hard for you to find a man in a bowler hat now. Sometimes around Pall Mall and St James's, you see the odd bowler-hat man coming out of one of the private drinking clubs, but there's not many in the bowler hats these days.

I'll tell you another example. You take it for granted now that everybody wears square glasses, you know the 1960s glasses are very trendy now. But when I started to wear those fourteen years ago in the City, no one was wearing that look. They were all wearing the little round Armani glasses. I was wearing black National Healths. Really throwing it out. Big glasses. Just throwing the look. Just sort of, I would say, Michael Caine. *The Ipcress File*, that sort of *Italian Job* look. He would have been an icon for me. Because he had the charm, the East End, south-east London roughness, you know, cockney charm, but with that smartness like, you know, streetwise, edgy, but definitely London. He's definitely London to me. Michael Caine is definitely London.

My DJ-ing and my club promoting at that period had grown very big. That's when I moved into the West End. I only wanted the biggest clubs in the West End to do my parties in. I had a strong crowd of about 500 or 600 people. I had a close friend at the time who was an actor who used to be in the TV programme *EastEnders* in the early days. He was a good-looking boy and the two of us together were, I suppose, a fantastic combination. There was me with my I-can-talk-for-England style, and my fun and love of music, and there was him with his good looks. He had a big following of women as well. There was me DJ-ing in these bars and I had a big following of girls, because girls loved my music. So with these nights we packed the clubs out and with us both working on the stock-market floor after his acting, he worked on the futures as well, we had a market place to sell our tickets for the parties. Before we even opened the door on our club nights, we'd sell 500 tickets in advance. So that would be revenue, even if the tickets say were £10 or £15 each. Somewhere between £5,000 to £6,000 before we even took any door money. Because we had the market. We had 3,500 people in a building, who all wanted to go out clubbing and partying. So we used that to our advantage. I remember our first club night. The club was called Tangerine Dream, because he had an obsession with this band that were from the Seventies called Tangerine Dream. Our first invite for our tickets were plastic credit cards, I'm sure you can work out what the credit cards were used for mostly; remember we were all stockbrokers. We were all in a trading environment, but there was obviously drugs going on at this period, too. A lot of cocaine was going on. And so we had credit-card invites for our parties and they were sold as tickets. Not paper tickets, you'd get a credit card for the party and Tangerine Dream in gold writing. No expense spared.

It was mad. Mad. I mean, when we used to do a party, people used to work in trading booths on the floor for different companies, say Goldman Sachs and Barclays, all the different banks, and you'd go round and you'd have runners. These were the ones that used to run round and get the cards from the traders in the pit to process the orders. Because nothing then was screen-based, you had to input the cards, the trading cards, in the computer to match the trades with other traders. So if we were advertising a party you might get one girl who wanted to bring twenty of her friends from outside the market to the party and she'd buy twenty tickets, thirty tickets, I want fifty tickets, so you could sell 500 tickets in no time because obviously if you had a girl who worked on the stock-market floor she might have 20 girlfriends who wanted to meet stockbrokers. They'd all want to come to the party in the hope they might meet a rich man. And the rich guys wanted to come to the parties, and the boys I knew who were from rougher areas wanted to come because they knew all the good-looking girls who worked in the City were coming. So they all fed off each other. My parties were legendary because at the first party we did, which was at the Turnmills Club in Clerkenwell, which is still there but it's now a restaurant, we had the dance studio at the back of Turnmills. We used to do that on a regular basis and we'd fill it out. We used to have two rooms: one was a house music room and the other room was my room, where I used to entertain my following of about 200 people with soul, disco and Balearic beats which was a mixture of rock dance music and Ibiza sounds. Early Ibiza music. It was 75 per cent girls at my parties.

What I suppose I wanted to try and create was, in a diluted way, a Studio 54 event of hedonism where all your fantasies could be relived. That John Travolta feeling: it's the weekend, let's go out and have fun. So dressing up, buying a new outfit, talking about it for a month before you go to the party, getting excited. People used to get excited about the night.

There was a lot of money around. We'd had another recession in the early Nineties, but when Tangerine Dream started in '95 and '96, there was a boom. That was when house prices were starting to rise. Stock markets were on a rollercoaster rally that really continued up to 9/11. The market was only one-way traffic. They were good times. No one worried. Everyone wanted to have fun. This, I think too, was really the peak of the designer thing. This was when all these labels that are now so famous like Vivienne Westwood, Comme des Garçons, they were at their height. People wanted the top clothes. It was all about buying expensive clothing from top designer stores that no one else could afford and wearing them to the parties.

The women wouldn't be wearing lots of clothes, but the Belgian designers were very big – Dries Van Noten, Ann Demeulemeester – Vivienne Westwood was very sexy clothing then. You had John Richmond, he was very big at that period. For menswear, Helmut Lang. Prada was starting to come in. Dolce & Gabbana before they were D&G, when it was very exclusive. Joseph. All the shops around Sloane Street were very popular. Harvey Nichols was an amphitheatre where people used to go.

It was a designer frenzy then, because there was so much money around. Everyone wanted to wear the top looks, wanted to go to top house music clubs and that's what brought on the superstar DJ thing. They had DJs like Paul Oakenfold, Danny Rampling, who was a friend of mine at the time, and then Boy George after Culture Club, he started to DJ, I knew him. They also started and it was all house music. There was warehouse parties, you know. It was slightly after acid house, which was really the late Eighties, early Nineties, it was now the garage scene. It was the superstar DJ thing and it was about expense. But, you know, there were some great warehouse and all-night parties. You had some big parties in London.

The new money was there. I think everything was driven from the futures market and this East End-made-rich type environment. There was still a lot of real Londoners around. I think the turning point was when Shoreditch became super-trendy, when the art crowd moved in after the Millennium. The art crowd came in, fashion started to move in. A lot of these Indian takeaways that were in Brick Lane, they were pushed out. The top end of Brick Lane if you go down there now, it's all fashion. The bottom end of Brick Lane is still all Indian, Bangladeshi restaurants, but in ten years' time they may push all the rest of the Indians out.

I loved the Shoreditch wave when it first started because it aped the real urban decay of the late Seventies and early Eighties. That's what I saw in the Shoreditch regeneration and the crowd moving there, but it's dead now. It's finished really. It's now a beano culture of let's get trashed. It's lovely for the kids, but I see the real happening places in London as being Kingsland Road, Stoke Newington. The other side of Dalston, which used to be the 'murder mile'. I see the new cultures moving to places like Stratford, maybe. Bow. And it may even go as far as a real run-down place, like Leytonstone.

So coming closer to me, I'm afraid, as the crowd gets pushed further out, as they look for the new thing, in the rougher parts of London. Again, it's the full circle of everything that was first started in that period of 1978 onwards. To me 1978 is the change because it was the Winter of Discontent and that's what changed everything. '78, '79, when Thatcher came, changed this country for ever really.

PART III

MAKING A LIFE

They stand near the bar. They'll eat their lunch elsewhere soon, Nick explains, somewhere in Liverpool city centre. They'll be working in the Wirral in the afternoon, so it's just a quick one or maybe one and a half before they get on with it. The half is looking more likely. Nick's companion, John, swills the remainder in his pint glass, round and round.

Nick holds his empty and says to me: 'Londoners. What they are ...'

'And you should listen to him,' John interjects, 'because he's been there, lived there.'

'What they are ...' Nick announces.

'He lived in some terrible places down there, had a terrible time.'

'They are so far up their own arses,' Nick says, above the clinking of the Blob Shop, which is full of a selection of Liverpool's afternoon drinkers. Older men shuffle up to the bar in succession. 'All that talk and talk and talk. They're so far up that it even shows with their football clubs – they can't help it. It's in their name. Arsenal. Arse.'

'To be fair, that's not the only club in the city,' says John.

'They've got Chelsea too. What's that got in it? Hell. Ch-hell-sea. You've got a Spur, an Arse, Hell. Millwall – another sort of hell.'

'West Ham,' John says.

'Ham,' Nick replies, disdainfully, but without explanation.

John drinks. Nick taps his empty glass on the bar to get the attention of the staff.

'He had something happen to him down there,' John explains.

'We don't need to go into that.'

'A terrible thing. Can't even talk about what happened.'

'Nothing happened,' says Nick.

'Won't even speak about it. He just hates the place, London.' On the television in the corner the 12.47 at Sunderland begins. Dogs erupt from the gates and charge across the screen.

'There's Crystal Palace too, you know,' John says. 'If you're thinking of all the clubs.'

'Sure,' Nick replies. 'Thing is, there's no Crystal Palace though, is there? There's no Crystal Palace in London. You can go down there and look for it but you're not going to find a Crystal Palace.'

'People say London was awful in the Seventies,' says Barbara as we drive to the fox hunt just outside Grantham. 'You couldn't get petrol after a certain time. But I remember it as a glamorous place. There was always someone's brother or someone's school friend who could get you a table at Annabel's. We wore long dresses when we went out. We wore long dresses for everything. They called us country. I'll never forget that. I suppose we were.'

It's a clear March day at Belvoir Castle, home of the Duke of Rutland, built in the nineteenth century and pronounced 'beaver'. Horseboxes are parked in rows in the parking lot so that 'Caution: Horse' is repeated in boldtype, over and over. An illustrated sign gives directions to Belvoir's adventure playground, the strip for jousting and the rose garden in the grounds, but the attraction today is the final hunt of the season. Hunters in gleaming black boots and jodhpurs trot up the hill past the snowdrops growing by the side of the road. Glasses of port are laid out on the table for the hunters. The challenge is to hold the port aloft, to sit comfortably, with elegance, and not gulp when the horse's head drops.

Hounds are scattered amongst the waiting horses and riders, sniffing each other. They nip at the empty platters of sausage rolls and perch their paws on the low stone wall, eager for the attention of the gathered crowd.

'I love seeing the hounds sitting around the feet of the hunters,' says a man behind me. 'He should really have more control,' says his companion. 'The huntsman should keep them near.' Both are middle-aged; both wear mud-spattered wellies; both are eating sausage rolls, handed to them by a well-dressed young woman with a metal tray.

'We are country,' the man furthest from me says a little later. 'We are not city.'

'I do go to London,' the other says. The word hangs in the air. 'I do go to London, yes. Under sufferance.'

JO THE GEORDIE

Who stayed in Newcastle

She has bleached blonde hair and seems to know everyone in Newcastle. She drinks tea after her morning coffee on a bright September day, the day Cheryl Cole got divorced and didn't go back to using 'Tweedy'.

London is a vast and lonely place. If you go there you have to take a bit of Newcastle with you. You have to export pet names for people you don't know. Pet, petal, flower, love, lover. My friend's mum, who is old-school Newcastle, calls everyone my little darling, even if she's just met them. In Newcastle, there's a base-level love. In London the base feeling is that you're either a terrorist, or a rapist, or both, until you've proven otherwise. You can feel a southern coldness on you when people look your way. Even if you come down with Newcastle words, they're not always enough to sustain you.

There is a Londoning process, a hardening that creeps up you. There was one man I knew, he came from a rough as arseholes neighbourhood and when he moved down he changed his accent. It happens. He came back up and said, [*her voice changes*] wow, this place has really changed. I remember when it was nowt but fields. *Oooh*, the quayside looks amazing, he says. He goes away, grows some pubes, and comes back to make that kind of comment. It's a bit fucking irritating.

There's this thing you're supposed to be part of in London. But what is it? That's the million-dollar question. Everyone's there because they're searching, aspiring. A very small percentage is actually living the dream. Ill, tired, unhappy, the rent is fucking loads, what is it you're getting? The idea of it, or something.

They say we've got the Tyne running through our veins and all that shit, it's so sentimental like. We're a bit of a cliché. It's rubbish but we love it. I was removed from a train by the police at 11 p.m. one night at Darlington Station for singing 'I'm Coming Home

Newcastle'. You know how it is – you're lighting up the carriage with your banter. It was Ladies' Day at the races at York. The whole carriage was full. It wasn't a conscious act of rebellion. The conductor came round. I couldn't understand why everyone didn't like it. I thought I was a bit of a legend.

There's a London type, ruthlessly aspirational, ambitious, cold-hearted, mid-forties, never had a long-term partner, bitter, hard-hearted, a terrible snob. The ones who are from where I'm from, but are so incredibly rude about Newcastle. Oh my god, don't you have dentists? The fucked-up thing is what happens to them when they give up Canary Wharf, or wherever. And there they are – so driven because they've been scared for so long of going under. All those people, grafting their ass off, turning into people who just know how to graft.

At 14 my oldest friend, my best friend Stacey, she ran away to London. She lived in a flat in Tower Bridge. I visited her, it was the first time I'd been to London. The escalators move quicker. It's a fact. It's like a fairground ride. I was with Stacey and it seemed the city was just as big as us. It all felt terribly grown-up. There I was staying at my friend's flat. She knew the Tubes. I knew the numbers of the buses in the North-East.

She was with a guy but it was hideously inappropriate – she was 13 when they started going out. I was very jealous. I had to go to school, get my GCSEs. I was going out with a pizza delivery boy with a metallic blue Ford Fiesta. When Stacey left it broke my heart. At various points our families had collapsed. Her mum was my mum. The street where she lived was called The Terraces – there was a metro station at the top of South Terrace. I was heartbroken after she left me at that metro station. I cried for a week. We'd ring each other; we'd watch *Neighbours* with each other on the phone. In London she was always on the back foot, always trying to act older, always trying not to be fazed. She acted as if it were nothing. Yeah, I'm in London, but whatever.

Stacey was in London doing that, so I thought, I'm going to stay in Newcastle and do this. Her rebellion was London. My London was going out with a crack addict in Newcastle. My London should have been London.

STACEY THE GEORDIE

Who came to London

By the time I was 13 I was regularly skiving off school and pinching money from my family to bugger off to London. My parents were splitting up and my brother, who was eleven years older than me, got into heroin and became psychotic, so things were really rough at home. And around about the same time that that was happening, my brother had been in London and he'd been in a band and one of the members of the band became my shoulder to cry on a bit. There wasn't really a lot happening for me in Newcastle, I was feeling miserable, and because my family was preoccupied with everything that was going on I just seemed to get away with slipping through the back door and disappearing off on the cheap old blue-line coach you used to be able to get down to London, which was fifteen quid for a return ticket. You could sit smoking fags in the back of the bus all the way down to London. I started doing that quite a lot.

It was a really strange thing, looking back. Jo and me pretty much grew up as siblings really, in and out of each other's homes. My mam was very much her mam, her mam was my mam. And we were both precocious and gobby and forthright, very opinionated. I remember one our catchphrases was like, 'God, I'm 13,' as if to say, like, 'Don't patronize me. I'm 13, for god sakes.' We were very, very sure that we knew it all.

I was 14 when I stopped going to school, and buggered off down there for good. The guy from the band was ten years older than me, and the whole band were on the dole and had absolutely nothing. And so I moved in with him. It's funny looking back to a time when you give no consideration at all to, like, how I'm going to pay the rent and look after myself or anything. I had my birthday money, which must have been all of 150 quid from various relatives. I was like, 'Ah, that's enough to see us through.'

I was looking at this person through the eyes of a teenage girl, and he was a lot older than me, which seemed really cool. And then their band went from being a band that nobody cared about to one that major labels were fighting over. They were getting flown off to New York, they were in the middle of a bit of a record-company bidding war. So not only was I in love with someone who was much older than me and more experienced than me and in a band, I was in love with somebody who it looked like was about to become a pop star, which added a whole other layer. They ended up getting a record deal, and going off on tour and into the studio. I spent quite a lot of time in a flat in Acton, smoking sixteen Marlboros a day, waiting for him to come home. I didn't really have any friends that weren't related to him. I didn't really have very much going on there at all.

Within the space of about six months my mum had left my dad, come down to London and moved in with us as well. So it was the three of us in this one-bedroom flat. I think my mam just thought, 'Stacey's in London. She seems to be all right. I'm going down there, that's all I've got.' So she hopped on the blue-line bus herself and sat in the back smoking fags and turned up. I went and picked her up at King's Cross. It was a hot summer's day, and I was wandering around in a really short skirt, fancying myself to be looking quite cool, and my mam got off the bus and said, 'God, you look really, really thin,' and I thought, '*Yes.*' That's the way things were at the time. That's my abiding memory of that day. The tragedy of the situation escaped us at the time.

★

After a year and a half, me and the older bloke eventually split up. But by that time, the singer of the band who was older again than him, he'd taken me under his wing a little bit. I was out on the streets, it was December, it was really snowy and I had nowhere to go. The singer had bought on the record company advance a penthouse apartment, just next to Tower Bridge. Like literally open your window and look out and there's London. He said to me and my mam, there's no way I'm seeing you out on the streets, it's Christmas. They were going off on tour the next day, and he just said, 'C'mon,' took us to his house, went out to the shops, bought us about 8,000 Marlboro Lights and a cupboard full of food, and off he went on tour for two weeks. It was completely bizarre. It snowed in London that Christmas, and it was just me and my mam. I was nearly 16 by this point. We were penniless, jobless, had no friends. I was heartbroken. My brother was going insane, somewhere, you know, a couple hundred miles north, yet we were living in this luxury penthouse apartment overlooking Tower Bridge, looking at this idyllic scene outside of the window. It was completely insane.

The thing about this penthouse on Tower Bridge, there wasn't even a bedroom. It was a living room, and the kitchen was just a space that you walked into where you had sort of like benches around you. It wasn't actually a room, it was just some work surfaces, and the washing machine tucked under, and the bathroom was just a tiny little room. That was it. There was three of us, and we lived like that for almost a year. We did nothing but laugh and laugh and laugh and play computer games. At the time of the record, like I guess most bands do, they had a drugs guy and you could just go around to his house and get a massive bag of weed and loads of LSD, and jeez, we would take loads of drugs and have a right laugh and we became completely nocturnal. It's funny because me and Jo grew up loving *Prisoner Cell Block H*, we were obsessed with it, and they started showing that again from the start. I think it started at a quarter past five in the morning, so we used to sit up for *Prisoner Cell Block H*. That was on for an hour, then we'd go to bed at a quarter past six.

I was having the time of my life because the singer had the biggest record collection you've ever seen, as well as a massive collection of films, and he opened my eyes to a lot of stuff. That was great, but at the same time I was desperately heartbroken about the relationship. It was this total mishmash of stuff going on. It was either an ecstatically happy time or a desperately sad time. I still haven't really made my mind up.

On New Year's Eve, standing on Tower Bridge, I remember looking out and thinking, what the hell is the next year going to bring us? I was feeling really jaded and cynical already. I remember there was a guy in front of us with this big coat on and a cigar in his mouth and he turned round and looked at us and said, 'Happy New Year!' in a broad New York accent. I thought, it doesn't really get any more surreal than this.

Eventually, the guy we were living with met a girl, and in about two days he said, 'Right, she's moving in.' We'd met her and she was quite hard work, and it was a one-room living space. Me and my mam thought, 'Shit.' By this point, my mam had actually got a job working in a market stall in Covent Garden and was sort of getting it together. Things were going a bit better. I was 16 at this point, and still had absolutely no idea of the concept of working or looking after myself at all. I was dossing about, basically. Spending most days just walking around London. I knew it all. The centre of London, from south-east London where we were, I could have mapped out the whole thing, I was just so used to pummelling it by foot, every day, wandering around like a little ghost feeling sad. A little ghost in a really short skirt with lots of make-up on.

So we ended up moving out. We had a friend who lived in Fulham, so we slept on her floor for a bit, and then I moved in with some friends in Camden. Eventually me and my mam ended up living with this lad we knew from Newcastle who had a spare room in his own home in Leytonstone. I wasn't bringing in any money at all, and my mam was working at this freezing-cold market stall, and this guy we were living with was a little bit bonkers, a little bit

'I've got a personality' exclamation mark! He would express that by painting the living room all fluorescent-marker-pen yellow, so we had these highlighter-yellow living-room walls. We were chronically depressed and by this point, really, really psychologically dependent on cannabis. Like, you know, food came second; we smoked dope from the second we woke up to the second we went to bed, and it was the only thing that was keeping us sane, or so we thought at the time. At this point I was estranged from the bloke we'd lived with in Tower Bridge. Their band was doing really well. They were on the front cover of the *NME* and I was sitting with fluorescent-yellow walls in a flat in Leytonstone, couldn't afford a travel card even to get out of Leytonstone, sometimes couldn't afford any dope for two days, crawling up the walls with this irritating flatmate and my mam, who was in the same state as me. It was desperately depressing, and made us realize the difference between how my life had been and the way my life was then. Basically no friends, no lifeline or link to the world outside of that highlighter-yellow room. It was absolutely horrendous.

Dog Man Star by Suede, that album absolutely encapsulates London for me. And *Sci-Fi Lullabies*, the B-sides album, cause there are so many lyrics and poignant tunes, swooping, swooning sort of sad strings and sounds that encapsulate being down and out in London. I mean, not just lyrically, just the sound of it as well, sort of the sound of your heart swooping around inside you. I quite enjoyed being miserable. There was a part of it that I really indulged in, having a good cry, walking around listening to the saddest music you can possibly imagine, thinking about how desperately sad I was.

I bought this beautiful pair of knee-high, white leather, 1960s-style platform-soled boots. I couldn't walk in them to save my life, they were crippling, but I loved them so much and I wore them with a white miniskirt and a black polo neck. I was quite into the Sixties sort of look. I was probably hobbling and teetering around London with blisters all over my feet. I must have cut quite a strange little figure, really.

Later that same year – this is awful, this is something that took us a long time to tell anyone, but I'm quite happy to tell people now because I'm old and I've done lots of nice things for people, so maybe it doesn't matter any more. But I was walking up Oxford Street, it was Christmas Eve, and I was in my trainers. I don't know what I was doing, I was on Oxford Street trying to get a bit of Christmas spirit. And I was running along and there was a man carrying a box with a television inside. I remember accidentally skidding on the ice and knocking into him, and I heard the television drop to the ground and smash, and so I ran and then I just kept running. And I remember having that moment where I thought, should I turn around, should I go back? Nah, I'm not going to do it, I'm just going to keep running. I spent all Christmas Day feeling sick cos I thought, I've deprived some family of their telly. I've ruined some family's Christmas. It took a long time for me to let myself off the hook for that one, and I still feel a bit sick when I think about it.

A few years later, when I was about 18, me and my mam came back to Newcastle to visit some friends. We stayed for a week, I think, and we got on the coach to come back to London, to go and stay in the hideous flat with the highlighter-yellow walls and the annoying flatmate. But, as soon as we'd sat down on the coach – I remember the moment as clear as day – we both just looked at each other and said, 'I don't really want to go back, do you?' 'No, I don't want to go back either.' We said, 'Should we move back to Newcastle?' And it was just decided there and then, we knew it was time to go back. It was a no-brainer, really. It totally, naturally and organically came to an end.

Maybe everyone should do what I did and go down to London when you're really young, really fucking irresponsible and really resilient. And really good-looking as well. Not to say that I was, but if you're an appealing young lass, who's quite gobby and attractive, people are more likely to look after you and see you're all right, than if you stagger down there when you're beaten by life and haven't got a lot of self-confidence. I mean, I was full of myself when I went down there, and that helped us along a little bit. You know, either that or if you're rich. I don't think there's any middle ground, really.

I do think that you have to have a lot of energy if you want to go and live in London. I can't be bloody bothered any more. A couple of days is all I can go for now. It's a bit of a drain. I feel like I've turned into one of those Northern clichés, like 'Ooh, that London, everyone's grasping down there and everyone's in on the rat race' and all that crap. You know, if we're watching the telly at home and if the news comes on, quite often there's a reporter stood there in front of Tower Bridge in London, and I think, god, I lived there.

GETTING ALONG

ED HUSAIN

Commentator

I remember when Wonderbra adverts came out. Outside the East London Mosque, Wonderbra adverts went up. It's all well and good advertising bras, but as we know in the lingerie industry more than bras get advertised, all sorts of other assets are displayed. So people inside the East London Mosque made sure that the adverts were taken down. And then, when they were put up again, they were painted over. I remember asking people, why don't we just leave them alone? I was born and raised here, so for me it wasn't such a big deal. But for many of these guys who were newcomers to Britain, who were Islamists trained in either Pakistan or Bangladesh, for them there were three levels of dislike – all based on the Prophet's teachings, but it's how they interpret it and implement it that's key. If you dislike something, according to their very strict interpretation of religion, you would physically change it with your hands. If you can't physically change it, you'd speak out against it. And if you can't speak out against it, then you must dislike it in your heart. That's the weakest of faith, and they want to be strongest of the strongest. So what are they doing? There they are, painting over Wonderbra ads. Guys, calm down. It's only there for two weeks, then the next fad will be up.

Another example is intimidating prostitutes in Brick Lane. If you speak to women in and around Jack the Ripper's old terrain, around Spitalfields and Brick Lane and Whitechapel, they will tell you that Asian, Muslim guys, mostly Islamists with big beards and what have you, have taken it on themselves to physically remove this vice. Talk about being bullies. Leave the women alone. What business is it of yours to go around intimidating those women? The same women will tell you that it's the uncles and the brothers of these guys who are their most regular clients. So it's just a world full of paradoxes and contradictions. For me, the most worrying bit is the element of bullying, imposing, physically trying to change what they consider to be wrong. In the world view of most people who choose to live in a liberal democracy, it's live and let live.

But Islamism is built on the fact that there is only one way of doing things – God's way. There are many ways of doing almost everything in life, and so the mission of the Islamist becomes to change all of that to bring it in accord with God's wishes. So there is that inner tension, the driving force to saying my responsibility, my duty to God, is not just to lead what I consider to be a loyal, godly life, but also to bring all of these people to God's path.

It depends on the personality, the level of extremism of an individual. Those that tend to be more accepting, compassionate, would have pity on people. You know, 'These poor, gay people,' or, 'These poor drug addicts. These poor single mothers, if only they were believers in God, all would be well or at least they would get rewarded in the afterlife. But these poor, pitied people aren't what they should be, because of me. I haven't done my proselytizing properly enough.' So there is that element of mental self-flagellation, that 'I should now go out and try to improve other people's lot.'

Most Muslims get on with life, but Islamists see themselves as the vanguard who are more than just Muslim. They have a responsibility to bring people to Islam, so there is this obsession of what they call *dowah* or proselytizing. You know, just being Muslim isn't good enough. You've got to be a shining example for everybody else. So there is that. Pity is a positive way of putting it, but it's damn patronizing that everyone else is somehow not on the straight and narrow and they have an attitude towards other Muslims, interestingly enough, it's not just non-Muslims, but towards other Muslims, they have this attitude that we need to do *dowah*. We need to bring them back to the straight and narrow. That's how they'd look at it.

In the 1990s the entire easyJet culture – the culture of having foreign holidays and travelling around – emerged. Islamists in London benefited from that in terms of being able to go to the Middle East to study. So they would go to Egypt and Syria to study and there they'd be shocked, because the very lewd women they were trying to run away from with the tight jeans and the low-cut tops, etc. – they were everywhere in the Middle East. The great Islamic lands, as they understood them to be, weren't so Islamic. It was just like everywhere else. Even the Prophet Mohammad's city, Medina, was like that. It was pluralist, you know, and we have the most reliable forms of the Prophet's sayings, we would call them *hadieth* material, where after the Prophet passed away, even during his early Caliphs, those who were in charge of the political entity after him, or the communal entity after him, there were bare-breasted women in Medina. No one freaked out. No one said, let's go and get these women clothed. You read even Ibn Khaldun's travels and he's talking about being in Africa as a Muslim scholar, traveller, dancing with women who are bare-breasted because it was the cultural norm. We don't see him trying to impose a veil on them. So my argument is not just that we should celebrate liberal democracy here and now, but also in ancient and medieval societies that was the norm. People let other people be. Especially on these women's rights issues. You can't contain the human spirit. You really can't. It always finds a way out.

In the early 2000s, when satellite television channels started to emerge, kids in places such as Tower Hamlets were surrounded at home by versions of either Pakistan or Bangladesh. The satellite television channels from those countries set up here in Urdu or Bengali are what the parents are watching, so rather than be connected, say, to a General Election campaign – in my case I remember Margaret Thatcher's and John Major's campaigns very clearly – kids in London now are being exposed to what's going on in Pakistan and what's going on in Bangladesh. Their focus is over there, because that's what their parents, first-generation immigrants, are interested in.

In an area like Tower Hamlets, your household is Bengali, your hospital nurse, doctor, comes from a Bangladeshi background. Mini-cab drivers have a Bangladeshi background. It's now Bangladesh in Britain round the East London Mosque, the restaurants are all from a Bangladeshi background. Bus drivers are from a Bangladeshi background. Stallholders in markets are from a Bangladeshi background. You're living in Little Bangladesh. The same in Southall with India. Same in parts of Brixton with black people.

Now it could be argued, what's wrong with it? Let a thousand cultures bloom. But what I find is that what ultimately happens is those people within those communities who we seek to honour and protect – in other words women, minorities, young teenagers born and raised in this country – are then forced to adhere to a collective notion of belonging to those communities that are culturally anchored in Pakistan or Bangladesh rather than have a strong, vibrant, individual identity here in a liberal democracy. So what happens is those women, thirty, forty years here in Britain, still don't speak English. Those women who experience, say, domestic violence or other difficulties at home, don't have the cultural confidence with which to speak to the local police or the social services. Those women don't work, so the rate of unemployment is much higher than your average white working-class English woman in this country. So in the name of trying to honour these communities and just let them be, you know, we're allowing male, middle-class, religiously defined men to control their women and to control the younger folk. I think there's something going wrong there that needs openly addressing.

There should be no expectation that schools and teachers will recruit interpreters for young kids who are arriving or for parents at parents' evenings. That would send a strong message that when you're here you learn the language of the land: English.

I think it can also be encouraged to change by the council housing structure that we have. You come to Britain and you expect the state – rightly – to accommodate people who don't have housing. I see nothing wrong with that. It's a noble aim and should continue. But that then does not mean that you're entitled to stay within two square miles in Tower Hamlets when there are empty houses, say, in Ilford further east or in northern cities or in and around the Home Counties. What's wrong with Milton Keynes? What's wrong with Luton? There are communities there. There are people there. In other words, we are allowing these clusters to build up simply because someone says, I want to be housed in Tower Hamlets next to my relative or next to a given butcher's shop or next to a community centre or an old people's home. Give people homes, by all means – that's a noble tradition and that speaks volumes about us here in this country – but not at the expense of damaging the fabric of people's lives, people's outlooks, the next generation.

I go into schools where kids speak to one another in languages other than English. That's where we are. You can accuse me of social engineering but in the absence of doing that, you know, by default it's the worst form of social engineering that's going on now, if you see what I mean – of exclusion, of 50 per cent of that population not working or women not speaking English, of children growing up with identity crises and then ultimately religious extremism and terrorism.

Don't tell me this is integration. Don't tell me this is what multiculturalism means. That's not what it was set out to mean. It's a noble aim and it was genuinely about how all the cultures enmesh and get along together. But something went wrong somewhere and we're living separately and apart.

ABUL AZAD

Social worker

He escorts me around Toynbee Hall in Whitechapel and explains its history of social reform and its current programmes. He volunteered here for two years and then, in 2001, started on one of the Hall's projects, Surma, which supports elderly Bangladeshi people in the community, some of whom trail him as we walk, smiling and peppering him with questions.

Around 35 per cent of the Tower Hamlets population is of Bangladeshi origin – perhaps as many as 70,000 people – and a lot of the older generation of Bangladeshis encounter language barriers. They are having problems and difficulties in every step of their life, because benefit issues and lifestyle issues can be complex. They encounter paperwork they don't understand, which leads to billing problems. So I help Bangladeshi people complete their benefit claim forms, I translate and interpret the letters given to them from various agencies and authorities, and help them navigate what to do next.

Bangladeshis started coming after the Second World War. Bangladesh is a member of the Commonwealth and so the UK government recruited Bangladeshis to come as labourers, to rebuild their homes and highways and Underground, then their shipping industry and also the trains, British Rail. When they arrived this country needed them, and they contributed to rebuilding the UK after the war. They worked sixty or seventy hours a week to earn money to send some back home again or to buy some land or build some houses, thinking they would go back for ever. That was their ambition when they arrived here. They came as a sort of economic migrant, worked hard in this country, and they wanted to earn their livelihood and then go back.

Since they brought their families here, their ideas of return have faded. They don't want to go back. They want to stay here because they've got friends here and with the system and the law – they find those things awkward when they go back to Bangladesh. Everybody wants to live in Tower Hamlets and Brick Lane because they feel at home; everywhere shops and restaurants are full of Bangladeshis. They feel safer and they can communicate, they feel better living with fellow people like them. I think mixing is very important, because if you're coming to a country to earn your livelihood or living for a long time, you should know the culture of the whole country. To be a Roman you have to act like a Roman, or if you're in Canada you have to act like a Canadian.

But the barriers are language skills and education, and they do not have these things. For them there are things that prevent them moving easily around London, including poverty. Most of them never worked in a high-profile job in the UK. They used to be labourers and they're treated as very low people. They are not rich. If you want to travel, if you want to learn something, you need money. If you want to go to the cinema, tickets are £20, you get me? If you want to go out eating it costs you money and they have to look after their families. They have to look after their ancestors in Bangladesh, and they've got limited income. So that is another thing. With the older people here we have two projects – one that consists mostly of white people and another that consists mostly of Bangladeshi people. The white group, most of them have got private pensions, they've got additional income or they've got bank savings. Only a few in our Bangladeshi group have got private pensions; most did not save for their retirement life. When they got older they didn't worry, because in our culture people think that when you're old the family will look after you.

I say to them sometimes they are isolating themselves. That is absolutely not a good thing to happen to generation after generation, because it is never good to be isolated from the mainstream. You are abandoned, you get me? If the minicab is Bengali, grocery shop is Bengali, everywhere is Bengali – so that means you are reducing your opportunities to learn more in your environment.

You are making yourself isolated, why don't you mix with the other people and things? Their answer is, well, my life is nearly ending. I am in the sunset period of my life. So there's no point to learn more. This is their answer because they are very old and they think they will not live much longer. And therefore they lose interest in mixing. They find it very comfortable to stay with what they know. I ask them, you have to come out from that mentality so you will be able to learn.

In my project, we've organized some joint outings together, like to the seaside at Brighton or safari park or Kew Gardens, and we've tried to mix and diversify them. When the Bangladeshis go in the bus they sit near the other Bangladeshis. The white people sit with white people. At Kew Gardens we went to see a lovely greenhouse environment. You've got palm trees, papayas, bananas. The Bangladeshis liked that. The white people also went but didn't stay long because they went to the aquarium. The Bangladeshis went to the aquarium too. They just didn't go together. Some mix because they can share ideas and be understood. For others it's hard. If you are not sharing with each other, talking with each other, what do you have? The older generation are not as in tune as the new generation are. They are not very much interested to know other cultures, to learn more about other people's interests. Older people say they aren't always interested to learn more. Younger generations, newer generations, are very much interested. They want to know the other people's culture, what you eat, all the things, certainly.

I want to be part of it. I want to keep my own culture in mind. I want my children to mix with the people here. I want them to learn the systems of the modern world but I don't want them to forget their culture. It's divided. London is a place of divided belongings.

NICOLA OWEN

Teacher

We meet at 7 p.m. Greenwich Mean Time, in Greenwich. When she arrives she looks so young I wonder for a moment if she is a student. She hasn't lived in Greenwich herself for many years, but already misses an older Greenwich, one with a woman in the market who just sold vintage bottles, tins emblazoned with the royals and images of Tower Bridge.

My first school was in south-east London. I had two days before any kids came on, two days just with the staff. My department had just moved office and there was dust all over everything. The women in my department were just bitching and moaning about all this dust being everywhere and I was like, okay, I'll go and get a cloth and then we'll clean it up ... And they said, oh, it's not our job to clean up the dust – Premises will come and clean it up. I realized that day why a lot of these schools are failing and the people in them have either been pushed to the point of not caring by overwork or weren't suited for it in the first place.

That first school was all girls, all girls from south-east London. A lot of Muslim girls because obviously that's the kind of family that desperately don't want their kids educated with boys. I think it was pretty much 50/50 white and non-whites. There were sixty-three languages spoken. I realized like twenty-five minutes into the lesson that one child didn't speak hardly any English at all. So I said, right, don't bother trying to do any of this, can you just write me something about yourself. Just a paragraph about you in English. Okay, she did that. And when I looked at it at the end of the day she'd written something about growing up in China and not knowing who her mum and dad were and then someone coming to her house one day and telling her that she had a mummy in Englishland and being put on a plane to Englishland and now living in Englishland with her mummy and her twin sister that she never knew existed.

We've had a kid bring a machete into school. Had a kid get stabbed in the vestibule. We have a knife arch pretty regularly: the police bring it down and put it at the front gates and the kids have to come through. But the kids just text each other first and go, there's a knife arch. Then all the black kids make a point of being twenty minutes late for school and they come in and they're like, yeah, yeah, I'm late because like there's a knife arch, so I couldn't come in.

There's a gang who wear one glove. That's their little gang sign and if it's on the right hand that shows they're evil, you know, 'I'm itchin' for a fight because then if I shoot someone with my gun hand they won't have any prints,' whereas on the left hand it means I'm not doing anything bad, I'm just moochin' about, being in a gang. So I take their gloves off. I say, I'll have your glove now. Just that one glove. And I call it a 'club', which they hate. 'It's not a club, miss.' Okay, all right. I had clubs when I was at school, too. They hate that. Because I think we glamorize gang culture when we say, oh, gangs are really dangerous, don't be in a gang. I think we run the risk of making it sound really cool and exciting. So I like to rip the piss a little bit.

Once a kid didn't do her homework and I was shouting at her about it. She said something about having to pick up her little brothers and sisters from school. I said, well, okay, that's a big responsibility and I know that must take a lot of your time, but you still need to do your homework. She was like, okay, okay. She was a very sweet girl, a lovely Muslim girl, and I went to the year office just to say, by the way, this kid is de facto caring for her siblings. I didn't know if they knew. And they said, yes, we do know. Her mother died last year and she's the oldest of ten or eleven kids. She'd taken on all the mother's responsibilities, including more traditional wifely responsibilities, and so they thought that not only was she caring for the children but effectively being raped by her father. I'm like, of course she hasn't done her homework. You know, why would you?

I can remember some pretty horrendous disasters. Like in my

first ever observations, where your tutor from Teach First comes and observes you. He came and observed me in the first or second week, and one of the kids was eating a lolly. I said, Lily, you need to put the lolly away. No, ain't doing it! Ain't doing nuffink, can't make me. I tried all these things, didn't know what to do, nothing worked. She had it in her hands at one point and I walked past and just snatched it out of her hand, at which point she just exploded and ran out. I was teaching in random huts near the bins in the playground, because there weren't enough classrooms, which was not pleasant in the summer when the smell drifted across the playground. So she ran out of this hut and started running around it and there's enough windows that all the rest of the kids were like zhoom!, watching her. Outside, she got her fingernails that were like these talons and scratched the side of her face and came back in and said, Miss, look what you done to me – I'm gonna sue. She'd drawn blood. My tutor's sitting in the back going, how are you going to deal with this? And I was like, fuck, that's it. That's the end of my teaching career. I've been in it a week and a half and I'm going to be sued. But just then some lovely very sweet girl in the front went, 'No you didn't. We all saw you scratch it.' And I thought, I love you, child, you can have an A. So I said, no, you scratched it yourself. You need to just go outside, Lily, and wait and then you can come in when you're calm. And she did.

The most demoralizing thing is that, five times a day, you stand in front of thirty people who don't listen to you and just sit and chat amongst themselves and you just have to keep doing it and doing it and doing it. I remember quite early in that week, after the lesson, going into the cupboard where we kept textbooks because I was so sure I was going to cry. And obviously you can't let kids see you crying, that's just the worst thing in the history of the world. I just sat in this dark cupboard going, it's okay, it's okay. They're just children, it's fine. It's like training animals, you only have to punish them five or six times before they realize that you mean it, and then they're like, right, I'll put my phone away now because otherwise you're going to take it and I believe you're going to take it and I believe you won't give it back to me. Also, you learn not to take it personally. They're so funny and they're so sweet. Even when they're shit to you they do apologize.

Sometimes it's really depressing. You see them in Year 7 and the little boys are just so cute, they're these tiny little kids and they've got their ties all done up beautifully, like top button, and their uniforms are a bit too big for them but they're really sweet and they're putting their hand up all the time and they're really excited. Maybe one in ten will stay like that. We've got some hugely successful black children and they've worked really hard and they've done really well and they're going to go off to university and become doctors and lawyers and stuff. But most of them just fall off. You can see them tussling with, I want to be clever and I want to do well, but actually I also want to be cool and I want to be liked and I want to say funny things. It's pretty heartbreaking.

Soon, the tie goes lower and lower and the knot gets bigger. The badder they are, the lower and bigger it is. I don't know how they tie them so big. Honestly, they're about the size of my hand. We have a rule in our school, you should be able to see three stripes on the tie and so they spend hours trying to get it as short as possible with still three stripes.

I've got a new tutor group this year, they're very very little because my old ones went off last year, after me filling out about twenty-five applications for plumbing and carpentry courses. I've got the bottom set again, even though they promised me that after my horrendous time with my last bottom set they would give me a top one. But they're like, oh, but you did it so well! Have another bunch of crazies. Anyway, I tie their ties for them as they go out in the morning, make it smaller and push it up and do their top button up and send them on their way. My A-level class are hanging outside going, Miss, you know they're just gonna untie it when they get to the end of the corridor – what are you bothering for?

Well, because, if people keep on saying to them, be smart, you can be smart, you can learn ... I don't know. Some sort of symbolism, I guess, about forcing them to be good. I don't make the knots too small, because I have to balance it out. I don't want them to be murdered.

Most other countries in the world have some sort of education for civics. A country that doesn't teach its kids about government or politics or sociology, that's mad. Finally it was introduced here in 2002 by Bernard Crick, who thought that it would combat apathy and disengagement from society and all that kind of stuff. So it's a bit of crime and law, a bit of politics and political organizations, a bit of society and sociology and social change. If you've done a unit on politics, you're meant to then go out and engage with local politicians, and if you do a unit on the environment you're meant to do some recycling campaigning at school or something. The kids love that bit because they feel like they're actually doing something. I was doing multiculturalism quite early on and I was talking about the BNP and the kids said, how can they justify their position? I said, let's just ring them and ask. This was quite a nice Year 10 class, I think, so about fifteen students. I put my phone on speaker-phone and rang the BNP Campaign Line and this poor woman on the end said to us, oh, you're asking me what is Britishness? The learning objective was what does it mean to be British, and we were talking about how the BNP define it as being white and how that's clearly wrong because we came from a million different places anyway in the first place. When the woman on the phone answered she said, someone who obviously was born in Britain and their family is all from Britain. My kids on the speaker-phone said, okay, how long do you have to have been in Britain for? Four generations? Five generations? And this woman said, a really long time, yeah, yeah. The kids said, how would you test if someone had been here long enough? The woman responded, oh, you just know, don't you? This veiled racist response. It got to the point when one of kids asked, so would you genetically test people? Would you look for their DNA to see if they were properly white enough?

But another time I gave them a map as I was trying to do some sort of 'Britain is multicultural' thing. I wanted to ask people where their families were from, and then get up and draw a line from that place to Britain. The idea was that at the end they'd all have a map that showed we've come from everywhere. But they couldn't do it because they didn't know where anywhere was. They were like, Miss, where's Germany? Miss, where's America? Miss, where's Britain? I said, can you sit back in your chairs? Let's have a little conversation. See this little island? Anyone? Britain. Where's London?

I love my debating club. They were on the television last Thursday – my debaters. I was very proud of them. They're really really good. I went to a normal comprehensive and I did debating and I was forced into it because I spoke a lot and someone said, oh my god, give that girl an outlet to go and do this. That was what made me apply to Oxford. I would never have applied to Oxford before, but I'd been there and I'd debated there and I'd beaten boys from Eton who had like really expensive ties, so I thought, okay, I'll try. So I started this debating club and I've got a really lovely mix in there. I've got one girl whose mum and dad are teachers, middle-class upbringing and really really lovely. And then I've got another girl whose mum was only 14 years old when she had her and was kicked out of school when she got pregnant with her and she gets drunk with her on the weekends. This girl is really clever and she's like, I'm going to be a lawyer and I'm going to use this debating skill.

Those two are really good mates and they debate in a pair. It's just the best feeling when they're debating against these posh, private-school boys. They had one on withdrawing from Afghanistan and so there's these two girls, very beautiful with this long blonde hair and these Eltham accents, and they're like, 'Ladies and gentleman, you should really fink about it, because like you ain't gonna know nuffink and like Ahmadinejad ain't gonna just like back off, he's gonna be like, no, I ain't backin' off.' The thing is, what they're saying is really clever, but they have these heavy accents and there's these boys across from them, you know, and they've got their floopy hair and their ridiculously expensive clothes and you can see that when they start talking the boys just think, ah, ha, well, we've obviously won this. It takes about two minutes into the speech and then you see it start to dawn on their faces while she's talking about like, I don't know, community fragmentation when you've got outside influences, or something. Then the boys suddenly start writing furiously.

There's about eight who come regularly to debating club. I had a three-year plan: in this first year I said I'm going to take you to loads of competitions and you're going to get beaten by sixth-formers – because they were Year 10. You're going to get beaten by kids much older than you, much posher than you, all the time and you've just got to keep going. That's fine, that's fine. Then obviously they started getting beaten by all these kids and they had a horrid time. I would buy them pizza afterwards and say, it's okay, come on, it's going to be good. And at the end of the year they won this competition for all the state schools in London.

The grand final was against a school in Enfield, on whether parents should be prosecuted for their kids truanting. And my kids obviously knew that they already are prosecuted for their kids truanting. As the motion was announced in this room, this girl whose mother was really young, said, 'That's status quo, innit, Miss?' I said, yes, yes it is. On you go. And they won.

It's amazing. Apart from getting your phone stolen every twelve weeks, this is the best job ever.

GUITY KEENS

Interpreter

I'm a foreigner here myself. I wasn't born here. It doesn't matter how many years I live here – and my son is English, my husband is

English – still I'm Iranian. But I know more about immigration law in England than any barrister. Every new bill, I'm aware of it. People call me from Iran, I say, you have to do this, that. I deal with a lot of immigrants coming from Iran or Afghanistan, because in part of Afghanistan they speak Farsi. They call it Dari, but it's an old form of Farsi. I go through interesting but very tough and sad things.

She's just come back to London from Cambridge, where she was working earlier today. She smokes behind the bike shed of the detention centre there, she says. She has painted fingernails and lively dark eyes that sometimes tear up as she speaks.

I had never worked in my whole life. I was a lady of leisure, I would lunch, you know. I went to university. I've got a degree. I got really bored. And a friend of mine, an Iranian, she had some dispute going to the court and she said, can you come with me? She can speak English, but not very well. So I went with her and her solicitor. It was like a magistrates court. Driving offence. And I said, can I interpret? So they said, okay, we'll use you. And so we did it and she won. We went and had a big drink and she said, Guity, why don't you do this job? I said, I don't have any experience. I haven't worked, you know. And then I came home and I thought about it and she keep pushing me and pushing me. Then I said to my husband, Michael, I can't work. I don't have confidence. He said, but you have been doing it for the last twenty years! When the Revolution happened, I was just married and my family, friends, everybody was coming here, so I had to take them to the Home Office, I had to take them to the solicitor, I had to take them to the hospital. I wasn't as good at English as I am now, but I was okay. My husband reminded me that I've been doing it for twenty years – without being paid! So I thought, okay, I'll try it. I started it and I love it.

I'm going to be quite honest with you now, okay? Afghanis don't have any political problems. They come for work. And some of them they lost their family to the Taliban as well. But they come here to work and some of them they come here to better themselves. Some of them they come to work for a few years and take their money – say, £5,000 is huge money in Afghanistan, they can go and start a business in Afghanistan. Iranians, they don't come here to work – there's lots of money in Iran. Iranian young people come here for freedom. They want to go to the pub. They want to have a girlfriend. They want to go to the disco. They want to go clubbing. That's why they want to come here.

They've been promised by the agents, the smugglers, a lot. Oh the pavement is gold, you know? They bring them here and take them for a nice shower, and the first thing I ask them is how is everything? And all the Afghanis say, it's fantastic. It's like a hotel here. They love it. Because nice bed, shower, food. And then they get very disappointed. Because there's the other side of it as well, and that's loneliness. They don't have anyone to talk to, they can't speak the language. People don't bother with you. And sometimes they don't like you. Obviously it depends which area you have been located. There are some areas, especially out of London, southern, the people they don't like them. You can't blame British people because it affects them as well. I go to these little market towns and you see this oldish couple, they're scared watching those immigrants. They think they're going to hurt them. They're scared. But the British are really really good people. I'm saying it as a foreigner. They are really generous. They are really tolerant comparing to the rest of the Europe. I've been to Germany and I've been to France and I see the way they treat the foreigners in the street. It's really horrible.

As soon as you say to them, 'social worker' or 'the police', they start crying. Doesn't matter how old they are: men, women, young. I mean, I had a 72-year-old Iranian man, he used to be one of the ministers in Iran during the Shah. He wanted residency. He doesn't want asylum, he's a multimillionaire, okay, but he wanted to get permission to stay here. His family, his children are living here and he used to come and go in Iran. Anyway, as soon as his solicitor starts talking, this man cried. I'm not joking, crying and wailing. Can you imagine me? So embarrassed. I didn't know what to do. I can't hold him. I can't hug him. He's older than my father. Everybody cries.

That tears was real, I tell you. That affected me because a man in his stage and in his position, to feel so broken, you know. That is a very very hard tear. That man, he was tough, I know his story. I know he's been fighting with this regime for quite some times. He's been in prison. *Real* prison, you know? And he said, you're the only woman to see my tears in my whole life.

Children cry. Women cry. Men cry. They all cry. There was this man, what do you call it? Geezer? Yeah. Very strong man. Tall, big, you know, Mr Muscles. I took him to solicitor and he says, you've been refused. Aaaah, the tears were coming and this man is looking at him. What's happened? Don't know. It's like a shock to them.

When they come they're very appreciative. They change their appearances because they know when they come here they don't look like everybody else, they look different. So they like to change and get mixed up with people and they are very much into girls. You can't even touch their hair. It's so sticky! I mean, when I see them it's like, nice, you know, natural hair. Next time I see them, it's spiky with lots of gel sticking up. What's happened? You have an electric shock or something? And the trainers, they are mad about trainers. Trainers, mobile phones and hair gel. These three things are very big.

As they stay longer and longer, then start moaning and complaining. Weather first. Then people. Not very nice things. I don't really want to repeat that because it makes me very upset because I'm very patriotic about Britain. As much as I like other people, I really love this country and I really get upset when people are ungrateful and they don't appreciate what people have gone and done for them. They think we're rich people. I say, no, you can't say that. None of them have British friends, that's another thing. I say, if you don't like it, piss off. Let's make room for another one.

The foreigners all see London as old-fashioned: the double-decker bus, black cab, the guards, Big Ben and all that. They don't know that London has changed. It's changed so much. They were so nice and polite; now it's dirty, rude, more vibrant. I used to live in Notting Hill Gate when I came here first. That was supposed to be multicultural then, and there was only one shop open until twelve o'clock. You could have a meal and then you go there. One shop. Everywhere was so dead. But now it's very lively, very upbeat.

Sometimes they get problems with police. I say, if you want to live here, you have to be law-abiding. Because the other thing is, you see, these people come from a very strict country which the police and the authorities have got very much control of. When they come here and see the policemen in the streets so nice and calm, they think, what a lovely place, we can get away with murder, you know? The first thing I tell them, I say, don't look at them, they are very nice now, but if you go to the police station that's a different matter, because I've been to the police station with them. So this is something I always tell them. This is the first guide or tip: do not even think about it, you cannot get away with doing something illegal if you want to stay here. Some of them are still waiting for the decision and if they commit any crime it affects their decision, you know, and they will deport them. So these are the things that I tell them to be careful of and if they don't do it I get really cheesed off.

This one Afghani boy, he was young, and he went from Afghanistan with his brother. It's something, they travel with brothers as well, the little ones, you know? They went to Iran. Stayed in Iran for a while, two or three years, saved his money. He was 15 and his brother was 11. They start coming to England. They came and they stopped in Calais. They couldn't get through there. They tried, tried and tried, every day. Somebody said to them, I don't know exactly, but there is like a little port where the ferry comes and then they transfer there to unload from the ferry coming out and he said to me, it's like a little island, all around is water. The truck was standing on the land

and there's the water between them and the truck. So somebody told them, if you can swim at night, go to that land, there's a truck there. You can get inside the truck. His brother said, I'm going first, I'm going first. He was 11, 12 years old. He jumped in the water at night and the older brother is standing there and trying to see the younger one going and the older brother feels like father, like mother, like everything. He brought up his younger brother. And as the younger brother is swimming, this ship is coming, and it hit his brother and he dies in front of him. Right in front of him. He went absolutely mad and other people really felt sorry for him. They collected money and gave it to agent because agent can really get on to bring him here. He came here, three times he tried to kill himself. Three times. And I don't know, he's like a cat with the lives. You know those bridges over the motorway. He jumped from one of them. Honestly, I'm not joking. He's not just in a rage, he hasn't grown up and now he must be 19, but he's tiny. Still he feels so guilty. He said, this is going to stay with me for the rest of my life, this guilt, because I came here. I brought my brother here. And I killed my brother. It's happened in front of me.

I mean, a British, they wouldn't know about this. They just think, they're coming here, taking our jobs, taking our benefits. All that. I have a friend, she's English. Old friend, she's very nice. She lives in Hampstead and every now and then we get together and see each other, go for coffee or lunch. I haven't seen her for ages because I've been busy, but recently she called me and said, 'Guity, I haven't seen you, come over to my house.' It's a very nice house in Hampstead Heath. And she start talking about these bloody foreigners coming here, you know, this, that, this, that. I didn't say anything. But we're having lots of wine and finally I said to her, I am so proud living in this country and choose this country as my country. You, as a British person, should be so proud. Don't knock it down. You have to be so proud that your government system is taking care of these people. And she started crying. Oh Guity, you're right!

It's because she didn't know. She only read the papers, she doesn't really know these people who are coming here. They're not all scroungers. Not all of them. Some of them really have problems. It's not easy to come here and it's not easy to live here. So you must really have had a very tough time back home to tolerate here.

LUCY SKILBECK

Mother

I meet her at Holborn station at 10 a.m. and we walk to a cafe around the corner with an upstairs room. She is focused. It's in the way she listens, in the way she dips into conversation, determined not to give anything away until finally the dam breaks and she speaks — about the necessary hustle of caring for a small child while trying to establish a career and then, soon after, caring for a mother caught in the throes of dementia. She speaks of her son and their peripatetic early years, moving from Australia to St Petersburg, Amsterdam, Denmark, to London, where he was placed in a crèche in Brixton.

I'm slightly famed in my family for every time we go somewhere nice, saying, let's move here. They get a bit fed up with my desire to move anywhere that looks nice for a day. We were once up in Hathersage in the Peak District and I'd done my 'let's move here' talk, this is lovely, etc. And then I saw these three teenagers, probably about my son Duncan's age, hanging out outside the petrol station on the main street in Haversidge looking about as bored as it's possible for a kid to look and I thought, if you're in Haversidge the only thing there is to do is climb. That's it. The whole town is about rock climbing because it's in a particular part of the Peak District where there's big climbs, and either you're a kid who does that or you've got nothing else to do. I looked at those kids and I just thought, there's no way I'd want my children to go through that interminable boredom. Obviously there's huge things to be said in favour of bringing your kids up in the country and I'm not knocking it, but it did just make me stop for a second.

In Hackney there's a really active cultural life. He also has friends that I think he wouldn't necessarily have somewhere else, friends with greatly divergent interests, so all his friends aren't like him, they're all really different and they all want to do really different things. Some of them want to be actors and some of them want to be economists and quite a few of them are musicians themselves and some of them are really sporty and there's just this breadth of experience because there's a breadth of opportunity where he lives. The people he hangs out with all have such an access to so many different things.

He's got this tremendous sense of confidence. He feels that he is part of a world full of possibility and opportunity. So he takes advantage of things that are on offer, so he does a lot of stuff. There's a climbing centre down the road he goes to. We had an equestrian centre ten minutes down the road from us and for years he rode. He also goes to Ministry of Sound club nights and stays out till five o'clock in the morning and then gets the Tube home.

In the secondary school he was at in Bethnal Green, there were lots of kids of black African origin. His best friend there was from a Nigerian family of like ten kids who kept going back and forth to Nigeria. He had Sikh friends, and friends from all over the place and he still does, you know, they come from different places and they go to different places and they want different things, but there is something about being central. And even things like the food. We're surrounded by Turkish shops and Indian shops.

He's really confident to take on the world as it is. I mean, I worry about things that he refuses to worry about to do with teenagehood. You hear about all the stabbings, and I think that there is a media storm about that, but I also think there are kids who are being seriously hurt and killed. That's terrible, but I don't know that moving to the country is the solution. I don't think that middle-class families saying, 'Well, we don't want our kids growing up in these neighbourhoods so we'll take them out of here' is actually the solution to any of the kinds of social problems that need addressing. I'm not saying that I'm staying as some kind of social martyr. We love being here because it is so diverse and so interesting and it seems to be the meeting place of so many cultures: there's the mosque at the top of our street, there's the big Turkish community, just up the road is one of the largest Hasidic Jewish communities in London, and then there's the African community which is split between Muslim and Christian faiths. All those communities actually all work together peaceably and I think there's something really important about that.

The other thing that happens when you grow up in London, and maybe Hackney in particular, is that you learn how to manage social tensions or cope with them or deal with them or avoid them. There are all sorts of signals that he will pick up that I wouldn't pick up. There are all sorts of coded things that I would be oblivious to. Simple things like where people are standing in relation to other people, for instance, and not getting too close. Or like what it is to disrespect someone and who it is you mustn't disrespect. Making eye contact or not making eye contact. There's all sorts of things that he just knows. It seems innate, but obviously it's learned through many years. I think it is a real skill and it's something that children who grow up here have a particular gift for or understanding of. It's a survival mechanism, of course, but it is transferable.

The other thing people don't realize is that the outside world is really accessible in London and particularly in Hackney where we've got the marshes and the canal and everything is at the end of our street. He grew up riding horses and he shared a pony so he was there three or four days a week, ten minutes' walk away. Sometimes I think it would be nice to get to the country more often but he also grew up doing Woodcraft Folk from when he was six. It's kind of like a hippy scouts, pacifist, left-wing, non-religious. Kind of an anti-Baden Powell equivalent, set up in order for kids in the city to get out into the country and do camping, build shelters, find edible berries, all those kinds of things. So it was all a bit different to the scouts, which was just like the training ground for the military.

Although everyone will tell you otherwise, there certainly is a class system, but here the class system is much more profound and deep-rooted and significant. I think accent is fundamentally attached to that, and that although regional dialects have become acceptable and in fact desirable in many ways, that London accent, with the *wiv*s and *whateva*s, still connotes a lack of facility with language or something, which in itself then suggests that you're not as intellectually adept. Of course that's not true, I know absolutely that's not true, but I think that that's how it's perceived. That's how it's heard. So with Duncan, what I found difficult was when he started picking up those bad habits, the *v* instead of the *th* and things. Because that, to me, signalled that he wouldn't be taken seriously as he got older. And so I just made this deal with him and he's kind of stuck to it, although he still needs prompting, but much less than he used to. He can talk however he needs to with his friends, but he also has to learn to talk more correctly so that he can be taken seriously when he's older. Whatever the rights and wrongs, it just seems to me the facts as they are. He's very bright and he wants to do engineering or possibly something in politics, not be a politician, but something, you know, like political commentary or political science. Just to pronounce his *th*s, that'll do. That's all.

KEEPING THE PEACE

PAUL JONES

Home security expert

There's like 28,500 streets in London, and there's very few of them that I haven't been to. Some streets you go to again and again and again and again. Some houses you go to again and again. A lot of the time it's the tenant's fault. He's just had his big plasma TV stolen, so he goes out and buys another one, and leaves the box in the front garden. Common sense. Stuff like that. Or the police know it's a house full of ratbags and they raid it on a regular basis. Or you see the handiwork of the other engineers who may have been there time and time again. You think, why didn't they do that properly? There's no limit to it. Every door that gets kicked in, it gets replaced. You can kick it in again. That's why this company has been going nearly twenty years.

We are in a pub in Homerton, the sound from the Chelsea match nearly drowning out his soft Liverpudlian accent. He was a builder for years before switching to motorcycle delivery and then damage control. He drinks Fosters as the Friday night disco is assembled around us, complete with flashing lights.

We get a lot of people saying, can you come and fit me a new door? All right, madam. How much is that going to be? Depends what door you want. There's thousands of types of doors. From a security point of view, you can go for the flat door blank, solid timber, which is safe and secure but doesn't have any lights through it. If you're going to go with a door with panels, go for very small panels. Because a door with bigger panels can easily admit access to a skinny junky.

Hardwood is what it says, it's hard wood. But it's very brittle. No one tells you that. So one kick on a hardwood door and they've broken it. People in this city are paying £300,000 for a one-bedroom flat, and don't realize that the door is made of the same stuff as their kitchen cabinets. And they will never know until that door's broken.

Some of them are like, I'd never have thought of that. Cor blimey, now you mention it, guvnor. Most of it's just blatantly obvious but only to people in the security industry. You could reduce burglary in London, especially during the night, by about 50 per cent at least, if insurance companies insisted on a better standard for doors.

A lot of people don't want to spend £100 when they get a new lock fitted. For a lot of people money is tight. Even the ones that own their own house, when they've been burgled, essentially they're not paying for it. The insurance does. Their insurance company will generally only pay like for like, so if they've got a cheap door with two locks on, that's what their insurance company's going to pay for. That's the ideal time to do an upgrade, but they don't want to spend that money. You can't make them spend it.

The older houses are generally protected, because the doors are made of a seasoned wood and properly constructed. But most of the doors in Docklands on the expensive flats, they're basically made of cheese. One kick, and they'll split in one of two ways: the door hinges will come off the side or they'll split in half. They'll say, 'Somebody's sawn my door off!' I'm sorry to tell you this, but no, they haven't. You have an incredibly cheap door. It's basically all built to minimum fire regulations, which state that an internal door needs to hold back fire for only thirty minutes.

Some of the richest people in London have the cheapest doors. I think that's called karma. A lot of these people are just so stupid. They live in a £2 million house in Islington, thirty yards up the road you've got one of the roughest council estates, so what's a really good idea? To have your keys visible on a rack in the hallway, all marked: back door, front door, windows. Within easy reach of the letterbox, with a little bit of bamboo with a hook on. Alternatively, the keys are in the kitchen drawer, the most obvious kitchen drawer, the one above the cleaning cupboard. They're too posh to have curtains. So you sit in your bay window with your £1,200 laptop on the desk, and someone can just look through the window …

There's a lot of converted Victorian houses with a little grey box on the inside with a wire so people can buzz you in. It's very popular. But even brand new, the little key thing has got about 3 or 4 millimetres of movement. One push and you're in. I have to tell these people that you were burgled because of that thing on the door downstairs. You can upgrade it. You can change the whole thing. Get a big grey lock rather than this weak little thing on your door frame. You'll be more safe. That's to the people who are nice. To the people who are not so nice … well, as a general rule if people weren't so fucking lazy that they couldn't walk down the stairs and open the door, they wouldn't have this problem.

COLIN HENDRICKS

Police officer

It's 2:30 p.m. in the parking lot of a North London police station. Two officers get into the front of a grey-green Ford Mondeo, an unmarked car well recognized in the estates of North London. There's a bit of tape stretched across the glove compartment, blue lights embedded in the grille – 'And this,' says Colin from the driver's seat, as he holds up the portable revolving halogen light he can affix to the car's roof.

'What's it called?' I ask him from the back seat.

'Kojak light,' he says.

The first call is a disturbance at a fried chicken restaurant in Swiss Cottage. There's no rush, so it's only later that he puts on the siren and the blue lights flash against the shopfronts. The traffic parts and for the first time I witness unfurling London streets free of impediment.

*

It'll be fifteen years full-time in September. I did two years before with the voluntary police – the special constables. I think I was about 13 when I decided I wanted to join. A lot of people grow out of it, don't they, but I was adamant I didn't want to go to university.

When you joined up, you'd go out with a very experienced police officer – an old sweat, an old crusty – who had probably been in fifteen years, twenty years, and knew everything and wouldn't even carry a pen. You'd be his bitch for ten weeks. They would deliberately take you to any grief that happened and you could guarantee he or she wouldn't get off late at the end of the day. They would stitch you up so you'd be doing horrendously long hours dealing with all the rubbish that no one else wants.

When I was 19 I was already turning up at people's houses, dealing with disputes. In those situations most of the time you're with experienced police officers, but you are just left to deal with it. You don't know what's going to happen when you go into that address. It could be a marital dispute and you're telling the bloke, you've got to leave or you're going to get nicked. And he says, really? I've got kids older than you, mate.

Now I've instructed young officers and I've been that experienced officer. We've found people hanging and I've gone in and said, OK, he's definitely dead. We're going to do this slow and I'm going to talk you through it. They've just gone green, turned round, gone outside and thrown their guts up all over the patio with all the neighbours looking and thinking, hmmm. People forget you are human and a lot of the time you go into situations and you're shitting yourself. You're scared, but when you've got the uniform on, you deal with it. You haven't got any choice. If there's someone in a house saying, if you come in here, you're going to get it, most people would like to call the police and then just step back and wait for the police to turn up. Can we do that?

The uniform is a bit of a shield. We've got these smart trousers and long sleeves. If you're a male officer you have to wear a long-sleeved shirt and a tie and your hat at every ceremonial event in London, regardless of the weather. Even when it's hot we often wear yellow jackets. Anywhere else in the world, they'd wear polo shirts and lightweight combat trousers and trainers and still look smart and official and efficient, but we're the Queen's police service, with the world's media on us. It's a big stage, as it were.

The Ford Mondeo comes to a stop on Euston Road. We inch forward. He honks his horn lightly and the woman in the car next to us looks over. 'Off. Your. Phone,' he mouths and the woman, with a guilty smile, takes the mobile from her ear.

I worked in Islington and dealt with a lot of horrible stuff. When I was out at parties with friends they'd say, Islington, what a lovely place, very posh. I'd just look at them. We've got two extremes – affluence and poverty – and there isn't the separation people might imagine. If I had the money now, I wouldn't live there if you gave me the house for half the price. I know what's on the doorstep. I've seen it.

Someone once said to me, three years in the Met and you'll get more experience than someone who stays in the Counties for ten years. Out there they could go through a night shift with maybe one, two, three calls, whereas in some boroughs it's just non-stop. You have to try not to be blasé when you turn up at calls, as if it's just another road accident where someone died, or it's just another dead person in a flat, but you do lapse into automatic mode: you turn up, your feelings are detached from it, you just do what you've got to do.

Police work isn't hard. You learn as you go along and bring your experiences from other parts of your life. Do what you honestly think is right or best for the victim, or what you think will make them feel like they've been helped. You turn up to a robbery victim who's just been mugged, who's been grabbed round the throat, dragged backwards in a dark street, had all her rings bitten off her fingers, which is quite a common thing in London. Do you stand there showing no empathy towards the person, not offering them an ambulance, not trying to get them off the street? No, you get them in somewhere warm, even it's a caff, tell the owner, I'm closing the caff, get all your customers out. That's just common sense. But some people would leave her sitting in the street on the pavement crying her eyes out, thinking, shit, what do I do now? She may just want an arm round her. You say, are you comfortable? And if she responds badly to that, then you adapt.

But then there's the unknown in London. One sleepy Sunday morning I wasn't really interested in being at work. I was with the guy who is now my best friend, who's quite a tough lad, does a lot of training, he's now a firearms officer and I dread to think what would have happened if he'd have had a gun on this day – in fact I know what would have happened. We get this call, a girl calls up and says, I've been assaulted by my boyfriend. We pulled up outside; she's there saying, my finger's hurting. I look at her finger and think it's nothing. It's a finger. Sunday morning, we thought, this is just rubbish. If it was a Friday night, I'd have been on more of a guard. I knocked on the door and a young black lad answers, very athletic, just in boxer shorts and not wearing anything else. He goes, what? We were in uniform, so he knew who we were. I said, hello, mate, we're from blah, blah, blah police station. We've been called here because your girlfriend says she's been attacked. He goes, well, that didn't happen, and tried to close the door. Straightaway, foot in the door. I said, hold on, mate, we're here to investigate. She's standing behind me going, uh, huh, my finger. I was thinking, I don't want to be here. We just need to deal with this and go back and have a coffee somewhere. Nothing else is happening. The streets are dead. We said to her, do you want to press charges? That's the phrase everyone knows. Do you want to make a statement? Do you want him arrested? She says, yes I do, and I want him out of my house. We said, right, we're coming in mate, got a Power of Entry now. He says, you're not coming in here. If you come in here, I'll kill you. I said, there's no need for that, mate. I've still got my hands in my pockets so I'm thinking, look at him, he's tiny. If he wants to have a go at us two, fine. So I'm standing in front and at this point I thought, I've had enough of this, so I push the door open and say, we're coming in, mate, and he says, I told you, I'll kill you. He starts walking backwards down a narrow hallway. At the end is a door. So we're walking down the hallway and I say, don't walk away from me, mate. I told you, I'll kill you, he says. I say, show me your hands, mate, and I'm still thinking, this is rubbish. He walks towards me and says, I fucking told you, I'll kill you, now get out. Then he pulls a gun and puts it straight to my head. Where did he pull it out from? I could feel it on my skin. I suddenly have a gun to my head. That was the one time I've ever had a firearm pulled on me. All I remember doing was saying, all right, mate, all right. I just slapped him as hard as I could with an open hand, the gun went flying and I punched him and it was all off.

I get dragged into a living room with this guy. On the floor was a claw hammer and one of those hand-held stun guns. There was a kitchen knife on the bed. It was horrendous. He reached for the stun gun and I thought, oh my god, now I'm really going to get done.

Then I managed to push him away from me. He was reaching for the hammer and the knife. We've got the metal batons now and I really thought, I'm going to be seriously injured here, so I flipped the baton out and I kept hitting him until he stopped moving, and I actually thought I'd killed him for a minute. My sergeant came in. We'd called up for urgent assistance, so everyone had heard it and the whole world was coming to us. He got to the front door. I was standing there, my shirt was ripped, I was covered in blood where I'd been scratched and cut to shreds, all my uniform was trashed. I'm standing over this man, completely out of breath, just staring at him with the stick still up. He's just lying motionless on the floor. My skipper just came up, literally turned round and said, out. Walk out. Go and stand outside. Not because I'd done anything wrong; he was just thinking, Jesus Christ, he's in shock. It was the only time in fifteen years I've really been worried. I've had other dodgy calls and I've been assaulted plenty of times, I've been knocked out two or three times, but that was the one time where

I sat there afterwards thinking, Jesus Christ. I sat at home that night and I was an emotional wreck, shaking. It turns out it was an imitation firearm.

At the Alexandra Road estate the two officers get out and climb the concrete steps to the address of a man who hasn't made an appearance in court. Colin peers through the letterbox. 'There's nothing in the world', he says, 'like a London letterbox. They're so useful. It gives you that extra bit of insight. You might look through and see if there are dust sheets on the floor. You might see the layout, a glimpse of a knife, a person.' The flat's occupant, a painfully thin, recently arrived Thai man, opens the door to reveal the narrow, dimly lit hall. It's not meant to be a set of flats but room numbers have been drawn on the doors. The man in question is nowhere to be seen; a dirty rice cooker sits in his room. Muted voices carry from the other rooms. After an inspection, the officers stand for what feels like a long time listening to the sounds of the flat. The Thai man shifts on his feet. 'Good luck with your studies,' Colin tells the man as they leave.

We used to be the Metropolitan Police Force. We were a *force*. We governed ourselves and we decided how we would do things. We weren't answerable to people. A lot of other forces are like that around the world. Then we became the Metropolitan Police Service. This is just my opinion, but they did that because it was a corporate relaunch of the Met. We want to be a service; we want to be showing that we're doing things for the community. It's all got very political. When we were the police force we told people, this is how we're going to do things – we're the experts. That's how it was done. We would discipline the police force. There were very strict rules, down to 'you will have your hair cut'. You joined the job and you were told how you were going to do it. Some things don't change. Guns: a lot of it is we're proud to publicize the fact that we're perhaps *the* only police force in the world, or country in the world – I think New Zealand don't as well – that don't. I wouldn't carry one. Unless it became compulsory.

With a gun you'd have to become less community-orientated and less polite to people because you'd have to be a lot more firm. None of this, hello, sir, would you mind stepping out the vehicle please. That's the polite way of the London police officer standing there in his nice, smart uniform. But things are changing, aren't they? Now, you don't know what the driver's got in the car, so we're more or less saying, hello, mate, out the car, we want to speak to you about your driving. It's the way you speak to people, isn't it? If we need to carry guns and you go to a car and you think they're armed, you're not going to be the polite London police officer any more.

With a gun you have to speak to people in a way that they will understand, so in that scenario I think it's right and proper that you'd be saying, hello, mate, get out the fucking car, now! You swear at them – our armed guys do that. It's different rules for them. They get a lot more respect.

I'm very much up for cameras for police officers – headcams are an absolutely fantastic idea. You get these people that have tried to kill police officers. They go to court and they wear the suit and say, I didn't do anything. The police officers say, OK, we'll just show you this video, and on the video you've got him going, I'm going to fucking stab you! It's the best thing ever.

A picture paints a thousand words and your video paints a million, doesn't it. What better evidence can you have than video – it's live, it shows facial expressions, you show it from your view; you can't get better evidence.

Later, at a flat on the Langdale Estate, he peers through a letterbox and then pushes through his extendable baton. They're here to look for another man who has missed a court date.

When the door finally opens, a woman with a Turkish accent says her brother isn't there. The two officers walk upstairs past framed paintings of roses, framed paintings of cats. A sweet, sickly smell permeates the flat.

'Who's in the loo?' he asks.

'My brother,' says the woman. 'But not the brother you're looking for,' she adds quickly.

'How do we know that?' asks Colin. There's a sound, a metallic clink, from behind the door. The sister looks confused. Colin steps away from the door.

'He's not going to jump out at me, is he?'

'He's not here.'

'Someone's here.'

'It's my other brother.'

'I don't know that until he comes out, do I?'

There's another metallic thump. Both officers suddenly have their batons in hand. Something has changed. On the North London landing, surrounded by paintings of roses, the situation swivels back and forth, innocence, threat, innocence.

The door opens.

'My brother isn't here,' says an overweight man draped in a dressing gown.

In the aftermath of the London bombings I was on the cordons at Warren Street for days afterwards. We were told to go out and do a lot of searches. Now that's typical of the Met. In the aftermath they decide to look for the horse after the stable door's shut and the horse has already bolted. We were going out doing stop-and-searches. I've never known whether we had intelligence. A lot of it is just public reassurance, which is good, but you've got to be careful that you don't discriminate, that you don't only stop Asians with backpacks. At the end of the day it was them that did the bombs, so it could have been intelligence-led stops really; so if you saw four Asian blokes with rucksacks, then yeah, perhaps they should be stopped. A lot of people stopped white businessmen. Now clearly that's going to wind white businessmen up, isn't it? But you've got to use common sense again, haven't you? I'm not saying a white man in a business suit couldn't be a bomber – he could be. But we were told to just go out, there was no profile of a suicide bomber. Stop-and-search is a very controversial power, but it is our best power – to stop and go through someone's pockets. Take their liberty away for five minutes and it makes them realize you're in charge. This is how it's going to be: we suspect you of something, we're going to do this to you whether you like it or not. We can use force on you if you don't comply with it. We'll give you the warning. If you kick off, then we will force you.

It becomes a problem when they tell you to go out and do these stop-and-searches and it becomes disproportionate to the amount of items found and the arrests. So, you know, borough X in London, they say, we've got an up-and-coming knife problem, so they draft in loads of resources to go and do stop-and-searches; inevitably, depending on the demographics of the borough, you're going to get problems where maybe during that week's operation you see a 50 per cent increase in young black youths being stopped, so straightaway their ethnic minority figures for stop-and-search go up and it distorts the figures. If you do fifty stops a day and don't find forty-nine weapons a day, then your figures are going to be disproportionate, and you've done a thousand stops this month, but you've only found three knives – how can that be right? And you say, hold on, we're responding to this crime or this crime. You have youth leaders, people like that, saying, our youths are always being stopped. That's because they're out at three o'clock in the morning standing around in gangs with their hoods or with these new jackets with the hood up with the big goggle eyes, and they can zip right up so their faces are concealed. So that's it from the police point of view. I can see why they think they're being unfairly targeted, but it has to be done.

We have to be nosy. We have to get in people's faces. You have to get in their pockets. You have to ask what they're doing, otherwise you're not doing your job.

It's nearly 10 p.m. when the final call comes over the radio. Waves of young Somalis wearing gang colours are travelling up the Northern Line from Charing Cross. 'Purple is what the Peckham Young Guns wear,' Colin says. They'll gather later in Leicester Square. They'll rendezvous at the Trocadero. All this aggression will be played out in the West End. 'A Section 60 has been granted by a supervisor,' he says. 'A Section 60 is authorized with good intelligence and it give us power to stop anyone in Camden borough without reasonable grounds. Usually a stop-and-search is only an option with reasonable grounds.' He reaches out and attaches the Kojak light. The car surges to life. The traffic parts.

When we arrive at Camden Town Tube station there are already a few black youths in the station with their arms spread wide in front of the officers. 'Put your hands down,' one officer says. 'This isn't America.'

'Why all this?' asks one youth.

'Leicester Square,' the officer replies.

'I never heard anything about anything,' says the youth.

'There's a Section 60,' the policeman says. 'How old are you?'

'Fourteen.'

He's wearing light blue shoes and what look to be lavender shoelaces but it's hard to know what constitutes purple in the bright lights of Camden Town Tube station. Handel's Water Music *is playing through the loudspeaker in an effort to calm the Camden crowds. Occasionally the voice of the Underground announces: 'Ladies and gentlemen there is a good service on the Northern Line.'*

When the search is finished, the youth lowers his arms and turns away from the wall.

Another police officer is patting down a tall Somali boy wearing a blue Adidas top with purple stripes on the side.

'What gang do you lot think you belong to?'

'I'm wearing a blue top,' says the youth to the wall.

'What does the purple mean?'

'It's blue. It's not purple.'

'We could have you remove these gang colours,' he says.

The youth straightens up and responds to each soft pat of his torso. Some of the officers are wearing violet-coloured plastic gloves. The violet gloves, the light purple of the stripes, the robin's-egg blue of the jumper.

'It's blue yeah?' says the youth. 'Not purple.'

NICK SMITH

Riot witness

The weather was good. It was early evening on a sunny day, so I was
in good spirits. When the sun shines in London people tend to be in
a good mood. There had been major trouble in Brixton the previous
night. Peckham had been hit as well, but none of that was on my
mind. I thought maybe it would be contained. I was thinking about
getting home and when a bus arrived, probably the 68, I was finally
able to get a seat upstairs. I was listening to music on my phone when
a call came through. My friend asked me how I was. Things were
happening in Peckham, he said. The bus continued through Elephant
and Castle. A few minutes later it was pulled over.

The engine went off. Straightaway a few people got off the bus
and a crowd gathered around the police officers who were standing
there. The crowd got bigger. It was strange, actually, seeing the buses
stopped before the crossroads. The police hadn't really organized
themselves. There were still cars coming out of the side streets,
beeping to get past. The roadblocks were quite far back. Cars were
trying to overtake the buses. There were people everywhere. There
was annoyance but no sign of trouble. There was no information.
People began questioning the police. Some people were curious,
others bewildered. None of the police were in riot gear. It was
August 2011.

I decided to walk down a side street to get past the police.
Another woman was doing the same. As we walked a guy casually
passed us walking the other way and holding a bunch of mobile-
phone equipment in his hands. He shouted something I didn't catch,
something boastful. I guess I assumed what was going on. I carried
on, straight into the middle of it.

The street led back to Walworth Road. It was quiet in that
stretch, eerie. I looked back at the police in the distance, the empty
buses. When I turned and looked the other way I saw groups of

people gathered near the shops on the corner. The glass doors of the pawnbrokers and the betting shop had been kicked in but the windows throughout were intact. The other shops had substantial damage. It looked like someone had used a brick. The cracked glass looked like a spider's web.

Ahead of me there was a reasonable-sized crowd working on the Foot Locker – around fifteen people repeatedly trying to force their way in, rattling the metal shutters, shaking them, prying them open. This group around the Foot Locker – a lot of them, like me, looked caught up in the wrong place. Some people were there for entertainment. They were not going anywhere. They were enjoying the scene.

It didn't feel aggressive; it felt controlled. I could have decided to go back to where the police were standing, but for some reason I didn't feel nervous walking through. It was broad daylight. There wasn't anger on display. It was greed and opportunity, a chance to steal. It's a lot scarier to be present when someone's being mugged. I didn't get that same feeling of fear. And there was no territorial aspect to it – people were helping each other out, black, white and brown. There was enough for everyone, and it was as if they all knew they needed the numbers. The numbers were important. The numbers allowed it to happen.

I'd never experienced anything like it before. I certainly didn't expect it in London. The people I saw – they didn't come from another country. They didn't just show up in London. They were the people who would, on any other day, be sitting next to me on the bus. They were smashing up shops.

I was trying to survey the scene, so I wasn't paying attention. I ran into a man quite hard. He had a scarf covering part of his face and didn't look like an innocent bystander. He was big. Even on a normal day you wouldn't want to smash into someone like that. I did and he was, I don't know, almost jovial. He couldn't care less. He had better things to do. I said sorry and he replied, 'Cool bredren', something like that. It felt, at that moment, like I was part of his gang. He didn't know who I was but I wasn't a police officer. I was on the same side. I felt as if I could have talked to anyone on the street – I could have said: 'Why don't we head to that shop next?' I didn't, but I could have.

I definitely had the feeling there were some bad people there, people known to the police. But there were others, people caught up, and I could understand them. The DVDs scattered on the floor outside Argos? Why wouldn't I pick them up? It was as if a great big box had split. There were too many DVDs for one person to carry. People were selecting which ones they wanted to pick up. I didn't want to get involved but I stood and watched as some women pulled up and began flinging them into their car. Those in bandanas; those smashing shops – that's not, and would never be, me. However, I think maybe if I'd been 16, 17, working part-time, I would have been tempted. I looked down at those DVDs and I thought, I've got a couple of box sets I haven't found time to watch. Why would I bother picking up DVDs when I haven't finished *The Wire*? But I wasn't worried about getting caught. I'm sure I could have got away with it.

Further along I saw a flatscreen lying on Walworth Road. I was actually tempted to pick up the flatscreen to see why it had been abandoned, but I was worried about how that would look. If I pick up a flatscreen, even to take a look, it's not something that's easily explained.

I felt quite calm. There had been fires burning the night before, fires in different parts of London, but while I was on the Walworth Road I felt calm, relaxed. It seemed like a lot of shops had already had their windows smashed. People were just working on the shutters of the Foot Locker. There was no conversation. They were working.

I left the Foot Locker and carried on walking home. It was hard to believe I'd just walked through that particular scene. The bus was stopped at seven and by the time I was home it was half eight. I live on my own. I called my friend back, told him I was all right. You see footage of the LA riots but that's just what happens in America. I know it's happened here but I was three years old in '81. It never seemed real. The mass scale, the way nobody cared about the police, the broken glass in broad daylight – it wasn't the London I knew. I didn't feel like I was in London.

MOHAMMED AL HASAN

Suspect

I got stopped and searched by the cops for terrorism. It was in Hounslow East Station, I was going to college in the morning, around 8.30, 8.15. They said, we're doing a random search so can we see your bag? They looked inside and they searched me and then they gave me a little receipt with a code that was the reason for the search. It was like C26 or whatever, and when I turned it around I saw that it meant terrorism. I was kind of shocked. Why am I getting searched for terrorism? You know, you say it's a random search but you grabbed me and let about ten people go. Obviously they saw my college ID with my name, and I've got a rucksack on and I'm Asian. It was like, what have I done? They didn't tell me.

I just had my school books in my bag, that's all it was. Just college books, my refill pad, pens and stuff like that. To get pulled out and searched like that, it's embarrassing. Everyone else is just going past, looking at you thinking, oh my god, what's he done? It made me feel like everybody is going to look at me like that now. And they didn't really handle it well, they did it out in the open.

We're in a youth centre in Hounslow. Tall, and hunched over his chair, he pulls on the collar of his T-shirt, which is emblazoned with a couple of stylized skulls.

★

I've always felt like I belong here. I was born in London and this is where I've been raised and this is my home town as much as it is anyone else's home town, you know. I mean like it's really weird because in Birmingham, when I go there to visit my cousins, if you tell them you're from London they're like, oh my god, he's from London! Yo! He's from London! To them, someone from London is a big thing. He's from London, he's all busy and stuff, man. Like, whoa, he's from London. For them to know someone from London it's like a big thing. Yeah, I know someone from London. They can tell it to their friends.

It's not like when people say that, I'm from some place and you're like, hold on, where's that? You know, when you say, I'm from London people know where it is, people know how it is, people know how busy it is, what the lifestyle's like and it's just acknowledged by everyone. It's amazing how just telling someone where you're from can spark a conversation and they just want to get to know more.

The funny thing about that day I got stopped and searched is that I got stopped and searched *again* on the way back home. Yeah, I got searched for terrorism on the way to college and then on the way back too. Years before, someone got stabbed in my college. So for extra security reasons they had a metal detector to go through before you touched your Oyster card in the Tube station. Well that day when I was going home, I had left my USB in my pocket. And the actual USB part is metal and the cover is metal as well, so when I went through, it beeped.

They took me aside, searched my bag, and asked me questions, like have you been searched before? I said, yeah – this morning. They just looked at me: are you being serious? So I showed them my receipt. They were like, twice in one day. You're a lucky one, aren't you? I'm like, yeah, you could say that. And then they let me go.

DAVID OBIRI, JEREMY RANGA AND KESHAV GUPTA

Barristers

They've gathered after work around a dinner table in front of a Thai green curry. Top buttons are undone. They're young; no one is dashing home to a family.

OBIRI: I got my first wig at Ede & Ravenscroft, the *only* place to go.

RANGA: Well, there's two. But you only get one wig, is the point.

GUPTA: I suppose it's *the* place, isn't it.

OBIRI: Yes. It's in Chancery Lane. You go and write down your name in a book.

RANGA: I've never understood that, because you can get your wig elsewhere. It's only there they've got the book and everything.

OBIRI: But the most eminent judges, Law Lords, barristers, they'll be in there. It's *Who's Who* in there.

RANGA: There used to be a tradition of keeping your wig immaculate to be handed down generation on generation. Juniors come in now and the idea is if you're going to be in court, stamp on your wig, make it break a little bit, because you want to look like you're not a newbie. You want to look like you've been around the block.

OBIRI: I didn't do that. It was way too bloody expensive to desecrate it.

RANGA: You know what you call a new barrister? A white wig. Because it's pristine and so is the barrister.

OBIRI: It's what Rumpole calls them.

GUPTA: There's also the traditional wig tins, aren't there? That was something that was quite coveted. One of the greatest things, I think, is to have your name on the board outside Chambers, so when you get taken on as a tenant finally your name appears. And then you've got the whole hierarchy, Silks at the top and it's all by call and then right at the top, if you get Silk early, you get bumped up to the QCs at the top. And apart from that, having your name on a wig tin *was* quite a cool thing.

OBIRI: Well, I like it.

GUPTA: Have you got a wig tin? It's like £150 for a piece of tin. I think the cool thing to do is to have like a biscuit tin.

OBIRI: Some people are really naff, they just keep the cardboard box.

GUPTA: I don't put mine in a tin at all, I just leave it out, you know, because it gets a little bit misshapen. I know where I am with that.

RANGA: There's a story about a senior member of the Bar, a Silk, who went off one day and his wife just thought she'd surprise him and had his wig cleaned and refurbished. He said, it took me twenty years to get my wig looking like that!

GUPTA: There's a guy in Chambers who is what they call the Old Bar. He's about thirty years called, or I think forty years called, anyway his wig is just in bits, it's yellow, it's misshapen, and the back of the wig, the thing they call the rat's tail, one side of it's completely severed, so it hangs down there. He didn't take Silk, so his gown is in tatters. There's rips through it and it's in a total and utter state. I was against him once and he just looked amazing. I thought, shit. I saw him wearing this and I put on my new gown, my new wig and I just thought …

OBIRI: I smell his newness.

GUPTA: I just look like I don't know what I'm doing and the judge is never going to listen to me.

RANGA: That is one thing I'll say about the wig, you put it on and you feel like an advocate. You have a bit more confidence in your submissions.

GUPTA: Yes. You put on a wig and gown and suddenly you get into the character of an orator.

RANGA: This is the other thing: nowadays more and more you get these sort of administrative hearings at county courts and they'll say, right, we're going to do it by telephone. So you get BT to set up a three-way thing and you've got your opponent from another Chambers, the judge and you, and you're there at your desk and you might be in your civvies sitting there and you've just come in, done a little bit of prep and all of a sudden you're speaking to a judge and there's this level of formality, and it doesn't feel right.

GUPTA: I remember somebody when I was doing a mini pupillage, like a sort of work experience, I remember this white guy saying there's an advantage if you ever come to the Bar, and I was like, why's that? He said, you'll look really cool in a wig. I still remember that. I hadn't gone to university yet. I'd just finished my A levels and this guy, a young criminal barrister, said to the clerk, don't black and Asian guys look so cool in their wigs? Yeah, they do. I've always thought about that.

OBIRI: It's like that bit in *Men in Black* when Will Smith puts on someone's stuff and just turns and goes, the difference between me and you is I make this look good.

OBIRI: When I first came to the Bar people would split London up into the different juries you'd get. So for instance if someone was running a racially aggravated offence prosecution, and the jury acquitted and that happened to be an East London jury, they'd say: yeah, oh yeah, an East London jury, they're never going to convict somebody of a racially aggravated Public Order Act offence. Or about a Knightsbridge jury, they'd say: black kid – robbery – yeah, guilty. I just remember thinking, whoa, I'd never thought of London that way. I overheard in Chambers someone saying, racially aggravated Public Order Act offence acquitted within, you know, half an hour, and it was like yeah: East London jury.

GUPTA: I went to a conference today and it came up on two or three occasions, amongst the speakers, a judge who sits at Woolwich Crown Court was criticized in the Court of Appeal for his case-management style, which boiled down to this: he would not allow the prosecution to bring cases where he felt a jury would never convict. There were a string of cases that my colleague in Chambers actually had to appeal, all racially aggravated Public Order Act offences and the judge had said, I'm not going to allow you to prosecute these because I know for a fact that a Woolwich jury will never convict on a racially aggravated offence.

OBIRI: So how would you divide London up? I mean, you know London courts better than I do.

GUPTA: Snaresbrook's good for handling stolen goods and a little bit of violence, they'll let you off. But kiddie fiddling, you're dead, all right? And if you go to Inner London, which is round Elephant and Castle, they don't mind a bit of drugs, a bit of violence, bit of gang-related stuff, kidnapping, you'll probably be okay. But then if you go to Blackfriars and their jury is drawn from Kensington and Chelsea, robberies they're probably not that cool with but they'll probably let off a sex offender on a rape. Date rape, they'll probably let you off, okay? Then you've got Southwark, that's frauds. Southwark, they usually draw people from the City. So you've got a run on a fraud at Southwark. But you're probably not going to get away with all the standard stuff like violence and drugs. But sex, again, date rape, you might get off. And then you go further south, you've got Croydon – drugs, you're never going to get off because they're right on the Gatwick corridor and they hate the concept that people are bringing drugs into the country up their streets effectively. It's the same as Isleworth, which is West London – drugs, you're never going to get off, but a bit of theft, dishonesty offences, mortgage fraud? You're probably going to be okay. But the one thing you won't get off on at any of those is false IDs and immigration offences, because it's right on their doorstep and they all work at Heathrow and Gatwick. Harrow, ugh, Harrow jury, you'll get off on sex, you'll get off on drugs, you'll get off on most things actually.

RANGA: Harrow juries are good juries. For a defence.

OBIRI: Generally, generally.

GUPTA: Because they're an understanding demographic.

OBIRI: Why?

RANGA: I don't know why. Maybe they're more understanding, but to get an acquittal you need someone who's strong and liberal on a jury, and I can't say that Harrow necessarily represents strong and liberal to me. It's a very heavily Asian demographic.

OBIRI: If I'm defending a black person or an Asian person I'm heartened by black or Asian faces on the jury.

RANGA: Yeah, me too.

OBIRI: Massively so. In fact I've almost got to the stage where I'll look as the jury come in and I go, I'm defending a black man, there are two young black men on the jury … *yes*.

RANGA: Yeah. I'd agree with that as well.

OBIRI: They're probably young Tories or something. Fresh from the Tory Party Conference.

RANGA: But the reality is, you know, it really depends on the facts of the case and the literacy of the jury. Sometimes there are cases that are very difficult to follow, maybe lost on a not very bright jury because they get bored and they'll just listen to what the judge tells them to do and convict or acquit accordingly. But sometimes the facts just don't add up to the offence.

OBIRI: And you never know. You never know.

RANGA: And also that demographic, going back to what David was saying, are going to be less likely to wholeheartedly believe what a policeman's saying or automatically accept the validity of a testimony.

OBIRI: Every juror's got prejudices, you know, whatever it is. I've sat on a jury, I've got my *Guardian/Observer*-reading, liberal, lefty prejudices. It's a prejudice, though. That's what I've brought to the table and there's a guy with the opposite, you know. We all have our prejudices. And juries have that, but I think you can find areas where there's going to be more of a preponderance of a certain kind of prejudice, so that's why I was saying in East London if you're prosecuting a guy for a racially aggravated Public Order Act offence where he's shouting, you fucking … or whatever, they're going to be less likely to convict a guy for that because they'll go, whoa.

GUPTA: I do that every Saturday night.

OBIRI: It's East London. They're white, they're working class or lower middle class or whatever …

RANGA: They probably see it all the time.

OBIRI: They know these people. They're going out with these people.

RANGA: They go and watch the footie with them.

OBIRI: They have something or they've come from this origin and it reflects the tensions in parts of East London. They are the disenfranchised white middle class or whatever, so they're thinking, we're not going to convict a guy for shouting racist abuse in public. Good lord. What's the world come to when we're criminalizing that? But you go to another jury in London where there's a make-up of ethnic minorities and whatever, and they're going to go, good lord, we can't have this. We can't have this in London.

RANGA: The worst part is when the jury's gone out to deliberate, you're waiting for them to come back, and you hear a tannoy saying: come to court whatever. You don't know whether the jury are back or whether the jury are asking a question or some other thing. So you go back and then you hear from the Clerk that there's a verdict. They won't tell you what the verdict is, just that there's a verdict. And you sit there and you wait and you feel horrible. You feel tense and your heart's racing and you have no idea and you think, like you're getting exam results, it's going to be the worst, it's going to be the worst, it's going to be the worst … And then you know. You know because they have to gather together in a room just before they come into court, and when the door opens that lets them into the court. Some will be chatting and you can hear the murmuring of their banter and the bubble of their chat. If you hear that, you know they're going to acquit. Juries that convict are really quiet, absolutely silent. They file in. Somebody said to me years ago, when they take their seats, if the jury looks over into the dock at the defendant, they're not going to convict him. They're going to acquit him, because you will never be able to look in the eye someone you're about to convict when you're on a jury. You will not want to. But then I realize before then by whether they're talking or not and if you hear silence you know. I was in court on Friday and the jury came back after four days of deliberations and I sat there. I was prosecuting but looking after a jury so I wasn't that bound up in the case, but having waited for four days.

OBIRI: What was the charge?

RANGA: Bizarrely, it was armed robbery. I got a bit caught up after waiting four or five days sort of wanting a conviction because that's my job and then …

OBIRI: Silence.

RANGA: … sure as anything. The jury assembled and then the Clerk opens the doors to lead them in − absolute silence. I knew from that point. They file in and as they are sitting down I look over and none of them are looking at the defendant. Yeah, double confirmation of guilt.

OBIRI: It's got to the stage now where I'm so alive to the fact that I'm nervous at that moment where they call the jury, that I don't look to see whether the jury are looking at my client, I just sit there. I don't even look. I just look down.

RANGA: I look at the judge.

OBIRI: I just look at the desk. If I look at the jury and see them not looking at my client I'll know. I just sit there and I look down and I hear the foreman go: 'Members of the Jury, have you reached a verdict upon which you are all agreed?' 'Yes.' 'Members of the Jury, what is that verdict?' 'Count 1 …' and you just kind of go and look at them. But the worst thing is now this person, years ago, told me this about the murmuring. I wouldn't have known about it if somebody hadn't told me. It sucks. It's true. It's so true. It's so true.

RANGA: You need a wig with some kind of earpiece that you can flick down. Yeah, I can imagine a barrister finally losing it and as the jury are filing in he's going, ahh, I can't hear you! I can't hear you!

CHARLES HENTY

Under-Sheriff and Secondary of London

We've had a prison on this site since about 1018 – if not before, because we've got a Roman wall downstairs. We've been here a while. Generally speaking we are dealing with Class 1 crimes, that's homicide and terrorism. That's our staple diet, if you like. Last year we had a record. We had seven High Court judges sitting here. So our resident judges had to go out on circuit. That shows the level of the cases that we're dealing with and that was pretty fierce. We don't tend to deal with anything minor here. You don't expect to come to the Old Bailey to be done for shoplifting.

He is an ex-military man, the youngest major ever he tells me, and he served in Northern Ireland in the 1980s and in the first Iraq War. He was married two and a half days before being sent to Iraq. His office in the Old Bailey is obsessively tidy and he sits in a chair close to the curtains covering a window looking out onto the courtyard. When he speaks about the armed security at the Old Bailey he mentions the armed guards stationed outside that window and seems vaguely worried when he pulls the curtains back and they're not there. We walk into a security room where a scrolling screen updates what's happening in each court. A white board lists the day's cases, with a small sword icon employed to denote where the senior judge will be. The white board lists shorthand for the crimes — murder, murder, accounting, terrorism, murder — as well as the list of names attached. Back in the office, he pulls back the curtains again and there are security officers outside — bald and bullish and ready.

My job is to make sure that this place runs smoothly. That everybody works together. Brand Old Bailey, as we call it. Because Joe Public comes in and sees a security officer at the front door, doesn't differentiate between him and anybody else, whether he works for me or the court service, it's Old Bailey. I have the usual electricians, boiler room, cleaners, security. I've got sixty-four security officers. Security is a very important point, obviously, at the Bailey because we have some pretty unpleasant people coming in. We've had the roads closed, the helicopter's up every day. We've had the cells searched on a daily basis, well overnight, because at the moment we have the highest-risk defendant in the country. I'm not going to tell you who it is, but the risk on him is massive. We have about 2,500 people coming through every day and yet it's not open to the public. So there's an awful lot of traffic here. I play the sort of guiding managing director's role, if you like. We've got to keep the courts in action. We don't want to lose time so we start early in the morning. We start at about six every morning and we're checking to make sure that each court is serviceable because you don't want a flickering light. We have a police team here, our City of London police, which is great and very reassuring. That said though, my team were the first in the country to be given a High Court Security Officer's status. In fact, today and tomorrow they'll be working on their armlocks and all the restraint positions. They have to have those skills because some people don't like coming here.

Each case will have a security assessment on it. If armed protection is required, that goes right up to allowing the deployment of armed police. It is decided by the Senior Presiding Judge and the police, but it has to go through the legal process for that to be deployed and they will be deployed under very strict guidelines. They're not here actually. I normally have a car out there full of armed police. That's a fact of life here. Last year was the first time that we overtly deployed weapons around the court. Normally they're bagged. We now have a chap actually in the court, a taser officer, so they don't need to use lethal force, but the risk is that high that a taser might be used before anything else. There are very very strict guidelines.

With each case, you've got the defendants coming in from whichever holding cell that they're going to be in. They all come through the same entrance and that, of course, is a risk in itself because you know that there's only one place that all the defendants will come in and they then go down into the cell area where, depending on which category, they'll get searched again. Their belongings, if they've got any with them, will be bagged, recorded and then they get put into the holding cell usually nearest where they'll be going up to court. We've got cells on three floors. We've got seventy-four of them. And we also have a Category A wing. Category A is high security. I can't go into too much detail about that, but put it this way, you can't put a telephone in there without cutting through steel. It is the Hannibal Lecter type. We've got nearly twenty Category A in today. Which is a lot. We also have vulnerable defendants and, sadly, we have an awful lot of youngsters. Last year, we had a boy who was sentenced for murder: he was 10 when he committed the crime. It was subsequently overturned to manslaughter, but we've had a couple of 14-year-olds who committed the most atrocious crimes, murder being part of it. I don't think one could necessarily say that murder's on the increase, but I think the age has dropped and that's the scary bit.

I'm very glad my children are not living in London, to be honest. It's not the London that I grew up in and I'm much more wary. But that may be a sign of me getting older. I'm not as comfortable with London as I used to be. And I think here in the City we're cocooned to a large extent because it's so well looked after and people are professional. We see what appears to be a fairly significant increase in the number of crimes committed by youngsters, that's the edge that worries me and how quickly it happens. You know, one bit of 'dis' and you've got a knife. There's one chap who's on trial at the moment because the other chap *looked* at him while getting on the bus and the guy just pulled out a knife and killed him. They'd never met before. And seeing some of the youngsters' attitude of 'I don't care', or 'So what? I'm in jail.' So I think we've made the right decision by not living in London.

BARBARA TUCKER

Protester

She prowls the pavement of Parliament Square, directly across the road from the Houses of Parliament. She smokes roll-ups and wears a light pink knitted hat that keeps slipping down. Nearby, a rumpled square of canvas covers a sleeping bag

I always say, every single building around here should be covered with the truth. It should be all over the place, you know? Then they'd soon stop, wouldn't they? Because what I've noticed is, they don't mind doing what they're doing, but they really don't do shame. What they're doing is really shameful. It beggars belief. You have to share that truth. The dynamic is brilliant here, because the global community of people come past, and we're giving them the opportunity to learn as much as they want. Not only to give you information, but to show you that yes, you can challenge your government. Yes, you can say no.

The people who are suffering and dying will never be forgotten while we're here. You know? And if that was happening to you or your family member you'd want somebody to speak out about it, wouldn't you, really?

The ground vibrates in Parliament Square thanks to the Tube trains below. In the spring I had watched the leaves of freshly planted pansies vibrate. Another group of protesters had planted crops in the square, including lettuce and carrots. There was a kitchen with drinking water in the Peace Camp, a table with painted rocks holding down pamphlets on Gaza. Tucker stayed apart from the camp. She walks her own patch of the pavement. Now, months later, the tents are gone. Metal barriers have been erected. Police in reflective vests walk the pavement in long lines, eyeing Tucker.

I say to people, 'Welcome to Westminster Village. The only thing we do well is making a killing out of the suffering of others.' I've been arrested thirty-nine times in five years. I've learnt that if you cannot stand your ground in a public space to tell the truth without violence, you shouldn't be doing what you're doing. It's those in government who duck and dive, and run and hide behind their gate, the weapons, the cheap sound bites in the TV studios and the corrupt courts.

Some nights when they have a late night getting out I stand here with the loudspeaker, and I say to them, as my little bedtime story: you are going to spend the rest of your miserable lives looking over your shoulders, checking your holiday itineraries, cos whether it's ten years, twenty years or thirty years from now, you know, people will hunt you down, bring you to justice – we're not saying we're going to murder you or slaughter you, but we'll bring you to justice and change the systems that have allowed this to happen where human life is not protected. It's my little bedtime story. It's like, go to sleep with that one.

Quite often on a Tuesday night or a Monday night, the MPs like to go out in a row, all at 10.30, bless their little cotton socks. So they all leave at once. One night the secretary of state for transport or something, you know, winds down his window and has the nerve to say to me, 'F off' and looks at the police to get rid of me, and they look back. They say to him, 'I think you'd better go.' That's your representatives.

I've got 'Arrest War Criminals' or 'Stop Killing Children' or other banners. They've got big tough machine guns. Protecting what? It just wakes up people. It was marvellous when I put up the banner outside Downing Street, cos you've got wonderful foot traffic, so it's brilliant for talking to people too. The tourists loved it. You know, the shot of Downing Street with banners in front saying here's the truth. What are these big tough guys protecting? You know? But they ended up with zero tolerance around Downing Street.

We are in the belly of the beast, really. We're surrounded. I say to people who pass by, I say on the loudspeaker, as long as this country will want to occupy other countries, then we're occupying the Westminster Village. We will occupy your minds, your time, your money, to remind the thousands of people that work in Westminster, that all you do is perpetuate the lies of this government that lead to the suffering of innocent civilians. And that when 90 per cent of the casualties of these legal wars are affecting civilians, it can't be war. Here's the levers of power, whatever you like to call it. Here's the people you need to wake up, the people you need to put pressure on.

They gave me a community order once, you know, oooh, bad, community order, saying I couldn't protest for a whole year without permission of the Commissioner of the Metropolitan Police. Well then, in my local community, shouldn't everybody know who the criminal is? So I went and put my community order on all the lampposts and said you must tell everybody that I'm this dreadful criminal. They went around ripping them down, and I said, excuse me, gentlemen, please. They would have sent me to prison on that one but they got a bit of cold feet, because it wasn't really compliant with the Human Rights Act to criminalize peaceful campaigning in that way, was it. But they are moving that way. It's got worse over the years here.

You can arrest us, you can put us in prison, you can hurt my body, but you'll never have my mind. You can kill me, but my spirit will live on. Because I think the human spirit in one way or another does. See, you can't kill people's human spirit. The state gets completely confused by the human spirit.

They sort of think of this road as a moat. It protects them from us.

You got to wake them up before you really get through to them, don't you? So this was the wake-up part. I'm trying to connect with their humanity. You got to look me in the face, you got to look this in the face.

The MPs complain about my loudspeaker. I've got a 25-watt loudspeaker. You know, I used it for three years, no problem. Well, that's not strictly true, I got arrested a few times but they never prosecuted me. It's a little 25-watt loudspeaker. From Edgware Road, £49. They got quite a good supply.

She looks back at the metal barricades surrounding the square.

I might remove the statues if I could. I just think it's really nice having Parliament Square as grass with a few seats around there. And just some more trees here would be quite pleasant, wouldn't it? But, to me, the most important thing is please put in proper crossings for people, and get over their phobia about members of the public crossing the street, the moat, meeting us and discovering we're actually quite normal, you know?

If we're going to have a normal world, let's bring people together. Because they try and portray it, 'Maaad people over there,' because that's the game, isn't it really. 'They're mad over there.' Let's make it as hard for you to go over there and discover that actually it's quite interesting, you know, who's doing what. I'd love to see this open, you know, as a sort of people's square. It's got to be kept open for everyone. What's the point of having a square if there's no access to it? It's got to be the people's square, you know. It should remain with the people for ever.

It is a really powerful place to campaign, because the government considers this to be their own village, really, so they don't want anybody here. It has always been zero tolerance. One of my friends, he was arrested outside Downing Street for having a George Orwell quote that said, 'In a time of universal deceit, telling the truth is a revolutionary act.' He was arrested. A guy has a criminal conviction for holding a George Orwell quote outside Downing Street! You have to swear, you know, in court, and he's swearing the affirmation and the judge says to him, what are you swearing on? And he says George Orwell, *1984.* The judge says, 'You're bringing the court into disrepute,' and he said, 'I don't think so. You are!'

The thing is, you never know who you are going to run into in the Westminster Village. They all make appearances. There used to be a little cafe on the corner where the Metropolitan Police Authority is. It's no longer around, but one day Lord Goldsmith was there. He's the one who provided the legal justification for the use of force in Iraq. And he saw me.

He was leaving and having a conversation with someone, but he saw me and I saw him. I thought to myself: the next few moments are going to be really important. I walked up to him. I knew I had to keep really, really calm. As a mother I felt a huge amount of anger and disgust. I looked him in the eyes and said, 'One day you'll stand trial for war crimes.'

The colour just drained from his face. To me, he knew what he'd done. He *knew.* He's surrounded by yes people, so he needed to hear it from someone else, from someone on the other side of the moat. When would he ever hear it otherwise, you know? But obviously he fled to his car.

These people walk the streets of Westminster. You need to understand who these people are and you can only do that by looking into their faces. I wanted to see who he was, really was. You know what I saw? A man who was scared. A man who knew that what he did was wrong. You don't see that around here much. He knew what he'd done. He can hide around here, but that's all he can do.

STAYING ON TOP

STUART FRASER

Chairman of the Policy and Resources Committee, City of London

I go to meet him in his office as he is trying to steward the City through the financial meltdown. A wooden door swings open to reveal a large flatscreen television against the wall, with President Obama's face moving on it. Fraser prepares himself and tries to turn it off but only succeeds in turning the channel to show the ragged ridges of an Asian stock market. 'Forty-five years,' he announces. He lowers his flattened hand toward the floor. 'I came here as a child prodigy.'

In terms of financial services, there are only two global cities in the world: New York and London. And frankly that's probably going to be the same case for another twenty-odd years, I don't see anybody else even coming near it from a global-city perspective. Other centres will become major hubs for their own savings market; probably. But to achieve a global position you have to go through many hoops, particularly the legal one for getting the legal contract in place and everything else, you've got to have transparency and you've got to be open to the rest of the world – any creed, colour, whatever you want, who come and work here. And to be brutally honest there aren't many places that are getting anywhere near that. I think this is the difference between the regional hub, the regional centre, maybe verging on small international – in other words, within the area – against a full global city.

I was in China last week discussing how they are trying to achieve that type of status in the years to come. It's very much of interest for us that the world's financial services industry does expand. We're not sitting here saying it can only be through London. I mean, it's been demonstrated many times in the past that if the cake rises sufficiently quick, then your share of it is growing at the same pace. So you know you don't necessarily have to create more market share, you just have to make sure that the cake keeps growing as quickly as it can.

I have reasonable confidence that the politicians do understand that this business is a large part of the UK economy. It's larger than the UK manufacturing base, but it might not be the case next year. But what would be the point in trying to destroy it? Surely you just rebuild it, make it better than it was and carry on and it's a great opportunity for the next fifty years. You've got billions of people who want to try and achieve the same living standards we enjoy in the West. They're all going to need financial services, they're all going to need more sophisticated financial markets, they're all going to want insurance products, they're going to want a whole host of financial areas as they move from a basic economy into a more sophisticated one. So if we can retain our markets and remain competitive and remain global and flexible, we'll benefit. And we do it quite well.

Don't get me wrong, it's no fault of its own, but financial services probably has become a somewhat overly large part of the UK economy. But then you've got to say as well, okay, so what else is going to take it over? Now, in the longer term, because we make deliberate efforts, our creative industries and research and technology and all those areas, yes, of course we can rebalance the economy. But if financial services went tomorrow there's nothing that's going to step into its place.

You've got to bear in mind most of the artistic field is paid for by the financial business. For every well-off banker we've got a whole host of industries that are supplying him with things, including his tickets to the theatre and the players that stand on the stage and everybody else like that. If somebody is earning a lot of money, they keep an awful lot of people employed directly or indirectly. If you took that out, there'd be a lot of unemployment in many areas: service industries, the arts and the media. People always seem to forget the arts were really actually spun off, if you like, from the wealth of business in the old days. Particularly artists and that who used to be sponsored by or looked after by some rich benefactor. So it is an integrator. I don't think you can just say, we can continue doing the arts to empty theatres.

I'm optimistic because I do think that the next upturn, when it comes, will be much more sustainable, because it will be built on much sounder foundations. And therefore if at the end of all this the City comes out of it retaining that degree of flexibility and innovation, if it is as attractive to outside people as it is today to come and work here, then one will be satisfied.

TOBY MURTHWAITE

Student

It's the day of a large student demonstration against university fees. We meet in a pub on Chandos Street.

To allow bankers to justify themselves. To normalize the language of banking, of usury, greed, of wealth, of ownership, of inviting men and woman who have pillaged elsewhere, who have stolen from the Russian public, or from the Arab world, who have thieved and lied, and moved money from tax haven to tax haven. To create a city for them to burrow into, to dig into the streets, to create caves of wealth down there, swimming pools and private cinemas? That's London. I love how one road in West London actually collapsed into one of these great empty holes. How could you not look at that photo in the paper and say, that's London. Wealth collapsed into its own hollow self. I loved it. Let it all come down, I say, all these big empty hollow houses.

You look at it and you think: honestly, it's a sad city, no pride. Here is this needy city that makes nothing of its own and relies on very questionable people spending their questionable money in questionable ways. And I'm not talking about crime. I'm talking about greed.

Let people speak and they will justify themselves. They should – it's their lives. They have to find a reason to live them. London always justifies itself in the voices of its people because it has to. It's not a religious city, it's not an arts city. So justify: the stakes are high. Too many of the world's young people show up here. Do these bright, highly educated children learn trades? Do they learn skills? Do they flock to work at climate-change charities? No. They learn numbers. They learn how to skim. They learn how to shift money. Skimming, shifting, shifty skimming. Of course they're going to make it sound important. That's what it runs on. And who uses their services? Who do you think? Oh, these people over here? They aren't crooks who have bled Russia dry. No, no, no. These are 'international businessmen'. How did they become international businessmen? Because we said, come over to London. Bring your flash, your wife's spending account, your mistress's credit card, bring all your troubles, bring your squabbles – remember that Russian who was poisoned? – bring it all here.

You can't cut the defiance out of London. The police force people to announce their protests now, announce their routes. And that works – it works until it doesn't. It works until something goes wrong. They kettle students, but someone's always going to be putting up a banner in this city, some stupid divorced father is going to be putting on the Spider-Man suit or Batman suit and hanging off Buckingham Palace. Someone's going to throw a johnny full of powder at the Prime Minister's head during question time. Brilliant. Because there are parts of the City, there are people in London, who look at Beijing with great envy. To be able to call in the tanks, to be able to push people around. That's the sort of thing that makes them salivate. Oh, the things we could do if we never had to worry about the streets, as if that was not the most important thing about this place – as if London was anything other than a place of defiance, a staging ground. The danger is that it gets turned into a nice day out. Remember Iraq? Come and protest, have a nice day out, chant, go home. What was the result? Nothing. You can get things done in London but it's not going to happen on a single afternoon in a nice orderly march.

PAUL HAWTIN

Hedge fund manager

Next to the Rolls-Royce showroom sits the cavernous entry hall of Berkeley Square House. Men in suits queue for security passes. There are nine floors of investment companies: capital management, capital management, capital management. Up an escalator, up in a lift, past hushed meeting rooms, I reach Hawtin's office. It is a single room with barely enough space for his desk and one for his partner – his brother. A small space heater behind them gently blows a Christmas card onto the floor.

Me and my brother, we're country boys from Derbyshire. Our parents live in a house in a field with sheep and cows and that's what we're used to. It's quite an isolated environment. I was so excited when I got the opportunity to be a trainee stockbroker in London, but it was very intimidating. I came on a Friday, and my job started the next Monday. Just: suit and tie, immaculate, turned up – it was a really smart building – and said, 'Oh, it's my first day.' You soon realize that it's a very aggressive environment. You're expecting everything to be laid out for you as the new boy but it wasn't at all. It was quite a small office, just a rack of desks down the middle with brokers sitting opposite each other; there was probably like eight on one side, eight on the other, the more senior ones at one end and the trainees at the other. The more senior chaps were earning a fortune, and they looked at us like tea boys.

It reminded me very much of boarding school, when you're one of the new boys in the lower years and the older boys beat you up. You become like a little unit and look after each other. We were given a list of thousands of names, and we'd pick up the phone at nine o'clock in the morning and just call these people non-stop. 'I'm calling from this company, are you interested in the stock market, do you buy shares?' These guys had just woken up, they were like, 'Shares? What are you talking about, I'm about to have my coffee.' It was hell. We must have been making hundreds of calls a day, most of them just putting the phone down on you. But it doesn't really effect you, it just becomes a spiel that comes out naturally. And eventually you'll get one that says, 'Oh, actually yeah, I am quite interested.' Then you're like, 'Christ, what do I say now?'

We'd probably make about 300 calls a day, and we sent about 10–15 packs out a day. Out of those packs you might get two or three that are remotely interested, and then you might get one out of every fifty packs that actually opens an account. So it's a real numbers game.

I progressed quite quickly actually, and I was able to become a trader. They wouldn't tell you what they were selling. They'd just come in one morning and say, 'Right, this is what we're selling, this is this company, this is the spiel.' You'd have a 7.30 meeting and you'd have to sell this at nine o'clock. 'Right, Paul, you're going to have fifty grand's worth of stock to sell,' and if I sold that, I'd get five grand. And I'm thinking, Jesus, five grand, for a day's work! This is what all this pain has been about.

They used to have a big white board on the wall with a list of all the brokers and the amount of stock that we've each got to shift on that day. Say it's fifty thousand: you make your calls and if someone buys five grand's worth, you put, '45 grand left', then, '35 grand', right to the bottom. You're competing with each other to see who can get rid of their stock fastest, and then when you get to the end they used to just put a smiley face, 'Done'. I remember a guy called Brian, a brilliant salesman, absolute genius, he used to be done within like two or three hours, and he'd just take the day off. Boss would say, 'Okay, well done Brian, go home,' and he's just made four grand or something. And then you could see the guys that were struggling, you can see their amounts going down in small amounts, taking a long time to get down. If you didn't shift it, you might be given the next day to try and get rid of it, or they'd take it off you and give it to another broker to sell it. It's very transparent, how you perform, in front of everybody, and very aggressive.

There was a guy called Phil, who was a real Essex boy, like, gold chain, no brains. He was just so vulgar on the phone. He used to really struggle. But he'd get there in the end, because he was a grinder. He'd just grind and grind and grind and finally get there, but he was always the last one. He'd get off the phone and pant like he was out of breath.

They had this thing where they cut your tie when you put your first trade through. I can't remember what company this was that I had to sell, but I'd built up this relationship with a guy, very wealthy guy, up in North London, Harrow he lived in, Asian chap, and I could tell he was a high net worth, so fifty grand to him was not a lot of money. He was a busy guy as well, and I remember calling him that morning and I thought, right, I'm going to try and sell the whole lot to this one guy, first call. Let's see if I can do it, cos it'll be brilliant. And I called him up, and I did my pitch, and he said, 'I'm actually just in the car, Paul, I'm about to go to work. I haven't really got time to listen to what you're saying, but I'm happy to give you a go. Let's just do whatever you're gonna say.' I was like, oh my god. I said, 'Okay, so we'll buy fifty thousand of da-da-da, this price,' gave him the risk warning. He was like, 'Yeah, fine, just do it.' I put the phone down and tried to keep myself really calm. And I went up to the board, it had fifty grand right at the top by my name, and I put a line straight through it, wrote '0' and a smiley face. And everyone was like, 'Fucking hell!'

You soon realize it's very lucrative, *but* you look at the performance of all these stocks, and they can just go to nothing. Clients can lose 80 per cent of their investment. You then try to pick up the phone and sell them again, and say, 'I'm sorry about the last one, it didn't work out but this one's even better,' and I just thought, I can't do this, this is not for me. That's when I moved on. I don't care how much they're paying me, I'm not interested in ripping people off.

When I started this business, I thought, well, I'll move to Sheffield: very low overheads. It doesn't matter how small I start, with how small a client base – if I can constantly deliver and look after them, things will grow organically. If someone gives you 10, 15 grand, 20 grand to invest, and in six months time you show them a 10 per cent, 15 per cent return, nice steady return, things are going to start loosening up. They're going to say, 'I like this, this is good, I'm going to give you a bit more'; 'I'm going to introduce you to a friend of mine who I play golf with'; 'This guy I go shooting with, he'd be interested in this,' and then it starts to expand. It's so much cheaper to grow your business like that, because a recommendation hasn't cost you a thing. Whereas these firms spend a fortune advertising because they are losing all their clients all the time, so they have to constantly keep getting fresh clients in.

But from a business point of view, I just don't think people take you seriously if you're in the provinces. If you have a Sheffield address – it's stupid, but people don't take it seriously. And it's a shame, because you can do a great job. For this kind of work, there is just a credibility to having a Berkeley Square, Mayfair address. Curzon Street, which is just down there – probably 70 per cent of the UK's hedge funds are based there, I'd say. It's a lot, just on that one strip. The money that's under management on that street is so powerful. If you combine them all together, you've probably got $150 billion there, which is being managed by maybe only forty or fifty people. So it's an extremely powerful entity. These guys can snap up a football club, they can buy a huge company. The big players in the game, the high net worth individuals, know that that's where the real expertise is. The way a hedge fund charges fees, it's called 2 and 20. You take a 2 per cent admin fee, so if you've got £100 under management, you take £2 a year, paid monthly. And then you take a 20 per cent performance fee, so whatever you make in profit you take 20 per cent. These hedge funds, some of them have got 10, 15 billion dollars under management. Say they've got a billion dollars, what's 2 per cent of that? That's $20 million a year. So they're getting $1.6 million a month guaranteed income, just as an admin fee. That's a lot of money. And then obviously they get their bonus at the end of the year. And this is split between maybe twelve, twenty guys in some instances. And obviously the bulk of that will go to the top four or five, because a lot of them are just support staff. They'll go to the Connaught or Claridge's and they'll just spend two, three thousand pounds on lunch; not even think twice about it. What's £4,000 over lunch? It's like, half an hour's work.

So I thought, if I get an address there, it's going to help our credibility. Berkeley Square, Mayfair? Oh great, that's a box ticked in their mind. If you said 'Ecclesall Road in Sheffield', not a clue. So that's why we've got the Berkeley Square address. If you look around here, every room there's traders and financial firms. Whereas in Sheffield, people were like, 'You what? You're − you're a trader? What do you trade, fruit?' 'No no, I trade the stock market, with derivatives.' 'Derivatives? What's a derivative?' They had no idea. That's not a bad thing, but it's just that you're thinking, how am I going to try and raise a network? A lot of our clients come from all sorts of social events that we do. Networking and talking to people, that's how we grow our business; in Sheffield it's very limited.

It's a relationship business, this. It's about getting on with people and they've got to trust you. And then you've got to deliver.

When I first came down here, Dad said, 'Don't ever change, don't let London change you.' He said, 'I'm really excited for you and it's a great opportunity but just don't let it change the person you are.'

Because London's like a pressure pot. He said, 'Don't get caught up in that style of life, and make sure you realize that life isn't all about making money.'

I'd like to get to the point where we generate good returns, so we've got happy clients, they trust us, that we can deliver; and we build this fund so our £10 million fund becomes £100 million, and then £500 million, and then a billion and so on. And then I'd like to give back, to do a lot of things that I feel the City hasn't been able to give me, out of my life. I mean at the end of the day, look at us, we sit in front of four screens ... What do we actually do for the world, to society? How do we contribute to the world? I don't think we contribute really. We don't build anything, we don't make anything, we're not helping people ... My girlfriend's a doctor. She helps people every day. I'd like to set up a charitable foundation, and maybe put a percentage of the profits that we make into that.

I'd also like to help small businesses. Entrepreneurship is so important – commerce wouldn't exist without those who go out and take a risk and set up a business. So I'd like to set up a fund where we help small businesses. Whether it's students or even younger than students, or older, who've got an idea, they can pitch it to us, we can help them. A £5,000 loan without any security, so if it doesn't work out, we lose it. If we can make money out of that fund, which I doubt, then great; but it's not really for that purpose, it's just to help start up businesses. Whereas if you go, traditionally, to a bank, they're never going to get any money. I'd love to do that. Seeing lots of bright enthusiastic people with great ideas and saying, 'Yeah, here's five grand.' Which is massive to them. I remember when I was trying to start businesses; five grand would be huge. To help them, and see it grow. That would be thrilling.

GEORGE IACOBESCU

Chief Executive Officer, Canary Wharf Group PLC

He is waiting for me in a marketing suite on the thirtieth floor of 1 Canada Square in Canary Wharf. There are models throughout the room: models of Canary Wharf now, models as it will be, models of the proposed Canary Wharf Crossrail station with a park installed on its top. On the walls are photoshopped images of Canary Wharf's development, peopled by the sort of well-dressed individuals who are rushing around Canary Wharf, thirty floors below. And old photographs of the Isle of Dogs, taken from the air: slack water, dirt piles, the remains of the docks, Canary Wharf in 1987 when it was still a brownsite. Pastries are laid out, coffee and water. An angular man in a crisp suit and striped shirt, he sits with his back to the window so that from one angle the Gherkin seems to rest like a charm on his shoulder. His legal counsel sits across the table, notepad in hand.

Probably from 1700, London was the biggest port in the world. But it was very slow to unload because all the boats were being unloaded at the edge of the water. And there was a lot of piracy, goods were stolen. All the ship-merchants got together and said we need to create a place which is very secure, so in 1802 they opened the London Docklands, which were locked. But by the mid-1960s to mid-Seventies, lots of the things that were produced by the British Empire or in the UK started being produced much cheaper in other parts of the world, so there was less export. And they discovered containers, which meant you could unload the boat in the sea – you could be in the sea and just take the container and that's it. In ten years the whole area died. The whole area had about 75,000 people working here, so there was huge despair and everyone was thinking, how do we bring the docks back to life?

I came to London and I couldn't see the logic of it. I got lost in the north-east area of Canary Wharf, which is mostly populated by Bangladeshi people. I had never been to London in my life, so it was for me a shock, to see more poverty there than anywhere else. In my mind, London was the London you see in the pictures, but you don't realize that you see a very limited part of London in the pictures. So my personal opinion was not to touch it. And most of the management was not thrilled with the idea. We were very doubtful about the project. Just to show how valuable our opinion was, that was in June; that July the 17th we signed the project.

The government said, we are opening the area for development, but by the way, there is no transport, there are no services, there are no streets. You know, small details. Normally you would expect the government to provide all the infrastructure. If you go and buy a piece of land in the City, you are surrounded by 500 years of infrastructure, by services, by history, by life. You didn't have all these benefits here, it was just a plain piece of land. There was no electricity, no water, there was no way to get here. Limehouse link did not exist, the DLR existed in that little form from Tower Hill to the tip of the island, but there were no trains running, and that was it. Ultimately it was agreed that we would pay £400 million towards the Jubilee Line, which was unexpected. It wasn't in the numbers and you wouldn't probably have started the project if it comes to the point where you have to pay for transport. Just imagine, in Toronto, New York, or Paris, where a developer has to pay for transport?

The principle is that it's very important for London, it's very important for us, it will transform the whole of London. I mean, the basic reason is that the government doesn't have the money. So what do you do, if the government says we cannot afford to build transport, but you know that London needs transport, you need transport, because the City Corp is contributing a similar amount of money – I think £200 million, and another £100 million from businesses. Because the City, the Square Mile, is in as much need of transport as we are – not for today, because today we have plenty of transport, with the upgrade of the DLR and the upgrade of the Jubilee Line we have all the transport we need for the next three or four or five years. But then development will stall and the same thing will happen in the City if the City wants to grow.

The Tower of London, that is the dividing line. William the Conqueror created the Tower: to the west was money and pleasure, and to the east was poverty, and it is still here. It tells the story of London, that for so long all this area had no transport. When we started building Canary Wharf in 1987, the Jubilee Line didn't exist, and the DLR was just one line here and a bit of line going to the Isle of Dogs. That was the whole transport. How could it be that a city as rich as London has the whole eastern part of the town with no transport? How could you expect all these people to go to work? I mean it was a reservoir of cheap labour, but you didn't even give them the opportunity to be slaves.

Today Canary Wharf is 15 million feet and there's another 10 million feet to go. So it's two and a half times the size that we looked at the first time. Canary Wharf is the most important thing to happen to London in the past hundred years, and probably Crossrail is going to be the next one. It has an extension that goes to London Bridge which makes a big difference, it starts creating the network of transport. We designed the Jubilee Line in such a way that it intersects with every other line. It is just two steps to come to Canary Wharf. Crossrail will change London for ever, because a lot of the companies in Canary Wharf or in the City would like to use a lot of the manpower coming from the east. They are more economical, not having to pay the rents of Kensington, Chelsea and Mayfair. And those areas have different salary expectations. So the labour force coming from the east is cheaper. The east of London will become the dormitory of London, because what London is missing is the Queens and the Brooklyn of New York. You don't have a place where the nurses and the teachers and the policemen and the firefighters can live very close to the city. If they all have to travel two or three hours to get to work, how productive are they and how tired are they by the time they get home? So the east of London is going to be where all these things happen.

The system is at breaking point, it hasn't been improved in the past 50–60 years. You have to go back sixty years to look at the last Tube that was built in London. Besides the Jubliee Line, and the improvements on the DLR and now Thameslink, and the East London Line, everything is very old. And you have to improve it, you have to build new stuff because the old stuff will go down, it will cease to perform. It's not only that Crossrail will create employment, not only that it will have a substantial investment return, which will be very good. It's 'what will it do for London?' And that's enormous.

My opinion is that the task of every government that comes to power is to maintain London as a financial centre. One day you have it, next day you don't. When you lose it, you lose it very quick. London should always be one of the major financial centres of the world, because of the language, because of the infrastructure in terms of lawyers and accountants and financial institutions, and because it's the crossroads for Asia, Africa and the Arab peninsula. It's in the right place, in the right language, with the right infrastructure, the right people. In all the studies that CBI or London First makes, London comes first with the exception of two things – transport and cost of housing. So you have to fix that.

The day when foreign companies tell you that the biggest problem London has is transport, it will take you twenty years to fix it. You cannot act quickly. What is the plan, where does London want to be in five years and in ten years? It's true that everybody is worried about the finances today. But if you look at the long term, where do you want to be? If you look at Brazil, it took them twenty years to try to fix the economy and today they are getting the benefit of it. But you cannot do it overnight. You have to look at the future and you have to prepare for the future, because when the future comes you don't have time to fix it.

When we did Canary Wharf, we came from New York and we knew exactly what the likes of Amex or Merrill Lynch or Dow Jones or Nomura or Oppenheim will need. So we applied what we learnt in New York to infrastructure and everything else. Nobody believed.

Everybody said Olympia Europe are crazy to do it and nobody wanted to bet on it. But it succeeded, and it will succeed in time as things develop, and it will link with the city. One day it will be forgotten as Canary Wharf. It will simply be part of London.

LIVING AND DYING

ALISON CATHCART

Superintendent Registrar, City of Westminster

As I enter the Old Marylebone Town Hall, a bride carefully negotiates the front steps while holding a bouquet of pink roses in her left hand and a bag from Office, the shoe shop, in her right. The photographer, edging backwards towards the kerb, has time to wait until the whole group is off the steps. Men in shiny suits surround her – a bride trying her best to look serene as buses roll down Marylebone Road. Inside, in an office down the hall from the board that displays wedding notices, Cathcart sits at her desk wearing a smart, conservative black suit.

Everyone, from princes and princesses right through to the guy who sweeps the streets, gets married here. Westminster is such a varied borough, it stretches out to Bayswater and Paddington, we cover Mayfair and Belgravia, so we have a huge spectrum of wealth or poverty, all coming to use our facilities. I even married a member of the Royal Family a couple of years ago. We had another chap who was a distant cousin of the Queen, but he looked just like Prince Charles, he even spoke like him, it was uncanny.

In this country you can't marry outside unless you're Jewish or Quaker. It's legislation that goes back to 1837, when civil registration began and registrar offices were established. Prior to that, it was the church or the registry office. And prior to all of that there were what we call clandestine marriages where prostitutes were marrying wealthy young men having got them drunk. They'd wake up the next day and they didn't even know they'd been through a wedding. Of course they had all sorts of inheritance rights and so forth, so to tidy up that sort of corruption weddings have to take place in approved premises or licensed-for-worship buildings, between the hours of eight and six, during daylight.

We are still using fountain pens and ink for registering marriages. Marriages are still written in registers and the format is exactly the same as it was in 1837. There's special ink provided to us by Her Majesty's Government, it's got special content in it that goes darker with age. A lot of inks fade over time, but this is called blue-black, it starts off blue and it goes black over time. If you get it on your clothes you haven't a hope of getting it out. You have to be really careful that you don't get it on a bride's dress. Sometimes people get a fountain pen, they're not used to using it, they can't get it to work and they'll go shake it, and of course the ink goes everywhere. Over the years they have tried to create biros with this specialist ink, but they've just never been able to develop it. So we are still using fountain pens. And we have a hotline to Her Majesty's Stationery Office.

Before 1995 you had to marry in your district of residence: if you lived in Westminster you married here, if you lived in Lambeth you married in Lambeth. It was quite restrictive. You could only get married in a church or a registry office, or a religious building that was licensed. And there wasn't much in the way of customizing ceremonies, the wording was very brief, it was all a bit perfunctory. And then in 1995 it all changed with the advent of the Approved Premises Act, so other venues could be licensed.

We started off with about thirty venues in Westminster. We thought we'd have to up our game here, we can't go out to Claridge's and do a ten-minute ceremony that we would have done in the registry office. So we had to look at all the options that we were offering couples in terms of choices and how to customize ceremonies, how to turn it into more of an event. We had to invest in uniforms for our staff, because if you're going out to a place like that you have to look presentable – not that people weren't, but it was all about the image and you're representing Westminster.

That was a huge change, and we're now at a point where we've got 130 venues and the list is growing. Claridge's is one of the most booked venues. There's a choice of rooms there, there's the ballroom and the drawing room and the French salon, if you've got loads of money. I've seen weddings there decked out with flowers and it's just pure romance. Or they've got smaller rooms up on the sixth floor for those who still want to say they got married at Claridge's but … you know what I mean. It's just got that sense of history about it. The Savoy, to be able to walk into venues like that. Or the Ritz – I'm a regular at the Ritz. The doorman knows me. That's a real buzz, to walk into places like that, that you would ordinarily never go to in your normal working life.

It should always be a seemly and dignified venue. I probably have turned down one or two just because they were really awful places. We do loads of weddings at London Zoo, in a nice little building near the Reptile House, actually. You can tell a Zoo wedding's going to be a certain type of person.

Civil partnerships was another major change. I would never have dreamt that we would have same-sex ceremonies when I first started out. And in fact some members of staff, not here but in other services, dropped out because they couldn't handle it. It was a step too far for some. Civil partnerships started in 2005. We hadn't a clue how that was going to be in terms of numbers, we just didn't know. We probably have done the most in the country. We did loads in the first year, there was such a huge backlog. A lot were older couples who had waited years for the legislation to change. They were in their seventies, had been together forty years, you know, they were together since before it became legal. So the very first day of civil partnerships was really emotional. We did twenty ceremonies that day, starting at eight o'clock in the morning right through to half past five in the evening. It was draining – draining in a nice way, because we were part of something really special.

It gets quite complex because of all the nationalities, all the per-mutations, divorce documents, you've got to give a lot of information to people to make sure that they've got it right, before the actual day.

It's not just about the hearts and the flowers and the catering and the car and this, that and the other. I mean, the legal bit is crucial – we're responsible for giving the right information, but the couple has a responsibility to take that on board and make sure that they know what they are doing as well. And it's quite complicated, depending on nationality, immigration status, marital status and so on. And whether they are coming from abroad, because we get a lot of people coming from abroad to get married here.

There is also the whole sham marriages thing, where they are clearly marrying to circumvent immigration. You can tell straight away. It's body language, it's not speaking the same language, it's some cultures that just wouldn't go together ordinarily, like Eastern European and Pakistanis. They don't have to say anything. You just watch how they interact with each other. I can't put my finger on it, I can't spell it out, but you know when it isn't a genuine marriage.

We are required to report to the Home Office if we have our suspicions. But we don't stop the wedding. If they are already married and we know that, or they are under age, or they haven't got the mental capacity or whatever, then you've got powers to stop the wedding. But if they haven't committed any outward offence then it's difficult. Because it's not a crime to not marry for love, is it?

We do encourage people to customize their ceremony. On the whole most people are fairly traditional, but occasionally you get something quirky, just as a bit of fun. I've had the *Match of the Day* theme played on a harp at a wedding, a concession to the groom. Recently my colleague came to me and said, would you do this ceremony, I think the bride was promising to do something with the groom's dirty underpants or something. I thought, no, that's not appropriate and we said no to that. Or there are readings that I cringe at every now and again. There's one, what is it, John Cooper Clarke, 'I wanna be your vacuum cleaner.' It goes on in that sort of vein … The problem is, when you're conducting a wedding, the bride and groom are facing you, the guests are facing you and you've got the person giving the reading facing out, so all eyes are on you and the person giving the reading. So you have to have this blank expression, and if you think something is cringeworthy you can't show your emotion. Or sometimes you'll have somebody who's been invited to give a reading and they don't have the skill to do it. That can be embarrassing. I can remember doing a wedding once where they had a family friend who was asked to sing, and she was out of tune and it went on and on and on, and again I had this bland look on my face because I couldn't show any emotion other than interest. So you have to be a bit of an actress.

I've had objections lodged before weddings but not on the actual day. Maybe that's something that's going to hit me, maybe it's around the corner, on the horizon, who knows? But I have never come across it. You get lots of people going 'Ahem, ahem' and all that, the usual jokes and the coughers, but not a proper legitimate objection on the day itself. I think I'd probably have a heart attack if it was real.

As I leave, I see an older man out on the steps with a hoover, cleaning up the confetti. He does the job a few times a day and says he can't talk now because he's missed a little down on the third step. He stretches the hoover and sucks up the clovers and the hearts.

ALEX BLAKE

Eyewitness

It was the Saturday before Christmas. I was living in Chalk Farm and I was going to meet some friends in South London, in Vauxhall, at a restaurant in Bonnington Square. Someone was having a birthday party there, fuck knows why.

I suppose I was 24, so you'd have a couple before you went out, d'you know what I mean? I was with two very good friends of mine at the time. One of whom I was living with and the other was a much closer, older friend of mine who was living in South London, but he'd come up that afternoon and we'd mucked around doing something and then I'm pretty sure we'd been to the pub near me up in Kentish Town and had a couple of pints.

We got on the Tube at Kentish Town to go down to Waterloo, or somewhere south, to get across to Vauxhall. So we did one stop to Camden Town and we were changing to get the Charing Cross rather than the Bank branch. It was the Saturday night before Christmas, it was eight o'clock at night, and it was chocka. Everyone was out, the Tube station was packed, all the way down the Tube platform was five-deep with people. Everyone had had a few drinks, Santa hats are out and the girls are in high heels. It's the Saturday night before Christmas and it's London and it's Camden. We were standing fairly close to where the train enters the platform, probably a carriage and a half's length. So not right at the end of the platform, but pretty close to it – I think we'd pushed all the way down to get some space; and we were standing there waiting for the train. As the train came into the platform I saw the front of the train coming in and it was coming in quickly, not abnormally quickly, but it was coming in quickly. The train came in from the right-hand side and then behind me, to my left-hand side, I heard a scream. A scream of determination and defiance. It wasn't bloodcurdling, but it was arresting. Not terror. Not surprise. It was … absolute determination is the best way I can put it. Out of the corner of my eye, coming from the back end of the platform – we were more or less at the front of the five-deep lot of people, we were quite close to the front and this girl came out of the edge of my vision, ran across the side of my vision and jumped off the edge of the platform right in the front of this oncoming train. She basically disintegrated on impact, is the bluntest way I can put it. I mean she disappeared. She became flesh and bone and blood instantly, absolutely instantly. God knows what it did to that Tube driver, because she landed right on top of him, more or less. The only thing between her and him would have been the glass. So she sort of popped, she exploded, do you know what I mean? And I didn't have any sense of anyone being covered in it. It didn't land on anyone or anything, because the train kept on going.

The immediate reaction was pandemonium at our end of the platform. I think it took a few seconds for it to get down to the other end of the platform. But the three of us just all turned and looked at each other, said, 'Let's get the fuck out of here,' and ran for the exit. But that was exactly what everybody else was doing. So I don't remember getting off the platform, but I do remember charging up the escalators to get out, up to Camden High Street. We were all really shocked. We jumped in a cab and carried on our journey, trying to work out what the fuck had just happened. The images that stay with me are the image of the train coming in, pretty quick, but not outrageously, and then this scream and then this person just running. I've always imagined she was probably quite an attractive girl, long blonde hair, but had been living on the streets for a while. She had a kind of down-at-heel look, with grotty jeans and a kind of dirty puffa jacket and trainers. She had a pallid complexion and blonde hair, but she might have been quite pretty once upon a time. And I just remember her screaming and running and jumping and then literally disintegrating.

I think there were so many different factors involved in the physics of it, you know, that anything's possible. But this girl just happened to get it right, if you see what I mean, and what stays with me is her determination not to fuck it up. She must have spent a certain amount of time watching other trains and working out what was going to be the best way of doing it, because if you're going to do it, the worst thing is that you end up under the train but still alive.

The combination of the speed of the train and the speed of her jump and the absolute clarity of her jump as well, it was a clear jump into the train. She jumped slightly at an angle towards it, rather than across it. She jumped into it. She hit the target.

For a long time after that happened, I would turn around and walk away down the platform when a train came into the station. I would be happily waiting for the train and then as the train came in

I would turn around and walk away to stop myself doing what she did. It was a kind of vertigo thing, you know that thing about vertigo where the fear is you're going to throw yourself off. Not that you're afraid of the height, but you're afraid of losing your own self-control.

I think these things, whether it's wanting to hurl yourself off the side of a mountain or in front of the Northern Line at Camden, from a psychological point of view, I think it's the trauma process. It's the rational mind slowly over time grappling with the irrational and the incomprehensible, throwing it up and confronting you with it, and you make the right choice, you keep on making the right choice and after time you've dealt with it.

I don't have any sense of her pushing people out of the way. She was probably sort of four or five people along from me down the platform. But I don't have any memory of her elbowing people out of the way. She just cleared a path, but it was the scream. Because she was right at the back of the platform, there was six, seven foot, two metres maybe, she'd got to cover. More maybe. And the scream started before she started to run and was extinguished when she hit the train.

The collective, undiscussed, instinctive reaction of everyone was just 'go'. Everyone wanted to get out of there as quickly as they possibly could. No one wanted to stay. The whole classic drive-by thing of you drive past a car accident, it was exactly the opposite. Everybody wanted to leave as quickly as they could.

I was 24 when that happened, and at that point in my life it was my most immediate experience of death and mortality. And then about eight years later, one of my best friends from school and then university was murdered in Kensal Green.

His name was Tom. It was January 2006, and he was jumped. He'd bought a flat on one of those roads that goes just north of Kensal Rise station. He was a young lawyer, 31 at the time, and he was on his way home from work. He was getting married in June that year and he was planning his wedding. I still know his girlfriend, his former fiancée, very well. In fact I introduced them, so I was friends with her before they got together.

He was on his way back to her, walking down Bathurst Gardens and he got jumped by two guys, 17 or 18 years old. And they cut him down. They just cut him down. He fought back, because he would have done that, d'you know what I mean? They challenged him; he gave them some money, he gave them his wallet. I can't remember the exact sequence of events, but they mugged him and I think he gave them some, but not all, of what he had on him and then they aggressed him again and he fought back, and they chased him down the street and cut him down. Cut him at the back of the legs, cut his hamstrings, and then stabbed him to death. For what in the end turned out to be £20 and an Oyster card. I mean, that was the value of the project, as it were.

What happened with Tom is not typical. You know, the idea we'd be safer if we weren't in London, that's actually nonsense. Statistically it's nonsense. But experientially it's nonsense as well. The media would have you believe it's typical and it could happen to you at any moment. I think we've got a massive problem in this city, much more than the country at large, with the media, the local media and the national media that is London-centric, at best using fear to sell newspapers and at worst being used as an organ for crowd control, in terms of limiting people's aspirations and hopes and self-confidence. I think experientially the chances of lightning striking twice, as it were, are next to nothing. The chances of a very close friend of mine being murdered in a street robbery are infinitesimally small. He didn't do anything stupid. It was just incredibly bad luck, and the chance of that happening again either to me or to someone I know is even smaller.

I think I went through a period after he died thinking, maybe I'll move out of London and go and live in the country. But that's the dream that nine-tenths of this city have, you know, nine-tenths of the time. It's ongoing. I'll do it one day. So that became intensified, but four years later I still haven't done it.

PERRY POWELL

Paramedic

We go everywhere, that's one of the perks of the job. I've done jobs in
bank vaults, I've done jobs in burger vans and cars and posh mansions.
Everywhere really. Parks – I delivered a baby in a park once, that was
an interesting job. Yeah, literally everywhere. You do get to see places
that other people just never see. The Eurostar terminal at St Pancras,
that was another one that was interesting. Interesting because the
French police weren't that happy about letting us through.

You get different types of jobs depending on where you work.
Certainly in Southall you get a lot of medical problems. South
Asian people are more prone to cardiac problems, for example, so
you do go to a lot of heart attacks, you go to a lot of respiratory
problems. In some of the most impoverished areas there's a lot more
drug use so you'll go to more heroin overdoses, which is unheard of
in somewhere like Ealing. And if you work up in town proper, say
Westminster and the West End, you go to a lot of tourists. I think
a lot of people from abroad are quite impressed with the service:
that an ambulance will turn up within eight minutes, that there's no
charge wherever you're from, whoever you are.

*We are sitting at a table just off Charlotte Street, surrounded by late morning
traffic – people in suits riding Boris bikes and pulling into nearby Scala
Street, where the rack is full of bikes, no empty spaces, cursing the mayor,
cursing the scheme. Nearby an Asian man finishes a whole egg and cress
sandwich in two bites, like he's been practising the move most of his working
life. Lorries rumble up Rathbone Place behind him.*

I think the main thing is talking to people, talking to all manner
of people, many types I'd never come across before. Talking to the
alcoholic who's lying in the gutter at three in the morning and wants
to lamp you. Talking to very elderly people who are terminally ill. I

found that really challenging. Dealing with kids. I had no experience
at all of dealing with kids and I think that for most ambulance staff,
really unwell children is their biggest fear because it's so difficult
to assess them and because they can go downhill very quickly, and
you're dealing with parents at the same time. Yeah, and people who
don't speak any English at all. Trying to reassure them and take a
history from them via a translator on the phone or via sign language
and still smiling.

I had an idea of how mixed London was but I didn't appreciate
the pockets you get. I spent my last years working in Hanwell, which
is Ealing way, you know, and we're on the doorstep of Southall,
which is just like another world. It's like nowhere I've ever seen in
London: you drive down the High Street and the Broadway and
you don't see a white face at all and you see all of these bazaars and
shops spilling out onto the streets and people hawking food from
open shop windows. It's fascinating. It's like nowhere else, it really
is. I didn't know that places like that existed. I always had this view
of London being terribly mixed and everyone living side by side. It
was an eye-opener. The same as when I was working in Oval, you do
get pockets of African-Caribbean people which are quite segregated
from the rest of the community.

I didn't find culture as much of an obstacle as I thought it might
be. You're spoken to about the issues of, for example, going into
mosques, people will expect you to take your footwear off and we're
not allowed to take our boots off because they're safety boots because
they're steel toe-cap, so they provided us with shoe covers in the end,
sort of like a bath hat really or a shower cap that you put on your
shoes. But I've never found that an issue. If an ambulance is called,
there's an understanding it's an emergency, people just say 'Come
through.' It's not been a problem. The same with male and female
segregated areas, that hasn't been an issue.

And also people talked about obstetrics and how in certain cultures
it's totally unacceptable for a man to deliver a baby or be involved in
any way. I've never found that either. I've delivered Muslim babies,

Hindu babies, white babies, black babies, and it's never really been a problem at all.

We generally take turns, we do a shift driving and a shift attending. I think most people become quite cynical about the number of jobs that we go to that we wouldn't perceive as emergencies or in need of an emergency. The sort of jobs that a patient could have gone to their GP about in four days' time or taken a couple of paracetamol and gone to bed and seen how they felt in the morning. Those sort of jobs start to wear you down and you spend a lot of time talking to these people in the back of the ambulance on the way to hospital and in their houses when you're attending, i.e. when you're not driving, and you spend a lot of time biting your tongue and maintaining a professional veneer when underneath you just want to say, come on, wake up, get a grip! They're holding calls across the sector, they're crying out for an ambulance which isn't available, to go to a 14-year-old who's stopped breathing, and we've got *you* in the back of our ambulance and I'm having to make polite conversation with you because you've stubbed your toe. You do want to smack them. I won't lie to you. When you drive, you kind of get away from all that. You can switch off, you don't have to listen to what they're saying. You don't have to bite your tongue. You can help out. You do a few obs and then you get in the front, drive to hospital, make the tea, clean the vehicle and go to the next one. Also there is the fact that driving on blue light just is quite good fun.

There's something like four times as many calls per day as there were ten years ago and the same number of ambulances to deal with them. So we're going from job to job to job most of the time. You get a few hours in the early morning where you green up, which means you push the button to say you're ready for the next job at hospital and you don't get a call straightaway, but that's the exception to the rule. So they are trying to make staff more and more productive, which is understandable in a way, but at the same time, by the time you've handed over your patient, you've finished writing your paperwork, which especially if they're quite unwell is very important, as it's a legal document and you want to make sure you've written everything you can think of about the patient. By the time you've done all that you can easily have spent half an hour. If you're a smoker and you want a fag as well, you're looking at 33–34 minutes. So yes, whereas they want you to turn around in no more than twenty minutes and they're constantly asking you to book delays if you're any longer than that and twenty-minute turnarounds are tight, especially when you're working a twelve-hour shift and the best you can hope for is a 45-minute break at some point, which maybe seven times out of ten you don't get because it's too busy. So these ten minutes or even five minutes after you've finished your paperwork here and there at hospital to eat a bit of lunch or to have a chat with your colleagues, it's important.

In terms of staff sanity as well, I think the few minutes at hospital where you can talk over a job with other crews are very important because we do go to some stressful situations and you do need to let off some steam occasionally and you do need a bit of reassurance that you did everything you could for a patient. Often that's all you need, but it is important especially now we rarely see station. There was a time when you would green up straightaway after a job and you'd go back to station and have a cup of tea, there'd be another crew there, you'd sit down, watch a bit of telly, make a few jokes, you know, and that was how it used be. But the busier it gets, the less frequently that happens.

I've never done a birth that was anything other than really straight-forward, thankfully, because we have two days' training in obstetrics: a day on the technician course and a day on the paramedic course. We know what to do if something goes wrong, but we never ever want to have to do it.

My first shift working with a student, I hadn't ever delivered a baby. We were on Richmond Park, I was driving and my crew mate was attending, and we went in and the woman was really nice, and said, really sorry to call you, I know it's not really an emergency but I have these really short labours. My last one was thirty minutes, so we didn't want to take any chances. We said, no, it's fine, it's fine, and we got all our stuff together. I let my crew mate have a look at the business end while I got some kit out and we decided we were going to have to stay where we were because she was crowning. There are certain indicators for when you go to the nearest obstetric unit or when you stay where you are. You don't want to have the baby in the back of an ambulance because it's just cramped and dirty. So we explained that she's doing well. She was very relaxed actually, there was no crying, no heavy breathing, it was all quite calm. She'd been there before, this was her third delivery. But then the husband turned to us and said, do you know the last time the crew came they'd never delivered a baby, can you believe that? So we kind of looked at each other and said, no, really? Shit. Well, it came out. Cut the cord, gave it to mum.

We waited until it was all over and said, you know, actually that was our first as well. The husband laughed. He said, well, you'd never have known it. That's a relief. The veneer of calm worked again.

There was a recent cardiac arrest I did. It came through as a chest pain, which can be anything from someone having a heart attack to someone with a cough – it's categorized the same. So we went there, a block of council flats somewhere in Southall. A grim old place actually. Just three floors of concrete flats in a long line. I think it was about ten or eleven at night. He was 40 and you do make assumptions based on what the computer tells you: 40-year-old male, chest pain. People don't generally have heart attacks in their forties so we're not expecting anything too serious but get there as quickly as we can. We go in and it turns out he has a long cardiac history, he's had three heart attacks in the past and he looks like death warmed up.

He's got the classic signs and symptoms of a heart attack, he's very pale. He was black but he barely looked it, if you know what I mean, he was that washed out, pouring with sweat, shivering, complaining of a tight, crushing pain in his chest radiating down both his arms. There was a paramedic on the Fast Response Unit in the car who was there before us. So we decided to do an ECG and give him aspirin GTN on the scene before we moved him, and the ECG showed quite clearly that he was having a heart attack. So we got him on our carry chair, carried him down the stairs puffing and panting all the way down because he wasn't a light bloke.

Some of our illest patients are very very heavy, which is no coincidence, you know, if you're twenty-five stone your heart's not going to be in the best shape and neither's the rest of you. So it's awkward. You can carry quite a heavy weight between the two of you down a straight flight of stairs but when you're in an old Victorian house with corners or, worse still, a fire escape in the rain in the dark, it's very hard work and there's the constant fear that you might actually drop the person. Thankfully I've never done that but I've come pretty close. All it takes is one stumble and then you unbalance a bit and your crew mate unbalances and down they go.

So we carried him down the stairs, got him in the back of the ambulance and I was just getting IV access to give him some morphine for the pain while my colleague was getting clopidogrel, which is an anti-platelet drug which works by stopping the platelets binding together and making the blockage in the heart worse, when he gargled and went into cardiac arrest then and there. And this was the first witnessed, monitored arrest that I'd done, i.e. he was wired up to the monitor and we saw him arrest. So we were able to give him a pre-cordial thump, which is something I haven't done before or since.

Basically it means punching them in the chest because that can sometimes create enough energy to restart the heart. Didn't work. So we got the de-fib on, shocked him straightaway and he reverted to a normal sinus rhythm. Because he was having a heart attack ordinarily we could have taken him to a specialist centre where they do primary angioplasty, the nearest one would have been Hammersmith Hospital, which was quite a long way away, but it means they can cure the problem straightaway. They go straight into a cath lab, they thread a wire up through the groin and clear the coronary artery that's caused the problem. It's all very clever, but because he was in cardiac arrest we couldn't do that because his airway was compromised. So we took him to the nearest hospital.

We managed to secure his airway but not until he'd vomited everywhere so there was a risk that he would have aspirated on his own vomit. As we were going into the A&E he regained consciousness and started to be aware of what was going on. But we got him in and the hospital were fantastic. Often district general hospitals dither. They have inexperienced staff. They don't have any specialists, especially at night. There are no consultants on so they'll take a few bloods, they'll confirm this, that or the other and it can be an hour, an hour and a half before they've actually come to a decision that the patient needs to be transferred, which is a decision we know we could have made in ten minutes. Anyway, they were very good. They saw he was up and about. The anaesthetist checked his airway, was happy with it and he was transferred within five minutes to the cath lab and then we heard that he'd made a full recovery and he'd gone home.

That was a really satisfying job. That's the kind of job that you join the Ambulance Service to do. It just feels fantastic when something like that happens.

At the end of a job there are three main types of fags, really. There's the euphoric fag when you've just delivered a baby or when you've just saved someone's life you really didn't think was going to make it, or you hear good news about a patient that you brought in earlier who's walked out of hospital. There's the run-of-the-mill fag, which you don't really need but you've taken someone with a cough into hospital and you're a bit bored and you want to smoke.

Finally, there's the fag to stop you crying. That's an important fag. I've only ever cried once at work and that was after a dead baby that we couldn't save. So we took it into Ealing. I was just kind of keeping it together. I was quite new at the time and working with someone that was also on my course, so neither of us had been there before. I booked the baby in and I just kind of went and lit up and that was ... yeah, that was a pretty grim fag.

JOHN HARRIS

Funeral director

In his office at his family's funeral home in Canning Town, there are two editions of The American Way of Death *on the bookshelves. The soft ring of the landline mixes with the clattering bell of his mobile phone. It's a clear, sunny day. We walk around outside and he turns on the small Chinese fountain near the stand of bamboo.*

My great-grandfather started this business. When he put his name above it, that was it. He was a stickler for things being absolutely right. He wasn't really a businessman; as a businessman you'd take him outside and shoot him tomorrow. He was a funeral director. You could rip him apart into as many pieces but every bit was a funeral director. If he thought to make the job wholly right he had to lose money at it, it was more important that the job was done right and that was the legacy he gave us. His actual saying was 'a funeral director is bred and born, not bread and butter', which means to say ... you're not there for the money, you're bred and born as a funeral director to do the job properly. The lovely part of that was in the end he built up such a reputation that if someone walked in they knew they would get a standard. That's actually quite good business. In the end he got to a stage with the business that in the morning all he had to do was open the door and sit back. The people would walk in. We didn't have to advertise because we had no mobility. If you was born in the East End you died in the East End. Everyone knew about funerals, everyone talked about funerals. Funerals were big then, you know.

The working classes, you had to go out with some style. We didn't need Yellow Pages, we didn't need fucking fancy adverts on the telly.

I came in when I was 18, so I've been down here thirty-seven years. You did your bit of church advertising but that was to keep you in with the church. The East End then was still very, very strong. The foreigners we had then were leftovers from the war or pre-war. We had a Polish community – always have had – because you got to remember this was a dock area. You pick out any dock area in the world and it has an immigrant population. Name a big city in the world that doesn't have a Chinese community, an enclave somewhere, the Vietnamese, the Poles, and some of the Caribbeans, and certainly in a port like London there would be little pockets. But they didn't make a significant amount.

Now you make this quantum leap to today. In just the time we've been speaking a few more Muslims will have moved into the area. They're coming over in vast numbers and they do make large ghettoes. The population is so mobile and the new people coming into the area are invariably foreign. They don't know what we stand for. All our people move out. I went to a house yesterday and the family had moved down to Clacton now. That was an old East End family but when this chappie died he had to be done by T. Cribb & Sons. That's why we've moved down. We've got an office in Benfleet and Leigh-on-Sea. We're following the East End out, because that's our strength. The first generation as they move out still come back to us, but the second generation ain't going to know T. Cribb & Sons. So we've got to strike there now while the first generation is still … We can open up an area in Essex which is strong, Pitsea, Basildon area, still a strong East End population. If we go down there now we will still get a lot of people walking through that door because it's T. Cribb & Sons. That's it. We have time to spread it to the next generation and we can continue that. If we don't strike now it's gone for ever. We've lost our window as it were.

And then we've got to look and think, here we are, we've built this monolith of a building. We still need to get people walking through that door, not a door we've got in Essex. We need people through that door. If you asked any funeral director: this is where your office is, so what are you hoping to do? You're hoping to administer to the people around you, aren't you? If half of that now is no good to you, we're left with this half. How do we get them?

Some of the Eastern Europeans we can work with. We're looking at the Polish community at the moment. We looked at it and saw that the Poles are just driving over, picking up the body and driving back. Polish immigrants we've got coming over here at the moment are a migrant workforce – the majority of houses around here, you've got 5–6 people living in a small unit. They come over, they'll probably have two or three jobs going, they can easily clear £300–£400. What happens when that 400 quid goes back to Poland? It is sixteen times more valuable back there. It doesn't sit in this economy. It goes back there. You see the amount of cars going backwards and forwards with three, four, five people in it, back to Poland every four or five weeks and the money migrates with it.

So I employed a Polish girl for a few months to contact all the Polish funeral directors – email, fax, whatever, phone. We offered them a service. They have to come over and they waste a day here because they've got to get up to the embassy, get the paperwork, all that. So what we said, phone us, we'll go pick up the body, we'll embalm it, get your paperwork, so you can come in, turn around. You may have three or four funeral directors all coming over here, we can get all the bodies back, you can send one man over and he can take four bodies back in one shot. We earn two bob out of it. You look at that and think, why the fuck would we bother for a couple of bob? But in 10–15 years' time the Polish community, a certain amount of them are going to be resident here. They still like their funerals, they have burials, they like nice coffins. That could be our mainstay for the next generation of T. Cribb & Sons. If you've established yourself in the Polish community or in the Lithuanian community, your name is there, isn't it?

The Hindus and Sikhs, a lot of the African countries, they do traditional washing. If you go to an average funeral directors it's around by their garage. We've done it in a clean area. They can use showers, they can use jugs, bowls, however they want to wash the body, it's all in there. We put a different god up on the wall for whoever's coming. It's not just pushed to the back to some work area.

When we have Chinese ashes staying here, they're not like you or I. Ashes are ashes. With them, they have a two-soul system so the soul that goes for rebirth is one and that's what we look after in there. But some of it stays in this country with the ashes, so if you're storing ashes here there is a spirit in those ashes. So we set this up for the Chinese so they can come. The spirit left here has to be tended, so they bring along drink, they light the joss sticks, which are a form of prayer. There's food and drink and prayer, which go to keep that spirit happy. When we have a Chinese service here now we'll get 60–80 people turn up. They'll see all this. I know they can't get looked after like this anywhere else.

The Filipino community, they like to do an all-night vigil. They sit with the body all night, they bring food in, and you can have 200–300 turn up. The average high-street funeral director ain't going to cope with that. Whereas they'll come down, they'll use our big service room in there. We can seat sixty to seventy in there to have a nice service. They can have that. Then they take over – because we're closed – they take over that reception, put tables all the way down, and then we have food all laid out like a buffet and they literally stay here all night and we stay with them and then they might stay all weekend and then on the Monday they all go home, we send the body off to the Philippines and that's it. It's quite a big population. But that might not last for ever because the new generation … will they want to fly the bodies back to the Philippines? No. The ones I'm sending back are 50-, 60-, 70-year-olds. They were born in the Philippines, their families are back there. The younger generations: they're English. They want burials here. We're doing a few Filipino burials already. It's a bit like the Africans. This generation, 95 per cent flown back. The next generations: not so many. By the time you get down to the third generation, they're all going to be buried here so that traffic will stop.

Will they know our name? That's what we're banking on.

I ain't going to give up, no. We just need to change things. I make it up as I go along. We're not double-glazing, we don't have a product we can export, we don't have something we can load into a lorry and ship up to Leeds. So how do we get people from a wider area through that door to still make this a functional business? We think, hold on, we've got to specialize in a way that's going to make people want to travel. Hence our involvement in Africa.

I got on a plane, went out to Ghana, had a look at the situation, and thought, we can have a go out here as well. And it was big, like when we started up with the horses. Dad, Graham and myself, we went out one Friday night to Holland to see if the breed was still there. By the time we came back on Sunday we had bought two horses. They were being quarantined by the time we come back. Within thirty days we was going to get them and we knew cock-all about it. Dad was brought up as a stable boy at 14. He knew what end of a horse was what. I knew a horse had a leg in each corner, but we knew the standard we wanted to get. The only reason we went out there was because we was tired of what was being offered in this country. My dad said when I was a boy, grandad's turnout was second to none and so we needed to get that quality, bring that back. Father was ashamed of what he was walking in front of. When someone was saying to us we want a horse-drawn funeral, we was going to a chap, a lovely old boy, supplied all the film trade, did all the Hammer Horrors, you know, but … If you looked at his turnout, it was great for your films. But to stand outside with a coffin on and people walking round it – it was shit. No disrespect to the old chap, he's died now. It was great for the job he was doing. But it wasn't … Grandfather's carriages were just pristine. The horses were immaculate. The harness was just right. Everyone was dressed right. There was this quality about everything. It was something.

When I went out to Ghana I was happy to link up with someone out there who could say, we could get bodies back to the villages, we could do all of that. But when I got out there … I realized within a couple of days of visiting mortuaries, this was just rubbish and there was no way we could link our name to it.

I knew absolutely fuck-all about Ghana, I didn't have a scooby. It was like landing on Mars, really. The first few journeys out there I was staying in a hotel. There were South Africans, Australians, most people were in mining, things like that. A lot of Lebanese, French, Belgians. A few Chinese too, they was into construction. The people I knew there, the Ghanaians I made contact with, they would say, yeah, we'll come pick you up at one o'clock. Three o'clock would arrive – typical African time. I got used to that over the years.

It takes them four or five months to arrange a funeral so the body is around for all this time. It gets deep-frozen. Here our fridges run at six degrees above freezing. They're running at six degrees below. It's like a branch of Iceland out there. Because once you take a body out of a freezer it will deteriorate quite quickly. Now bearing in mind they have their traditional washing, they will have the body on show during the wake. There's a notice on every fridge I ever went to in any hospital – you need to give them three days. That's one to find the body and two to defreeze it. And more often than not they've found and defrosted the wrong one. If you don't keep up your payments they take the body out.

I went into one mortuary and there were bodies laying on the floor at various stages of decomposition when they'd not kept up the payments. It was like Beirut on a Friday night. There were bodies everywhere. It was surreal. You had to see this happening. The state of the bodies – as they are defrosting they'd have their ritual washing and dressing. It's a two-, three-, four-hour operation depending on who's doing it. Once they've dressed them in these robes and have got seven bits of kente around them and all this other stuff – by the time they finished it was soaking wet and and bloodstained. Horrible.

You think to yourself, I can make a difference here. The premises that was doing it was just awful. We went and found this piece of ground. This is what we built out there ... [*He tilts his PC monitor out of the March sunlight to show me snapshots of the new facility; in one shot he stands in ceremonial dress, wrapped in fabric with one shoulder showing.*] This is a restaurant and bar area for people travelling. This is the actual chapel. This building here is the washrooms and mortuary. We've done all the landscaping now. This would be set on three and a half acres. We are T. Cribb & Sons. That's the business that's set up and running, T. Cribb & Sons, Ghana Ltd.

SPENCER LEE

Crematorium technician

Londoners are weird. Very, very, very strange. But I've come to the conclusion that everyone, every area has a strange side to it. Every person has something that's, you know, 'Hang on, that's strange.' It's only because it's different to what I know. They might think *I'm* strange. 'Look at this weird guy who works in a crematorium.' You know? 'What's wrong with him, why can't he just go and work in an office like everyone else?'

There are a few cremators on the north side of the building made by Toibo in Stockholm.

Nearby is the cremulator, which is 'like a big tumble dryer with seven ceramic balls of different sizes', he says. 'It's used to break down the brittle bone.' To the right of the cremulator are trays of ferrous and non-ferrous metals. 'That's a hip,' he says. 'That's a bigger hip replacement. That's the socket.' Most are collected by a Dutch company but other pieces are picked up by friends and relatives. 'They'll say, it was part of him. It used to wind up the bloody security at Heathrow. I want it back. And they'll come in and claim it.'

It's surprisingly cold because it's unethical to heat a room with remains. His
gloves have a Hessian outer layer, like an oven-glove. Nearby is a collection of
blue boxes made from recycled cardboard. Each blue box carries the 2–3 kg of
ash. 'I notice the names that are disappearing from London,' he says. 'Violet,
Hilda, Beatrice, Edgar, Percy, Gladys, Edith, Ethel, Eliza.'

Go back seven years, when I started here, we used to do twenty-eight
services a day. Now, the average is about twelve or thirteen. It's just
the death rate has fallen. They predicted it would. Cos you've got
the generations, and when one generation begins to, they all die out.
And then you have a gap before the next generation starts to get to
that age. So it has peaks and troughs, the death rate. And also, a lot
of people move out of the area. It's becoming more of a Muslim
community, and their way of burial is different. We're on the down
part of the death rate. Soon it's gonna be picking up.

It's a strange thing when you think about it, because the industry
talk about 'Oh, you busy?' And you go, 'No …' That's a good thing,
isn't it?! It means less people are dying, you know? But as an industry,
people worry about it. The funeral directors, a lot of them are private
concerns, it's their livelihood. So it's quite stressful.

Repatriation is a big business at the moment, for the funeral
directors. There's all different types of paperwork needs to be
completed. I mean, I don't make out to understand it completely.
In the Muslim community, their burials have to take place within
twenty-four hours, that's their culture. So everything's got to be done
quick, paperwork's got to be gathered together, and you've got to
contact the cemetery, they've got to dig the graves very quickly. It's
amazing how they turn it around.

We don't offer a section, as such, for the Muslim community. We're
not saying they're not welcome to use our cemetery. But they kind of
like to have an area of their own where they're all buried together, in
that area. But we just haven't got that sort of space available. And it's
not a policy of ours to offer specific areas for specific denominations
or religions. This is, you know, for everyone. But we're not going to

say, 'You can't have yours there because you're not this specific faith.' That's something that we wouldn't go for, at all.

Always the worrying thing, which obviously you don't want to happen, is your pandemics and your epidemics. You know, you've got the bird flu worry. Once one gets it and it's airborne, that's it – that's a major problem. I mean, when I think when we did like 5,700 cremations in one year, I think that was an epidemic. But with a *pandemic*, you can need to do that in six *weeks*. Each crematorium may need to do 5,000 cremations in six weeks.

The last stage of a pandemic is that all funeral services are cancelled. If you want a service, you have a quick service in a church. And then basically we would just have hearses bringing coffins. Straight in, straight down to the basement, ready to cremate. Straight in, another one, next one that come in. Maybe we would have a minister for each chapel, so as we received the coffins, couple of prayers, send it down. Just a nice touch.

The very final stage of that plan would be that services would have to cease, and we would just have to receive coffins. Almost just be bringing them in by the car-load, if you like. Leaving many bodies around in unrefrigerated areas is a major problem, specially if it's a pandemic and it's airborne. You've got a worry that they need to go straightaway. Then of course you have to plan in that it could be us that's got it. We might not die as a result of it, but we could be so ill we can't come to work. So: 'Who else can we use; who else can we get trained? Let's get someone that knows how to work them machines.' There's a couple of intense courses that you need to go on, and you need to pass exams in order to be able to use them machines. There's five of us that can use 'em here. Say three of us are taken ill, and we've got to operate twenty-four hours a day? You can't have one in during the day and one in during the night, it's just not possible. You need two people at all times.

The bird flu is the worry. It hasn't happened. Let's keep our fingers crossed it doesn't happen. But it's nice to know that we can deal with it if it does happen. Because that's obviously the biggest worry, is how do you get rid of the … how do you stop bodies piling up, almost like the old plague?

London has been through that many times before. Hopefully never again. Hopefully our medicine is at a level where we can stop that. But any virus that's nasty like that does take out your vulnerable age groups, the very young and the very old. But in the city there's nowhere to store them. Because there are some crematoriums that have just one cremator, and they might need to rely on me. I've got four cremators. But I might need to rely on someone who has eight. You see what I mean?

DEPARTING

MICHAEL LININGTON

Seeker

The funny thing about London is how everything feels like it's trying to push you out. So all these people are trying to get in, but the city itself and the infrastructures that have been created and the social issues, everything is trying to push you straight back out. Everyone's trying to fight to get into the middle, but then there's something in the middle that's just trying to force everyone out and it's saying, you've got to earn your place. But if you get pushed out then someone else instantly fills your space. We feel a bit disposable.

You can have all the knowledge in the world but if you don't know how to function within the city and learn the language and the codes, you're fucked. You have to learn how things work here, for a start. First you learn the language of the city anyway, in terms of architecture and transport and things like that. You work out that Tube map and that tells you where stuff is, but actually it's not like that at all. There's all these other things going on. It compresses distance. I can remember thinking, okay, that's just down the road. Covent Garden is right next to Leicester Square. But then you start to learn the languages of subcultures and ways of meeting people and finding things that are going on.

In London, everything *feels* like it's on offer. If I can have anything, what is it that I actually want? Even choice in the supermarkets I find a nightmare. How am I meant to choose what I want for lunch, let alone what I want to do for the rest of my life or who I want to go out with? You could go out with someone and then there's going to be a thousand other people that are ten times hotter and ten times more connected with ten times more interesting stories.

It changes you. It changes the way you deal with things. You're presented with things changing so quick all the time and with new things being on offer and possibility. Possibility is the problem, when everything presents an opportunity. There's a possibility within everything. Living like that is horrible, I think, because how are you ever going to be happy? You're not, you're just not. Because you're always going to be considering the other options. When do you get to the zenith? When are you in a place where you're not wanting something else, you know? I'm living in one place now, but I think I'd really love to live in blah, blah … and then I'd probably move there and be like, this is nice and everything but I could be in a penthouse in EC1 and that would be much nicer and it'd be closer to the Tube. So when's the top point? When are you actually happy and satisfied with what you've got? I guess you're not and maybe London just likes to rub it in.

And the thing about the city as well is that it glamorizes everything. It glamorizes the full breadth of humanity. It can glamorize drug use. It can glamorize sickness. It can glamorize poverty. That's weird, right? It can glamorize the high life but it can also glamorize the low life. It's a meaning-making machine.

I hate that London never satisfies me. Nothing is ever enough. So it's like always looking for the next thing or waiting for the next place to go to. It would be nice if things just stopped for a while. I just don't feel like I could ever be satisfied here because there's too much on offer. When do you stop desiring? You don't, and I think I'm too stuck in the system to stop wanting.

When I was 13 or 14 I can remember coming here with my parents on a day trip and thinking, oh my god, this is amazing. Look at all these people. Everything must be happening here, this is where I'm going to end up. There's no other option than that I'll live in London. But then when it got to making decisions I was like, maybe I'm not good enough to go. Maybe it's too full-on. How do you start with nothing? But now it's like, I want more. There's something bigger and better, but then again starting with nothing's a horrible thought and yet living here I'm always trying to get back to the neutral, as in trying to strip away all the wanting stuff all the time. I don't want for things materially, I want for things experientially and maybe that's a London thing as well.

You're never full up. You can't ever have enough sex. You can't ever eat enough food. You can't ever be excited enough. It satisfies you for a bit and then you have to start over again, and I think looking at that as a long-term projection is quite disheartening. I'm stuck in this cycle. Something that keeps delivering but can't satisfy.

I wonder if London will ever stop existing, because you know when you look back in history there's cities that rose and fell. Is there a limit to how many people an infrastructure can support? I just think, where does all this waste go? How can you just keep building buildings on top of buildings?

ROB DE GROOT

Antique clock restorer

Give me a smoke and I'll tell you this mad story. Right ... okay, I work in Portobello Road, and every day I see people who are so filthy rich it's out of control, just insane. Often you don't even see them. Someone will come in and say, 'Hello, yeah, I've been sent to pick this thing up,' right? And they've got this massive fucking luxury supercar and this entourage. But one time this dude came in with his wife, right? I suppose he was trying to impress her. She looks at this thing that's like ten thousand quid and says, 'That looks cool.' He goes, 'Yeah, okay, let's buy it.' And right on the spot, without even thinking about it, he says to me, 'I'll have that.' I said, 'Well, how'd you want this thing shipped?' And the guy's like, 'Oh, no problem, I'll get my pilot to like take it over in a helicopter.'

I hate living here. I can't stand it any more, I just absolutely hate it, every single minute is like living torture. It's bullshit, I loathe it. You always think to yourself, there's some sorta thing I might be able to chisel into. It's like a fruit machine. You think, how hard can it be to wind up with three fucking pies?

But you are losing money every day you are here. It's always that thing: if I hang in here just a little bit longer, things may happen. I'll be hanging out with somebody in the pub, right, and they answer the phone and they'll go, 'Yeah, shit, no problem,' and they'll go, 'Yeah, someone I know just called, it's a video director, they need somebody to just hang out for half an hour and they'll give you 400 quid: can you do that tomorrow?' and I'm like, 'Yeah, all right.' And it's just enough little carrots that dangle in front of you every so often where you think, I am gonna really get something out of this experience.

No matter what you want to do in London, there's a million others who are in the queue ahead of you. Everything is always a hassle, because there is just so many people wanting to do the same shit at the same time. No matter what it is. And no matter what cool idea you've had, there's somebody else who's already done it. And they're usually younger, richer and more well-connected than you. In New York you'd know that certain places would be jammed all the time, but if you didn't like it you could go somewhere else. Right? But that's because it's a little bit more individualistic, most everybody's working on their own schedule. Whereas in London, there's times when it isn't crowded, but then there's nothing open so you can't get nothing done. It's like you can only do things at certain times. And that's when everyone's gonna be doing it. Like shopping for groceries. At certain times of the day everybody is getting them. Even when you go at the weirdest possible time, it doesn't matter. It's still gonna be the same queues because all the shelves are empty and they've only got one person working on the till. Another typical thing. You have to bring books in to the library when they're open.

I find the manager, and say, 'Why don't you have a slot like video shops?' 'Oh, because people put burning newspapers through it.' What is it with the destructiveness of people here?

London is like any other kind of addiction, really. You get 5 per cent entertainment out of it, and that makes you suffer through the other 95 per cent of it. I'm at the breaking point now, though, I figure. I've done enough, nobody sane stays in the city for longer than that.

It's a very punitive culture here. In London there's more signs telling you not to do shit than anywhere I've ever seen in my life. About a decade ago, there was an extreme crime problem on the street, it was really violent. I mean, it used to be just insane. There used to be so much fighting and antisocial behaviour all the time. What they decided to do was, plaster CCTVs all over the city. And now, everywhere you go there's signs saying YOU ARE BEING WATCHED. Or on the Tube, every ten seconds there's these announcements: 'For your safety and security, you are being watched on camera all the time.' Why do we need to spy on the entire population? Does anybody ever ask why there is such a need for everybody to be under 24-hour surveillance? Like, why is it that half the population feel at constant threat from the other half?

Basically, I'm a lazy sack of shit, right? I hate work. I don't mean my job, I mean any job. I'll tell you what I hate, I don't like getting the Tube in the morning with, you know, you know who's on the Tube. Loads of tourists who are mindless, they don't know anything and they bump into you all the time and they step on your feet and they're just idiots walking at three inches an hour in front of you. Or else the mindless robot zombie drones going to their nine-to-fives, right, and you just … I don't like getting up in the morning and going on the Tube.

Rob goes to buy a drink. The owners have only recently placed candles on the tables of this Dalston pub. One flickers in front of me. The price tag is still on the candleholder.

*

Having to go to Portobello from where I live in the East End, I hate that. I always think to myself, okay, what would happen if I left slightly earlier? It doesn't matter. I will always be late, no matter what time I leave the house. If I get to the Tube station at eight, there'll be one tube leaving every ten minutes. And if I get there at half nine, there'll be one leaving every two minutes, but there'll be people backed all the way up the stairs. I'm starting to think the people who actually run this idiot circus actually love it. They love watching people suffer. This is the whole English thing, isn't it? Make people suffer. How do we conquer the world? By making our infantry in the colonial wars take cold baths for nine years. Everything is to do with suffering.

It's like George Orwell said: war is peace, ignorance is strength. In London, happiness is misery. A friend of mine was going on this art course and one of their assignments was to come up with a new advertising campaign for London, like. He asked me for a slogan. I told him the best slogan for London would be, 'It just gets worse.' [*Laughs.*] Well, that just sums it up.

Dave takes a toilet break.

The image of London that you get around the world is far different than the reality. Like, okay: you see the image of London in films and in television and you figure, it must be so beautiful and everybody is very mannerly. Right, this is the paradox of London. It's like Japan, there's a code of manners, and etiquette, and protocol, and everybody is mannered. But also everybody is violent and everybody is rude and everybody is willing to fucking kill everybody for the smallest thing. I couldn't work out this contradiction in my head, right, for the longest time. And then I figured it out. I thought, there's a public face and a private face, right, and the public face is always opposite, it's the demi-urge, right? And the reason that people are so preoccupied with manners and etiquette in London is because if you do not *show* the right etiquette it might – possibly – get you killed. And this works on all levels of society.

All evil originates here. Well it does, really. I mean … industrial-ization, capitalism, imperialism, the whole idea of enslaving people for their resources and turning everybody into zombies and robots and, you know, raping the earth and raping the world's population and … they all start here.

I got to get out of this fucking city.

ETHEL HARDY

Old-age pensioner

I had a caravan down in West Mersea, on the beach. And we used to go down there every weekend nearly. But whenever I got there I'd want to come back to London. I don't know why, but I always want to get back.

Oh, but there's something that gets you in London. There's something here that makes you want to stay in London. A lot of people don't want it. If they've got a house, they want to live on their own. They don't want other people to live near them. It's funny. I've got a neighbour, she doesn't like certain people, but when she was ill they come in and helped her, didn't they? She doesn't want them to live near her, but I'm pleased to have them live near me in case. All different nationalities, all different people mixed up. They help me a lot, these people. I go in every day and they help me up the stairs. I've got my key but they open the door, and it's a very heavy door. I've had so many offers to move out, to places like Hertford and that, but …

She taps her finger against her mug of tea. It's just been delivered to her by a volunteer at the community centre.

*

I've packed up three times and each time I had to tell my grandson, I'm sorry, I don't want to go. I don't want to move. I'm staying where I am now. My son-in-law, he died. They've got a plant-hire business down Broxbourne way, but he died, and my daughter was left on her own. They'd bought me a flat down there, a lovely flat, near the river at Broxbourne. I had packed everything. But I said to him, I don't really want to move. I want to stay in London. It was a flat by the river in Broxbourne, a nice building, two or three flats in it. It was very nice. They were buying it for me, and it was going cheap because a nurse and her son was selling it. But I told him I wanted to stay where I am. So I unpacked. He was a bit annoyed.

Another time, my children come here and they say, we'll be taking you out on the Sunday. Where are we going? Come on, we'll go. And I went with them. Did I ever. And they took me to a flat also in Broxbourne. It was a nice flat with old ladies and that. They said, you can move out with the ladies. I didn't feel as if I wanted to go. I didn't want to move at all. But I talked to the ladies, or I tried to. I went downstairs and had a cup of tea. There you were, sat on a settee with a book, and they didn't talk. I looked around at these ladies in Broxbourne. I looked back and forth. I looked at this flat. I thought, they're not very friendly here. It was so quiet. It might have been painful for them to even say a word. But an old lady with a walker was there. I went over and talked to her. She was looking for company and that. She spoke very slowly. But anyway, I didn't take it, not that flat.

There's something that gets you in London and you don't want to let go. It's so quiet in the country, isn't it? Too quiet. You meet so many people here that you get to talk to and that. I've been here so many years, I've picked up so many friends. I think there's something here in the East End. It's all different nationalities. You get mixed up with them, don't you? When I ran the little charity shop round there, I used to meet all sorts of people, mostly Asians. My best customers, the Asians. Plenty of men round there had no places to live and that.

And they used to come in to buy bits of furniture. They must have been given little flats eventually, and they'd take their little bits of furniture.

Oh, London. You never know if you're going to be ill or fall. I did fall years ago and I crawled to the door and I opened the door and I called help. Two Asian boys that live upstairs, they come and they got me help. They phoned the ambulance, got my son for me, helped me right to the last, right until I got into the ambulance. You wouldn't think that, but they did. They stayed with me until the ambulance come and my son come. They held my hand.

All the things that have happened to you, all them years. Where you've been and who you've been with. All the different people I've met. I always seem to get on with them. If I see people I always talk to people. That's just what I do.

I wouldn't move. I wouldn't go out again. I like London. I wouldn't like to live in the country. All that quiet.

LUDMILA OLSZEWSKA

Former Londoner

She has recently returned to Warsaw after spending a year working in a pub in Kilburn. Her voice through the telephone is raspy, and I can hear her daughter playing contentedly behind her.

I remember the English weather, English cigarettes, grey skies, but sometimes beautiful skies, Oxford Street, Topshop. Irish men in my pub all day. They were so sad but also very funny, and also very respectful. They ask me what I was in London for. I said to them: money. I asked them why they came to London for. They said: money. They sit still for so long, all day, and some tell you things at the end of the night that you don't want to hear. I remember the music, the light of the pub, the Guinness, the waiting for the Guinness. That was one of the first things I learned in London: to wait for the Guinness with them.

I would make time each day to call my daughter, Alexandra, who was 4 and living with my mother in Warsaw. I would text my mother to make sure it was a good time. It was hard to hear my daughter from so far away. She comes on the phone, she doesn't always speak to me and I said, come on, say something, and there was her breathing and other small sounds but sometimes no words, and that is so hard to hear. Just sounds. It made me wonder if she knew it was me. She did. That is when you think, what am I doing in London? How much do I make? What do I have to do before I go home?

I remember the old churches, the London Eye, Shoot Up Hill, and many women who are well dressed, though not in Kilburn. My money, my toothbrush, my mobile phone, my sim card, my make-up, my shampoo, some clothes, some clothes I never took out of my bag. Primrose Hill once for an afternoon. I ate my lunch there. The buses. Always listening to Polish people on the buses. They think that no one understands them.

Where are you going, they asked at the pub when I left, and I said, I am going home. They knew about my daughter because they sat in the pub all day. Don't leave us, one man said to me. What will we ever do without you? But they also told me going home was very important. They would like to go home to Ireland. Some had been in London for forty years. I said to them, go. I am going. I am finished with London. You should go too. They said, no, they could not go.

I miss the freedom of London. I do miss the mixture. I think I will go back sometime with Alexandra and show her the city. She will understand why I went. And perhaps why I came back.

SMARTIE

Taxi driver

The light has changed again. The afternoon has moved on, as have the young mothers, pushing their prams ahead. There are empty cups in front of us. There is less din in the Costa Coffee. 'I'm great for reminiscing,' he says. 'I always think about the past and my wife sometimes tells me off. She says, move forward. I say, the future is the past.'

I stopped working in the City for good about ten years ago, and I started the Knowledge to be a London taxi driver. I know a lot of people who were traders in the City who are now taxi drivers.

Basically, I met somebody who I really wanted to be with. I met her through my DJ-ing, she was a friend of the guy who owned the bar that I was DJ-ing in. We met from there and we formed a relationship and she lived with me. And now we're married, we have a son, and I became a taxi driver. I can honestly say that doing the Knowledge is the hardest thing I've ever done in my life.

I love driving a London taxi. It's the diesel engine really, the sound of the diesel. It doesn't sound like any other vehicle. I suppose it sounds like an old chugger, an old banger, it's just a diesel engine turning over. It's a real individual sound. I mean the only other sound of a vehicle that I think is really individual is a Porsche engine. I used to have a Porsche Carrera before I had my son and that engine, when you started the engine over, there's no other sound like it. It's a purr. But the taxi engine it's a real rattly sound, I love it. You can sense it chugging down the road. It's just your normal diesel engine, but it's a big engine. All London taxis were originally made in Coventry by the LTI, London Taxi International, and it was a British-made vehicle, so it's all British parts and pieces. It's an iconic vehicle. It's a bit like the Mini car or the red phone box. If they ever got rid of the London taxi it wouldn't be London.

If somebody said to me, what things remind you of New York, I would think, the Empire State Building, yellow cabs, Times Square. An American who'd never been to London, they'll say Buckingham Palace, they'll say Big Ben, they'll say Trafalgar Square, maybe. They're the things that remind you of London. Not many of them would say the London Eye, you know, the big wheel built for the Millennium. It's not an icon in the way that people remember London. It's just a big Ferris wheel, isn't it?

There's a lot of people out there that want to make London like Paris. They want coffee-bar culture, but this is London. When people come to London, they want the London they see in the films. They want the old-fashioned boozers. They want Jack the Ripper. They want Sherlock Holmes. Don't ever try and be Paris; if you want Paris you go to Paris. If you want London you go to London. So that individual niche sound of the London taxi should never ever go, because yes, you can hear it, and so many people turn around when I drive down the road in my taxi and they hear the engine and they know it's me coming to their rescue when they're stranded in some back road. There's a taxi coming.

Every Sunday night I work from eight o'clock at night to about one o'clock or 1.30 in the morning. I really enjoy it because I get the chance to see real London. I like looking at buildings. When I look at architecture, I look at how buildings have changed. I see things that remind me of when I was growing up. I look at areas that I used to hang around in as a kid, I might have been on a Red Bus Rover or I might have run through those streets being chased by a gang of kids.

Places like, for instance, the South Bank or London Bridge, which were full of burnt-out buildings back then. Places that I grew up with in Leyton that were derelict and we used to run through these houses at night knocking on people's doors, buildings that were derelict where we used to let off fireworks and stuff. Those places are now all housing developments.

When I go out on a Sunday, I see all parts of London, I drive everywhere and I go everywhere, I still see a lot of things that remind

me of its past. I go to places which are run-down, and I think, I
wonder what that will be like in five years' time? Will that still be the
same or will it be different? It excites me. I still get excitement out
of London. I suppose the day I don't get excitement out of London
will be the day I leave it, you know. My wife always says she'd love to
live in the countryside. I like the idea of escaping all the nonsense of
London, but you know what? My heart and soul are here in the city,
really. So I think that's where I'll always be.

KEVIN POVER

Commercial airline pilot

The best part about viewing London is when you do what they call
a Lambourne departure, when you leave from Heathrow. You take
off on the westerlies, you hang a right immediately, turn back 180
degrees, fly downwind and then you make a climbing left turn and
as you climb in the left turn you climb above London. That's when
you get this awesome view of the whole of London and you can
see the view of the Thames coming in – just like the opening on
EastEnders – and then it horseshoes round the London Eye and you
look further on towards Canary Wharf and you see everything. It's
incredible. Sometimes they keep you slightly low over there as well,
and if they've not got any London City or Biggin Hill airport traffic
then you've got a fabulous view, you really have. Every single time
you're just staring at it. Obviously you're flying the aeroplane as well,
but you can't help but have a quick glance because it's just one of
those places where there's so many things going on. There's so many
different things to look at. You can see why London's been developed
in such a way, really, because obviously back in the day it was all
centred around the river Thames coming in and that's the main
reason why it's all built up in that area and as it spreads outwards

you can see the concrete fading away into the greenery. You can see Wembley for miles.

When you do a departure along the northerly from Gatwick, you get a real sense of humanity. As you climb out over the city, you can see masses of people down there, all the buildings and all the built-up area are lit up. And at night-time you've got the M25, which circles London, and you can see all these little beady lights that are dotted around in a very windy circle and you realize that it's six o'clock and all those little beady lights are actual cars, and they're all queuing around the M25. Day by day they're down there and you just think of the effort, all the effort, just to get by. It's a tough city. All those little dots, those beads of light, like a rosary, all those people, wanting to get in, wanting to get out.

The best thing in the world, I find, is where it's a grim day downstairs and there's a layer of cloud, let's say at 5,000 feet or something like that, and so it's dark and gloomy. You take off, you can see a little bit below, might be a bit of rain, a bit of drizzle, not a particularly great day in London. The climb out of London is tricky, but then you fly through this cloud, which takes almost five seconds to get through, and all of a sudden upstairs is blue skies, brilliant sunshine. You're still listening to the London frequency but there's this sunshine. You can see the dots of other airplanes. You do feel as though you're leaving behind the beehive. You change to another frequency and you know it's going to get quieter. But then, of course it would. You're leaving the energy behind.

ACKNOWLEDGEMENTS

Thank you to each of the interviewees who found the time to speak to me.

Thanks also to:

Bella Lacey, Tracy Bohan, Euan Thorneycroft, Sara Holloway, Kelly Pike, Brigid Macleod, Michael Salu, Benjamin Buchan, Stephen Guise, Christine Lo, Anne Meadows and all the other excellent employees at Granta Books.

Matt Weiland, Shanna Milkey, Libby Edelson, Barry Harbaugh, Daniel Halpern and all at Ecco who brought this book to the US.

Orla Hickey, Paul Murashe, Leah Kirkland, Elliott Jack, Eliot Sandiford, Kuldip Sandhu, Candy Burnaine, Neal Price, Maria Stephens, Kate at Kalayaan, Stephen Kennard, Alexa Seligman, Joseph Chen, Rashad Ali, Abigail Stepnitz at Eaves and Max Knight.

Roger Warhurst, Kimberley Martin and Roger Protz at CAMRA.

Heather Richardson, Claire Henty, Sarah Darby, and a few other hardworking members of the NHS.

Vicky Harrison, Kathy Wade and Madeline Denny at Toynbee Hall.

Shamsul Islam, Davide Pascarella and Martin Gavin at Brent Council.

Bill Fishman, Sam at Hope Not Hate, Anne Kershen, Parvati Nair, Steve Livett, Ron Livett, Bruce Panday, Virginie Bigand, Catherine Byrne, Stephen Kennard, Victoria Lenzoi-Lee and Catherine West.

Heather Monley, Harriet Bird, Stephanie Cross and Alison Sieff.

Henry Besant, James Walker Osborn, Nicki Whitworth, Stephen Ferguson, Bill Clegg, Almir Biba, Carly Graham and Vicky Elliott.

Olivia Ware at NACRO, Jane at African Women's Care, Mark Clayton, Anastasia Lenglet, Lucy Gilliam, Marie Phillips and Michal Skop.

Simon Prosser, Anna Kelly, Juliette Mitchell, Josephine Greywoode, Helen Conford, Sophie Robinson, Rosamund Hutchison, Ellie Hutchison, Jenny Lord, Jon Elek, Sophie Missing, Lottie Moggach, Tom Moggach, Matt Clacher, Paul Ewen, Jamie Fewery, Jean Goldsmith, Stuart Hammond, Lynsey Hanley, Jamie O'Brien, Philippa Harrison, Jessica Jackson, Erica Jarnes, Muzaffar Khan, Georgia Lee, Barry Lewis, Hannah Charlton, Adam Conn, Alberta Matarutse, Sarah Maule, the staff of the London Library, Ian McKellen, Michael Schmelling, Leanne Shapton, Deirdre Dolan, Jerome Silva, Laurence Howarth, DW Gibson and the staff of Ledig House, and Deborah Moggach, who made many excellent mid-book suggestions.

Dan Hancox, Phil Oltermann, Jakob von Baeyer, Des Yankson and Chris Lochery.

Liam Crosby, Peter Murray, Lucy Wilson, Lucy Harrison, Sian Anderson, Tim O'Carroll, Naomi Kerbel, Alex Young, Anthony Clark, Paul Wallman and Cassandra Hamblett.

Katy Baggott, Lelia Ferro, Hattie Crisell, Harvey Darke, Hamid Kabir, Romola Garai, Hamish McDougall and Andrew Buckingham.

Karl Robertson at Hawk Force, Nepal Asatthawasi, Funke Aleshe, Dean Allen, Gail Armstrong, Pam Baguley, Julie Bridgewater, David Charkham, Chipo Chung, Wendy Coumantaros, David Hawkins, Paul Davis, Jo de Frias, Michael de la Lama, Joe Dunthorne, Molly Murray, Patrick Neate, Cavey Nick, Sarah Neufeld, Phil Holly and Rosalind Porter.

Merope Mills, Katharine Viner, Becky Barnicoat and the staff of the *Guardian Weekend* magazine.

Paul Tough, for allowing me to reprint sections of the introduction, which appears in a different form on the website Open Letters.

My parents, Marian Luxton and Clare Taylor, and my brother, Skott.

Brian Haw, whose presence will be missed in London.

Jo Ralling, Paula Prynn, Juliet Munro and Geoff Guy, who picked me up in his car from Clapham Junction in September, 2000.

INDEX